Rational Choice and Politics

PREFERENCE FORMATION 8, 144,
INFORMATION AVAILABLE TO THE ACCT 17
BELIEFS ABOUT HOW WE
UNCERTAINTY CONDS –
METHODOLOGICAL PRIVI

WHY PHENOMENON COM
LEXICOGRAPHIC PREF
SOCIAL NORMS 141 (+FORCE OF NORMS 142) + COMPAT WITH RCT 144
DUTY TO VOTE 170
PREDICTION DIFFS OF NON-INSTRUMENTALLY RATIONAL ACTION 170
FRAMING EFFECTS 155
VOTER PARADOX 161
CONTEXT–RELATIVENESS OF PREFERENCES 144 (SOCIETY)
SOCIAL NORMS AS LINGUISTIC RULES (GIDDENS?) 146
CONTEXTUAL KNOWLEDGE & TRUTH CONDS OF SENTENCES 146
    (OPACITY OF CHOICE SITUATION 146–7)
PREFERENCES, CHOICES & IDENTITY 147–8
– CENTRAL PARTS OF POLITICAL PHENOMENA? 148
QN OF INFO ACQUISITION & RCT 1–2
ELSTER VS 'PREDICTIVE SUCCESS' 69
'A' REASON VS. 'THE' REASON 164

Critical Political Studies Series

Series Editor: Jules Townshend

Rational Choice and Politics

A Critical Introduction

Stephen Parsons

continuum
LONDON • NEW YORK

Continuum International Publishing Group
The Tower Building   15 East 26th Street
11 York Road   New York
London SE1 7NX   NY 10010

www.continuumbooks.com

British Library Cataloguing-in-Publication Data
A catalogue record for this book is available from the British Library.

ISBN 0 8264 7721 6 (hardback)
    0 8264 7722 4 (paperback)

Library of Congress Cataloging-in-Publication Data
A catalogue record for this book is available from the Library of Congress.

Typeset by RefineCatch Limited, Bungay, Suffolk
Printed and bound in Great Britain by Cromwell Press, Trowbridge, Wilts

CONTENTS

FOR MY PARENTS

Introduction

Why do peasants revolt, individuals vote, politicians campaign, or governments exist? These are some of the questions explored in the rational choice literature. Over the last couple of decades, rational choice theory has become increasingly influential as a method for explaining political phenomena. However, for a variety of reasons this growth in the use of rational choice methods of explaining political phenomena is somewhat surprising. For instance, the literature can exhibit a tendency to be highly technical, it seems to reduce the study of political phenomena to becoming no more than a sub-branch of economics, and its success rate in explaining certain political phenomena is, to put it mildly, somewhat disappointing.

Nevertheless the growth in the use of rational choice theories in political investigations shows no sign of abating – quite the opposite. This book is hence intended to give students an insight into the main issues and controversies surrounding the use of rational choice theory in politics. Of course, as there is a vast literature on the subject of rational choice explanations in politics, the examples investigated can only be highly selective. However, hopefully the book will provide an appreciation of the potential strengths and limitations of the theory, and give students a basic understanding of the literature.

Although rational choice theory is closely related in various ways to certain economic theories, the book does not assume that students have any knowledge of either economic theory or decision theory, and students without such knowledge should not suffer any disadvantage when approaching the book. If anything, the opposite could be the case, as the book is somewhat sceptical about a number of claims advanced in conventional economic textbooks. There is a rationale for this scepticism, which the following is intended to illustrate.

One of the issues that surfaces repeatedly in the discussions in the book concerns the attempt to incorporate the subject of information acquisition into rational choice theory. This issue is explored partly because it is far from clear that rational choice theories have successfully dealt with the complexities and problems surrounding the question of information. This might not be surprising, as informational issues are highly contentious in economic theories. For example, questions such as what is information, is it the same for everyone, how does an individual know the value of something they have not yet obtained, etc., do not seem to be as easily resolved as is often assumed.

In order to gain an appreciation of some of the issues involved here, assume that one of your fellow students, prior to an important exam, offered to sell you a copy of the exam paper. Leaving moral scruples aside (as economists tend to), would you be prepared to buy the claimed copy? Well, it may depend upon whether you thought that the copy contained 'information': you will only know if the claimed copy is a genuine copy when you eventually enter the exam and read the actual exam paper, by which time it may well be too late. So would your decision depend to some extent upon your view of your fellow student: would they consider selling you a false copy in the hope that you would believe it genuine, hence making money for little effort, or even making it more than likely that you fail the exam? What if you knew that the student was also offering to sell the claimed copy to your fellow students? If so, and if the copy is a genuine copy, then you would not gain any advantage by purchasing it. However, if all your fellow students purchase it, and you do not, this might well entail that you would be disadvantaged.

As the following chapters will reveal, this form of reasoning, where each attempts to anticipate what the other will do, is quite common in explanations based on rational choice theories. It is also quite commonly assumed that individuals are not motivated by any form of ethical or moral worries: lying may be the norm, if it gains the liar an advantage.[1] Yet informational issues raise severe problems in economic theories generally, especially when coupled with the assumption that individuals may attempt to manipulate others, using information that they possess but that the other individual does not.

Some examples should clarify this point. Until fairly recently, economists could happily relate explanations as to how individuals and firms would behave under various market conditions. They could also explain how, given certain conditions, the decisions of all participants in the market would intermesh. However, these explanations assumed that individuals had perfect, or near perfect, information (knew all relevant information) and that individuals were basically 'honest brokers' – if they made a contract, they would keep to the terms of the contract.

However, these forms of explanation are not possible when it is assumed that individuals do not possess full information and will, if possible, break contracts if it is in their interests to do so. Hence economists are currently facing difficulties in explaining how the actions of all can be co-ordinated via the market. Further, the more informational problems are admitted, the more difficult it becomes to mathematically model the relevant processes, and the more intransigent becomes the problem of predicting what will happen.

Moreover, the 'informational issue' is by no means politically neutral. For example, for the majority of the previous century, many economists were quite happy advancing models explaining how centrally planned economies of the sort prevalent, in various forms, in the old Soviet Union and elsewhere, both could and would work. A number of criticisms of these models, such as those advanced by Hayek, focused precisely on the assumptions about information that the models contained (Hayek, 1949). It remains a moot point to what extent the break up of the Soviet Union can be traced back to informational problems that were assumed not to exist. In general, it could be considered somewhat ironic that investigations into political phenomena are fascinated by economic forms of explanation at the very time that economic forms of explanation are encountering something of a crisis.

Having hopefully explained part of the rationale for the subjects investigated, it may be useful to provide a brief résumé of the following chapters. Chapter 1 sets out the basic model of individual choice that is utilized in rational choice theories. It introduces the basic ideas germane to the model, and seeks to explore how and why it may, or may not, be useful in explaining political phenomena.

Chapter 2 investigates five seminal models which apply rational choice theory to the study of various political processes. The models investigated were among the first to utilize rational choice theory in connection with studies of political phenomena, and have proved highly influential for later investigations. The topics investigated here include voting behaviour and party policy formation, problems of collective action, relationships between bureaucracies and governments, democratic decision-making and constitutional choice.

Chapter 3 explores the nature and problems of rational choice theory in more detail. It also explores two further authors whose ideas have become influential in political studies. The first author is Schelling, who was one of the first authors to attempt to use game theory to provide explanations in certain areas significant in the study of international relations. The second author is Arrow, whose theory questions the possibility of arriving at decisions through democratic processes.

Chapter 4 examines further models which use rational choice theory in politic investigations, the majority of which build upon the ideas investigated in Chapter 2. The chapter thus investigates attempts to utilize rational choice theory in exploring the ideas of classic writers such as Hobbes and Marx, and in exploring politically significant factors such as institutions, revolutions, voting behaviour and procedures, agenda setting, and logrolling, amongst others.

The final two chapters are concerned, in somewhat different ways, with the scientific status of rational choice theory, a status which, for many of its advocates, is one of the main reasons why the theory should form the basis for explanations of political phenomena and processes. Chapter 5 examines the recent controversies surrounding the use of rational choice theory in politics. It investigates some of the criticisms that have been levelled against the theory, and some of the defences advanced by its adherents. Particular attention is given to the question of voting behaviour. Chapter 6 extends this inquiry in two ways. Firstly, it investigates the question as to how successful the theory has been in explaining choice in general, not just with regard to political phenomena. Secondly, it examines to what extent the basic 'building blocks' of the theory are sufficient in offering a coherent general explanation of individual choice. The conclusion to the book attempts to summarize the advantages and disadvantages of utilizing rational choice theory in politics.

Two apologies seem in order. Firstly, apart from the investigation of Schelling, the book does not explicitly investigate the use of rational choice theory in the study of international relations. Although I am aware of a number of relevant studies in this area, I do not feel competent enough to assess their potential usefulness or otherwise in this regard. Further, the studies I am aware of do appear to build upon the basic models outlined in the book. Secondly, the book is concerned with rational choice models and the appropriateness or otherwise of their use in the investigation of political phenomena. It thus seeks to explore the internal coherence of the various models, and critically assess the various claims that have been advanced by advocates – for example, that the models can provide adequate explanations or predictions in politics. I have thus not investigated the various criticisms of the theory that have been advanced from external perspectives.

The book thus does not engage with criticisms that have been advanced from a Habermasean perspective that rational choice theory does not exhaust the concept of rationality, and other areas of rationality, for example communicative rationality, are of equal, or even of primary, importance. Nor does the book engage with the various criticisms that have been advanced concerning the reliance on the idea of rationality, whether the criticisms emanate from post-modernist or feminist perspectives. This neglect should not be understood as a rejection of these forms of criticisms – far from it. Rather, given the scope of the book, it seemed preferable to concentrate on the questions and issues that can be raised about rational choice theories when these theories are taken on their own terms.

Notes

1. Unfortunately, this apparent lack of ethical and moral worries frequently appears to be shared by individuals who study economics. A few years ago I had to stop recommending that third year undergraduate students looked at specific journal articles as, whenever I recommended an article, it was rapidly and forcibly removed from the journal – by the use of a Stanley knife, apparently. I was unable to discover whether the article was removed so that the offending student

thus did not have to pay photocopying fees, or whether it was removed so that other students could not read it. There is some debate as to whether economics students choose the subject because they already behave in the manner that economic models assume, hence find the subject congenial, or whether they come to behave in the manner of the model the more they study it. I believe the latter understanding is currently the prevalent explanation.

CHAPTER 1

An Introduction to Rational Choice Theory

We make choices throughout our lives. Some of these choices are relatively commonplace, such as choosing whether or not to make a drink, whilst others, such as choosing whether to attend university, are essentially 'one off' choices which can have a dramatic affect on our lives. We make choices about whether to vote in elections, whether to have children, whether to keep promises we have made. Initially, it might seem that these different examples of choices do not share much in common: the sudden choice to make a drink does not appear comparable to agonizing for months over the choice as to whether or not to attend university, or which to attend.

However, Rational Choice Theory (RCT) claims to be able to explain not just how some choices are made, but how *all* choices are made. Thus, according to the theory, there is no difference in principle between choosing whether to buy apples rather than bananas, and choosing whether to join a political revolution or stay at home and watch television. Further, it claims to explain how *all* individuals make all of their choices. The theory is thus regarded as being equally applicable to the lord and the peasant, the genius and the not so bright.

One of the basic ideas behind RCT is both simple and rather elegant, characteristics which no doubt help explain the appeal of the theory. If I am choosing whether to make a drink for myself, then I must weigh up the benefits of performing this action (satisfying my thirst) against the costs (time and trouble of performing the action). Similarly, when deciding whether to vote, all individuals calculate the benefits of their voting (potentially influencing the outcome of an election) against the costs (the time and trouble involved in going to the polling station).

Given the reference to 'costs' and 'benefits', it is perhaps not surprising to find that the most avid supporters of RCT tend to be found amongst economists. As a first approximation, RCT can thus be viewed as the application of an economic model of human action to the political sphere. In the words of Monroe's book title, it involves 'the economic approach to politics' (Monroe, 1991). The claim is that, as the individual who makes a choice in the economic sphere is the same individual who makes a choice in the political sphere, why should there be different forms of explanation for each sphere?[1] Why should the way an individual makes choices in political matters, or indeed any choice at all, be any different from the way the same individual makes choices in economic matters? Thus the claim is that, as RCT has been successful in explaining economic phenomena, there appears to be no obvious reason why it should not also be successful in explaining political phenomena. The theory claims to explain all choices, for everyone, and thus advocates of RCT deny that the theory is only applicable to economic choices. Thus the economist Gary Becker argues that:

> I have come to the position that the economic approach is a comprehensive one that is applicable to all human behaviour, be it behaviour involving money prices or imputed shadow prices, repeated or infrequent decisions, emotional or mechanical ends, rich or poor persons, . . . brilliant or stupid persons. (Becker, 1976: 8)

Given this claim to universal applicability, it is perhaps not surprising to find that over the last three or four decades RCT has become increasingly influential as a means of providing explanations in politics. Green and Shapiro (1994: 2) note 'scarcely an area of political science has remained untouched by its influence', whilst Shepsle notes that 'in political science, rational choice has moved from minor tributary to main stream' (Shepsle, 2001: 1). This growth in the use of RCT models in politics is inclusive of the area of international relations. Thus, at the beginning of a critical review of the use of RCT in the area of security studies, Walt notes that the popularity of RCT 'has grown significantly in recent years' (Walt, 2000:1).

The predominance of RCT forms of explanation in the social sciences generally is acknowledged in the question asked in the title of Mark Lichbach's recent book: 'Is Rational Choice Theory all of Social Science?' (Lichbach, 2003). It is worth noting, however, that geographical boundaries may well be relevant here. Hence the majority of the examples discussed in the literature are frequently drawn from investigations into political phenomena in the United States, and Dryzek has noted that RCT 'is the most powerful paradigm in the political science discipline, especially in the United States' (Dryzek, 2000: 31).

Although few people doubt the tremendous influence RCT has exercised over political studies in recent decades, for some there is something rather puzzling about this. Lane captures the view of a number of political scientists when he observes that 'in spite of its failure to predict or explain the phenomena it addresses, most commentators believe it will persist undaunted' (Lane, 1996: 124). The adoption of RCT in political studies is thus seen by many as a mistaken adoption of a theory incapable of either predicting what will happen or explaining what is happening or has happened. Yet despite this, most commentators also agree that the use of RCT in political studies will

continue, if not increase. Thus, in political studies, RCT has its proponents and its opponents. However, both agree that it will continue to
be an influential form of investigation. It is thus possible to be either
sympathetic or hostile to the use of RCT in political studies. However,
it appears increasingly unlikely that anyone can simply ignore it.

Yet beyond the basic ideas of weighing costs and benefits of choices,
what is RCT? Unfortunately, there is no single or unitary system of
ideas forming RCT, and practitioners adopt various different types
of analysis. Further, even the term 'rational choice theory' is somewhat
contentious, as some authors have indicated a preference for the term
'rational action theories'. However, as the term 'rational choice theory'
is well entrenched in the relevant literature, it seems advisable to adopt
it here.

THE BASIS OF THE RCT MODEL

Despite the differences amongst RCT approaches, they can all be
identified as derived, in different yet important ways, from the
philosopher Hume. Basically, individuals are regarded as possessing
desires and beliefs, and actions are explained in terms of these desires
and beliefs. Desires are neither rational nor irrational: adopting Hume's
(in)famous example, there is nothing wrong with my desiring the
destruction of the world rather than a cut on my finger. In RCT
models desires are termed 'preferences', and hence an individual, say,
indicates a preference for apples over bananas (desires apples rather than
bananas).

An individual's preferences are commonly regarded as being 'given'.
To say that preferences are 'given' can indicate a number of factors.
Firstly, it can indicate that they are not subject to any judgement by
the investigator. Thus, if an individual does prefer the destruction of
the world to the cutting of their finger, this is quite acceptable. If an
individual prefers to make as much money as they can, rather than assist
the underprivileged, this is of no concern to the investigator. Secondly,
to say that preferences are 'given' also tends to indicate that the investigator is uninterested in the source of these preferences, or why an
individual has the preferences that they do have. Economists thus
tend to treat issues concerning the formation of preferences, or why
individuals have the preferences that they do, as one of no particular
interest, a question to be investigated in other disciplines. As explored
in more detail later, this tendency to neglect questions concerning
preference formation can raise a number of issues when the analysis is
applied to political phenomena. An economist may merely note that
an individual prefers one thing to another: however, in politics, a
researcher may be interested in how it comes about that an individual,

say, decides that they prefer party x to party y. Thirdly, it can indicate that preferences are viewed as being constant, or unchanging. Although economists tend to be uncomfortable with the term 'needs', it has been suggested that the tendency to treat preferences as constant is analogous to treating them as 'human needs'.

Whereas the investigator is disinterested in judging an individual's preferences, this is not generally the case with an individual's beliefs. Although preferences are neither rational nor irrational, it is assumed that there is a 'need to stipulate that beliefs themselves are rational' (Elster, 2000: 29).[2] The difference between desires or preferences can thus be viewed in terms of the differences in the way that they relate to the world. In the case of desires or preferences, an individual is viewed as trying to accommodate the world to their desires. Thus if I desire to quench my thirst, I will try and bring it about that my thirst is quenched.

In contrast, in the case of beliefs, an individual is viewed as trying to accommodate their beliefs to the world. Thus if I desire to quench my thirst, and believe that consuming a cup of salt will lead to my thirst being quenched, there seems a good chance that my belief, but not my desire, is false. There is nothing wrong with an individual desiring that the moon be made of green cheese. However, there almost certainly is something wrong if an individual believes that the moon is made of green cheese. Note also that desires are not assumed to directly affect beliefs: my desire that the moon is made of green cheese should not lead me to believe that it is so made.[3]

In this basic form, the relationship between desires or preferences, beliefs, and action can be put in the form of a practical syllogism thus:

Premise One: I desire to eat something sweet.
Premise Two: I believe that the eating of this bar of chocolate will be
    the eating of something sweet.
Conclusion: Therefore, I eat the bar of chocolate.

Action is thus identified as the conclusion of the syllogism, where desires and beliefs form the premises. Hence it is argued that we can explain the individual's choice to eat the bar of chocolate simply in terms of the individual's desires or preferences and beliefs. At this stage, the idea of costs and benefits has not yet been integrated into this basic model, and hence the model is not necessarily restricted to RCT, and may be advocated by individuals not necessarily committed to RCT. For example, the model, typically referred to as the model of instrumentally rational action, may be adopted by writers concerned with exploring the philosophy of action. The model does appear to offer a fairly simple explanation of individual action. Indeed, it will be argued later that this explanation is too simple when we try and explain certain more complex forms of action. However, it serves as a sufficient basis for exploring the basics of RCT.

THE BASIC MODEL

As noted, on a strict Humean view, desires are neither rational nor irrational. However, in incorporating desires as 'preferences', the RCT model does introduce certain qualifications. Firstly, it tends to be assumed that preferences are 'well ordered'. Thus, an individual cannot both prefer apples to bananas and bananas to apples. Secondly, preferences are regarded as being transitive.[4] Thus if an individual prefers apples to bananas, and bananas to pears, it is assumed that the individual will prefer apples to pears. Hence: If A > B, and B > C, then A > C.

Many economists regard this restriction in preferences as entirely legitimate, as it is argued that if preferences were not of this form, individual actions would exhibit irrationality. This claimed irrationality is frequently illustrated in terms of a 'money pump'. If an individual prefers A to B, it is assumed that they would be prepared to pay a sum of money, however small, in order to obtain A rather than B. Similarly, if the individual prefers B to C, they would be willing to forgo a sum of money in order to obtain B rather than C. Hence the individual would be willing to pay to obtain B rather than C, and willing to pay again to obtain A rather than B. However, if the individual also states that they prefer C to A, then they would also be prepared to pay to obtain C rather than A. Consequently the individual would pay for B rather than C, A rather than B, yet C rather than A. The individual would thus continue to be willing to pay money to arrive at the desired state, and the exchange process would thus continue until the individual has spent all their money.

However, two things are worth observing. Firstly, as Sugden (1991) has noted, there is nothing in the basic 'Humean model' that allows these restrictions. As desires are neither rational nor irrational, and beliefs are not allowed to directly affect desires, it is not clear which component of the model is responsible for this ordering. Secondly, it is assumed either that the reference is to preferences at any one point of time, or to unchanging preferences over time. There is no inconsistency involved in an individual preferring A to B and B to C one day, yet the next day states they now prefer C to A because, in the intervening period, their preferences have changed.

The individual thus has well-ordered preferences, and these preferences serve as a guide to action. Essentially, the individual acts in a way that attempts to satisfy preferences, and does so on the basis of the beliefs, especially their beliefs concerning the opportunities for action available to them. In attempting to satisfy their preferences, individuals in the basic model are regarded as 'utility maximizers'. This term is used in a restricted, technical sense in contemporary microeconomics, and another source of contention concerns the degree to which this technical sense can be carried over into political models.

At a first approximation, to say that an individual is a 'utility maximizer' simply means that individuals satisfy their preferences as well as they can, given their beliefs about the actions available to them. They choose the action whose outcome, or consequence, is the most preferred. Hence 'given the set of available actions, the agent chooses rationally if there is no other action available to him the consequences of which he prefers to that of the chosen action' (Hollis and Hahn, 1979: 4). The term 'utility' hence simply denotes an individual's preferences: it summarizes how the individual ranks the items under consideration. Hence if the utility of A is greater than the utility of B, the individual prefers A to B.

It is with this move from preferences and beliefs to actions and their consequences that the idea of the 'costs' and 'benefits' of actions is relevant. The benefits of any action are given by the preference that is thus satisfied as a consequence of completing the action. However, individuals are viewed as making choices under conditions of scarcity. Hence one condition for preference satisfaction concerns the resources, or means, available to the individual. An individual may prefer a Porsche car to a Fiat Uno. However, if the individual does not possess sufficient funds to purchase the Porsche, then this action is not available to them, and preference satisfaction would seem to require that the Fiat Uno is purchased instead. Individuals are thus viewed as making choices under conditions of scarcity, where scarce resources are not restricted to money, but may also include factors such as time and effort.

Consequently in the general RCT model actions are viewed as having certain potential benefits (e.g. the preferences that will be satisfied as a consequence of completing the action) and certain potential costs (the time and money it takes to complete the action). Individuals are thus characterized as calculators, who weigh up the benefits and costs of various courses of action available to them. The individual assesses the various actions open to them, and chooses the one giving the greater benefit. As actions are made under conditions of scarcity, the set of actions available to the individual is constrained by their resources. For example, consumers are 'constrained' by their time and budgets, firms by their capital and labour.

In economic theories, these constraints, like preferences, are also frequently taken as 'given'. Hence consumers are viewed as having a 'given' budget. The actions available to the individual are frequently termed the 'feasibility set' (Elster, 1985a: 9). The feasibility set is viewed as being non-empty, so individuals can always make a choice. Actions thus have outcomes, or consequences, and individuals are viewed as performing that action from all available actions whose outcome is the most preferred.

Although economic theories frequently take constraints as being 'given', when RCT models are applied in the study of political phenomena then the question as to why certain constraints are or would be chosen can also be addressed. Why would individuals choose to be ruled by states that constrain their actions, rather than live in a state of anarchy? Why should individuals choose that decisions are to be made by majority voting rather than other forms of voting? As explored in the following chapters, different voting procedures may well produce different outcomes, even if the preferences of the individuals voting remain unaltered. As the voting procedure chosen hence constrains the outcomes that are possible, then the reasons for the choice of this form of constraint is regarded as a legitimate question for exploring through the use of RCT models.

Given scarcity, then one consequence of choosing to perform one action rather than another is that other actions and their outcomes are thus foregone. For example, if an individual chooses to read a newspaper rather than go for a walk in the park, this may well result in the consequence that the individual is better informed about current events than previously. However, a further consequence of selecting the act of reading is that the individual forgoes the exercise that would have been attained through walking. The consequences of any action may well extend over time. Thus an individual may be able to afford a Porsche rather than a Fiat Uno, but purchasing the Porsche entails that they will be unable to go on holiday next summer.

There are thus 'opportunity costs' to any action, where the cost of undertaking one course of action is the cost of the next best available action forgone. If I am deciding between purchasing a car and extending my kitchen, then the 'cost' of my purchasing the car is the kitchen extension I thus miss out on. Similarly, the 'cost' of my going to vote in an election is given by next best action I no longer have the time to undertake.

However, this way of formulating the costs of an action, although common, reveals another assumption that the model makes. Say I am contemplating the decision between the car and the kitchen extension, and opt for the car. The 'opportunity cost' of this decision is thus the kitchen extension that I forgo. However, as I now do not have the kitchen extension, how can I know what I have forgone? I can imagine what the cost of not having a larger kitchen is, but I can never know what it is, because I will not have it. The tendency is thus to treat the benefits and costs of actions as something that can be clearly known in advance, although this assumption is often dubious (Buchanan, 1969).

As the actual benefits and costs of any action can only be known after the action has been completed, reference is often made to 'expected costs' and 'expected benefits'. Again, the assumption is that these expected costs and benefits can be calculated, although, as noted, it is not clear how an individual could calculate, rather than merely imagine, the expected benefits of something that they will never have. However, according to the model, an individual choosing whether to commit funds to a car or a kitchen extension calculates, prior to choosing, what they expect the costs and benefits of each action to be. However, how does an individual calculate the expected costs and benefits of any action? As beliefs are rational, then the individual necessarily has rational beliefs about these expected costs and benefits.

In the case of the choice between the car and the kitchen, it is assumed that the individual will formulate their choice through obtaining information concerning the opportunities available. Hence the individual will undertake activities such as gaining estimates from different builders, search for different car prices, etc. As beliefs, unlike preferences, are regarded as capable of being rational or not, then, as Elster notes, for a belief to be rational it must be 'grounded in the information that is available to the agent' (Elster, 2000: 29). Initially, this seems quite plausible, and it would seem rather perverse to believe in something when all the information available to the agent indicates that this belief is wrong. If an individual discovers, after obtaining estimates, that the cost of the kitchen will be considerably more than originally thought, it would seem an exercise in wishful thinking to believe that it can, after all, be built for considerably less. However, there are, of course, various areas where the information between beliefs and information is far from clear. For example, is a belief in the curative powers of acupuncture mistaken in the light of current 'information available'?

However, the main problem for the model arises through linking the idea of rational beliefs to the assumption of utility maximization. Say I desire to purchase some apples, and visit the local market to do so. I am aware of various stalls that sell apples, and thus of various opportunities open to me. The model assumes that I make the best of the opportunities open to me. Thus I must know the prices of all the apples at all of the stalls and calculate which purchase would represent making the best of the opportunities available.

However, it could also be that there are various shops nearby selling apples, and thus I need to know the prices of these apples as well. Thus in order to make the best of the opportunities available to me, I must have information concerning all of the possible alternatives. Thus in many economic models, the assumption is made that individuals have perfect, or complete, information about all the relevant alternatives, and can perform the adequate calculations. Economists acknowledge that this assumption is not entirely realistic:

> The idea that the typical individual is capable of making the best of the opportunities available to him is a common one in economics . . . In demand theory . . . the mathematics behind this choice strategy is highly sophisticated and for the vast majority of people completely unintelligible. Yet it is assumed that people act as if they understand it . . . No one believes that the typical consumer or firm really could explain the

13

mathematical complexities involved in making the best of the opportunities open to them. (Attfield *et al.*, 1985: 22)

In order to make the best of their opportunities, the individual must have extensive knowledge of the various opportunities available to them and be able to perform complex calculations concerning these opportunities. Unless it is assumed that individuals do possess this information, and can perform the requisite calculations, then the individual is not making the best of their opportunities, and is thus not a utility maximizer.

Given the stringency of this assumption, a number (although by no means all) advocates of RCT in political studies relax the assumption somewhat. Thus Elster notes that:

We need to take account of the fact that the full set of objective opportunities available to the agent may not be known to him ... Applied to this situation, the theory says that people do as well as they believe they can. (Elster, 2000: 29)

Rather than individuals being viewed as doing the best that they can, they are now viewed as doing the best that they *believe* that they can. The individual is now no longer assumed to have complete knowledge of all the opportunities available to them. However, this qualification merely introduces other problems. If the individual no longer has full information, how much information do they require in order to 'do as well as they believe they can'? Take the market situation again. It is now no longer necessary to assume I must have information about all relevant alternatives. However, it is still the case that I must have information about some of the alternatives, and thus it is necessary for me to discover relevant information. I must still, therefore, spend time and energy finding out the different prices at different stalls.

However, if I am no longer required to have full information about alternatives, how many alternatives do I need information about? How much time and energy should I spend gathering information about these alternatives? In this instance, Elster speaks of the individual collecting an 'optimal amount of information'. This idea of an 'optimal amount' is often, perhaps not surprisingly, fleshed out in terms of costs and benefits: the individual searches for information until the expected costs of gaining more information exceed the expected benefits to be gained from the information. Thus, in the market situation, I may investigate the price of apples at various stalls, decide the prices are more or less equal, and thus it does not seem worth searching any further. I thus calculate that the expected benefits of continuing to search are likely to be outweighed by the time and energy (costs) that further searching will take. I thus make my purchase.

Information is thus regarded just like any other commodity, and as such is subject to what is termed 'diminishing marginal utility'. The basic assumption underpinning this idea is that the more of an item the individual consumes, the less benefit they receive. Thus if an individual is thirsty, they will receive more benefit from the first glass of water than the second, and more from the second than the third. As they receive successively less benefit from each glass of water, so they will be willing to forgo less to purchase successive glasses. The individual may be prepared to go to a lot of time and trouble to obtain the first glass of water, but not the second and subsequent glasses. The individual is thus assumed to be willing to exchange benefits for costs, but only up to a point, and stops the relevant action when the marginal contribution (to their utility) of the last unit of the good in question is close to, although without being less than, the marginal cost incurred (utility lost) in obtaining the good.[5]

This assumption may well be questioned in the case of normal goods or commodities, especially if linked to the idea of preference change. For example, an individual may sip their first alcoholic drink of the day with a feeling of some enjoyment, offset by feeling of guilt. However, the effects of the alcohol consumed are such that the feeling of guilt gradually disappears, and the second drink is consumed with relish. The individual thus enjoys the second drink more than the first. The consumption of the first drink thus alters the preference structure of the individual.

However, let us accept that preferences do not change. This does not remove the fact that the assumption appears to be even more questionable in the case of information. The claim is that the more information an individual collects, the less benefit is received from each additional source of information, until eventually the expected benefits of gaining more information do not seem worth the effort. However, although an individual may thus arrive at a decision, this does not mean that the individual has made this decision with an 'optimal amount of information'. Say the individual enters the market from the southern entrance, and initially restricts their search to the immediate vicinity. Having completed the purchase they suddenly realize that they need to visit a shop that is best reached through exiting the market at the northern entrance. However, in making their way to the northern entrance they notice a stall selling apples identical to the ones they have just purchased, but at a considerably lower price.

In this case, the individual clearly has not made the best of the opportunities available to them. However, neither, in retrospect, have they done as well as they believed that they could. With hindsight, they realize they had not, in fact, collected the optimal amount of information. It would have only taken a couple of minutes to discover the cheaper stall, and the resulting benefits, in the form of a lower price, would have been considerable. Here, the belief that they had collected the optimal amount of information was mistaken. However, if their action was based upon false beliefs then, according to RCT, it was not rational, even although at the time they believed that it was rational.

Recall that, in the strong version, individuals do the best that they can in any situation and, in the weak version, do the best they believe that they can. In order to act in these ways, individuals must have 'well-grounded' beliefs about the opportunities that are, in fact, available to them. Beliefs can only be of this character if they are based on information and, in the strong version, individuals possess all relevant information. In contrast, in the weak version, rational individuals are viewed as being engaged in obtaining an 'optimal amount' of information. However, in this latter case, it would thus appear that the only way an individual can establish if they have obtained an optimal amount of information is for them to obtain all possible information, then calculate what the optimal amount would be, which is absurd (Elster, 1986).

As the following chapters will reveal, informational issues are highly significant in RCT. Nevertheless, it is worth noting here that there are a couple of other issues that are relevant to the question of information acquisition. For example, information may be continually changing, and thus any information I already possess may have become obsolete by the time I acquire further information. Hence in the market situation, sellers may be continually altering the prices of their apples (this may be especially so if the market is about to close for the day). Further, information I collect may be contradictory. The tendency is to assume that information is always a 'good': however, if further information collected contradicts earlier information, confusion may result.

Hence it is far from clear how information can be subject to the 'diminishing utility' idea. In the case of drinking water, the assumption is that each glass of water is qualitatively identical: the sixth glass is exactly like the first glass, and all that has changed is my enjoyment of it. However, in the case of information, this assumption of qualitative identity does not seem warranted. An individual may collect a lot of information about some matter, then come across a piece of information that calls into question *all* the information they have collected so far. The problem with information is that you do not know what it is until you have obtained it, and hence you can never know in advance how it will relate to any information you already possess.

Another aspect of this process that the model tends to ignore is the fact that calculating the expected costs and benefits of acquiring information is itself a process that takes time, and is thus costly. The model assumes that individuals make choices in a certain way. What is not considered is the fact that individuals may regard themselves as choosing whether to behave according to the model, and disregarding certain actions because of the costs involved. Thus, I may arrive at the market and decide that attempting to calculate the expected costs and benefits of gathering the 'optimal' information is simply not worth the time and trouble. I may, for instance, merely go to a certain stall, possibly one I have used before, and purchase the goods. Here, it is not the case that I have calculated it is too costly to gather more information from other stalls. Rather, I simply cannot be bothered engaging in any such calculation.

In this case, I have not chosen the action that gains me the best advantage, but one that I regard as being 'good enough'. It might well be possible for me to have done the best that I can for myself by choosing another course of action. In fact, I do not even believe that I have done as well as I can. However, as far as I am concerned, I have achieved a satisfactory result.

Because of the rather formidable informational requirements that the pure model requires, a number of studies in politics relax the assumption that individuals maximize. It is argued that, instead, individuals frequently act in ways that bring about what they regard as a satisfactory, rather than an optimal, outcome. In such models, individuals are thus regarded as being satisficers, rather than maximizers.

It is important to note that the claim that individuals are prepared to consume an item until there is equality between the satisfaction of preferences thus obtained and the costs thus forgone need not imply that therefore preferences are somehow being measured. What is of interest is the ordering of preferences, not their strength. All that is required is that an individual ranks their preferences, say as preferring apples to bananas. It is not required that the individual can thus measure, or knows by how much, they prefer apples to bananas. It is the order, not strength, of preferences that matters. Technically, the model only assumes that preferences are ordinal, not cardinal.

There is an analogy here with most electoral systems, which are also only concerned with an ordinal ranking. Thus one individual may strongly support party x, and be vehemently opposed to party y, and thus cast their vote for party x. In contrast, another individual may be fairly indifferent between parties x and y, yet decide, although without any strong conviction, to vote for party y. Under a simple majority electoral system, these votes will cancel each other out. There is thus no way that the electoral system can measure the strength of individual preferences. However, whilst this may be regarded as a weakness in electoral systems, most economists are happy to work with ordinal, rather than cardinal, rankings.[6]

The issue as to how individual preferences are viewed in RCT warrants further exploration. In the basic model, as noted, no assumption about the content of preferences is necessarily entailed. An individual may seek to become as rich as possible, or to devote their lives to charitable works. However, in the main, RCT tends to assume that the preferences of an individual are self-regarding. The individual is thus characterized as being self-interested, and so predominantly concerned with their own or their immediate family's welfare. Various defences have been offered for this assumption. Elster claims that it has 'methodological priority', whilst others have argued that it is a realistic assumption, and individuals are basically self-interested, others that the assumption simplifies the analysis.[7]

Whatever the justification for the self-interest assumption, it does tend to be widely incorporated in the model. Indeed, without this assumption, many of the analyses that practitioners advance are simply not viable. It is thus not so much that practitioners choose to assume self-interest, but that they must assume self-interest. This assumption again raises questions about the relevance of RCT for studies of politics. Even if individuals do act according to self-interest in economic matters, it cannot simply be assumed that they will also act in this manner in political matters. Whereas an individual would hardly claim that they had purchased an apple from a sense of 'public duty', a politician may well offer this sense of duty as an explanation for their actions. Of course, the politician's explanation may not be truthful. However, this example does seem to suggest that the assumption that all behaviour is self-interested, although possibly warranted in economics, may be a more dubious assumption in politics.

We thus have an individual who maximizes their utility subject to constraints and is guided by self-interest. The individual makes the best use of the opportunities available in order to satisfy well ordered, probably self-interested, preferences, and uses the various resources available to them efficiently in order to satisfy their preferences. The individual has consistent preferences, and is concerned with choosing the appropriate means of satisfying them, given their beliefs, including their beliefs about the opportunities available, given constraints. Instrumental rationality is thus frequently referred to as means/ends rationality, where the question concerns the suitable selection of means to satisfy ends given by preferences. If an individual prefers to be rich rather than poor, giving all their wealth to charity is possibly not the best means of satisfying this end.

GAME THEORY

The investigation conducted so far concerns the individual making choices according to RCT. It is now necessary to investigate what occurs when two or more individuals interact with each other, where each is acting according to RCT. The interaction of two or more individuals is investigated in game theory. These interactions between individuals may be viewed in terms of a co-operative game. For example, two motorists approaching a narrow section of the road from opposite directions may have to co-operate in order to co-ordinate their actions so they can each pass each other. However, many of the games examined are examples of non-cooperative game theory, the broad outlines of which can be illustrated with the following prisoners' dilemma (PD).

An officer of the law arrests and imprisons two individuals, both of whom are suspected of partaking in a major crime. The prisoners are given the following scenarios. If both confess to the crime, they each receive a prison sentence of three years. If only one prisoner confesses, then this unfortunate individual receives ten years in prison, whilst the other prisoner is released. However, if neither prisoner confesses, then the law officer, strongly suspecting that both are lying, gives them an eight-year prison sentence each.[8] The possible punishments are represented in Figure 1.1, where C = confess (co-operate), D = not confess (defect), and prisoner 2's payoffs are given first in each box. The negative signs indicate that the payoffs are viewed as costs, not benefits.

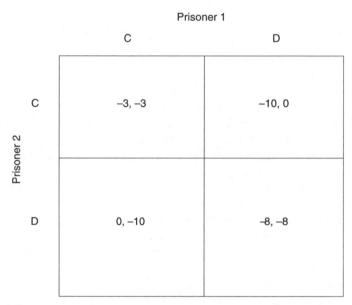

Figure 1.1

The total years spent in prison are thus six (if both confess), ten (if only one confesses) or sixteen (if neither confesses). It would thus seem that the best move, or strategy, for each prisoner to adopt is confess, as this results in the lowest total number of years spent in prison.[9] However, according to game theory, the actual result of this scenario would be that each prisoner would adopt the strategy of defecting, hence each would go to prison for eight years (the worst possible overall result). Why is this?

Imagine you are prisoner 1, pondering whether to select the strategy of confessing or defecting. If your fellow prisoner chooses to confess, then if you also choose to confess, you will go to prison for three years (as will your fellow prisoner). However, if you choose not to confess, to defect, you will be released, and not have to go to prison at all. Hence, if your fellow prisoner chooses to confess, it is better for you to choose to defect. Alternatively, if your fellow prisoner chooses to defect, whilst you choose to confess, you will go to prison for ten years, whilst if you choose to defect you will only go to prison for eight years. Hence, if your fellow prisoner chooses to defect, it is better for you to defect also. Consequently, you are better choosing to defect if your fellow prisoner chooses either to confess or defect. Defect is thus your *dominant strategy*: it is the strategy you should pursue whatever strategy the other chooses. However, the scenario is exactly the same for prisoner 2. The dominant strategy for each player is thus to defect, with the end result that both prisoners spend eight years in prison. The position of both defecting is known as a Nash equilibrium, after the mathematician John Nash, as it represents each player's best response given expectations as to how the other will respond (defect). Alternatively, the equilibrium position signifies that each player has no incentive to deviate from their strategy given that other players do not deviate.

In the prisoners' dilemma, even if both prisoners discuss the situation beforehand, and come to an agreement that both will confess (co-operate), defection still remains the dominant strategy for each. This is because each would be better off if the other upheld the agreement and confessed, whilst they themselves defected. Hence, in game theory, it is not regarded as rational to keep promises if an individual can secure an advantage through breaking a promise.[10]

In the prisoners' dilemma, each individual is regarded as behaving according to RCT. Thus each is trying to do the best for themselves, given the opportunities available to them. However, as the game involves an interaction between two rational individuals, a further dimension of RCT is brought into focus. Not only is it assumed that each individual is rational, it is also assumed that each individual knows that other individuals are also rational: prisoner 1 knows that prisoner 2 is rational, and vice-versa. Thus each individual in the prisoners' dilemma not only knows that defection is the rational choice for themselves, they also know that it is the rational choice for the other prisoner. Further, each prisoner knows that the other prisoner knows that they themselves are rational: prisoner 1 knows that prisoner 2 knows that prisoner 1 is rational. Game theory thus tends to assume a common knowledge of rationality (CKR):

1) Each player is rational;
2) Each player knows all other players are rational;
3) Each player knows all other players know all players are rational.[11]

It is worth noting that the prisoners' dilemma has been drawn upon in order to illustrate a number of issues in politics. For example, why do we need states? Why cannot individuals simply organize their own affairs in the absence of a government? Say we assume that a number of individuals join together, and decide to organize their affairs without any government. Assume further that all individuals agree that their community requires some form of defence force, in order to counter any aggression from other communities, and each individual is willing to pay a certain contribution in order to provide this defence. However, when the time comes to pay the contribution, each individual thinks that they would be better off not contributing, as they will still benefit from the defence force. Yet as all individuals will so think, then contributions will not be forthcoming, and the defence force will not materialize.

Consequently, even though each agrees there should be a defence force, and each is willing to contribute, the end result is that each tries to 'free ride', with the result that no defence force is established. Hence the state is necessary in order to tax people, thus ensuring that the defence force that each wants is actually provided. The state is thus required in order to ensure a $(-3,-3)$ outcome rather than a $(-8,-8)$ outcome, given that each individual would prefer a $(0,-10)$ situation.

The question of whether to contribute becomes even more unlikely if the CKR condition is invoked. In this case, not only does each think that it is irrational for themselves to contribute, they also realize that every other individual will arrive at the same conclusion. This gives each individual a further incentive not to contribute, as no individual wants to appear to be a 'sucker' by being the only person to contribute. The prisoners' dilemma can thus be used to illustrate two problems potentially relevant in the investigation of political phenomena (Schmidtz, 1991). Firstly, there is the free rider problem: if I can benefit, why contribute (why confess because, if the other does, I am released)? Secondly, there is an assurance problem: why contribute, or no-one else will (why confess because, as the other will not, I would be a fool to do so)?

As the investigations in the following chapters will indicate, although the free rider problem has received considerable attention in the RCT literature, the assurance problem has not tended to be regarded as equally relevant. The colloquial manner of referring to the assurance problem is captured in the response to the question: 'what if everyone thought like that?' with the reply 'well, I would be stupid not to, wouldn't I'. A good example as to how the assurance problem can be resolved is provided – in the United Kingdom, at least – by the example of a televised evening devoted to raising money for charities. In the course of the evening viewers are continually reminded as to how much money has already been raised by numerous individuals, in order to provide assurance that anyone willing to contribute will not be alone, a situation whereby they may feel that they appear rather silly.

CONCLUSION

The use of RCT models in order to explore political phenomena has been subject to a number of criticisms, and the nature of some of these criticisms will be investigated in the following chapters. However, it is undoubtedly the case that the use of RCT in politics has increased significantly over the last few decades. Hence an appreciation of the theory can indicate both the strengths and limitations of the theory in political contexts. Essentially, RCT models individuals as rational calculators, carrying out complex calculations in order to do the best that they can, given their preferences and the opportunities available to them. This requirement may sometimes be relaxed, however, and individuals are assumed merely to do the best that they believe that they can.

In order to do the best that they can, individuals must be in possession of information concerning all the opportunities available to them, and be able to perform complex mathematical feats in assessing these opportunities. These informational requirements can be relaxed if individuals are only viewed as doing the best that they believe they can. However, if individuals do not possess complete information about the opportunities available, there is a difficult issue concerning how much information individuals can be assumed to have in order to act rationally. The assumption that individuals will collect the 'optimal amount' of information is itself fraught with difficulties. In the case of interactive behaviour, as outlined in the prisoners' dilemma, it is assumed that individuals have complete information concerning the pay-offs available, and can also predict how, given these pay-offs, other players will act.

This chapter has outlined the basic assumptions of the RCT model. There are, however, some further assumptions intrinsic to the model that require investigation. Yet as any further investigation of these assumptions can only be assisted by first investigating the use of the model in investigating political phenomena, the following chapter will examine some of these uses, before returning in Chapter 3 to further investigations into the nature of the assumptions that the model makes.

Notes

1. This, essentially, is an adoption of the argument advanced in Tullock, 1976: 5.
2. Some economists (e.g. Mises, 1949) argue that all behaviour is rational from the perspective of the acting individual, which implies that all beliefs are rational.
3. The problem with desires directly affecting beliefs is hence that of 'wishful thinking' (Elster, 2000: 31).

4. There are further conditions, and the two listed are merely listed here. Further conditions will be explored in the subsequent chapters.
5. This idea, frequently referred to as the 'equi-marginal principle', tends to be taken as a 'self-evident truth'.
6. As explored in Chapter 3, the ordinal assumption is modified when choice under uncertainty is addressed.
7. The self-interested assumption is explored further in Chapter 3.
8. Note that it does not matter whether they have committed the crime or not.
9. The situation where both confess is known as the Pareto optimal position. It is the position where neither can benefit without the other being in a worse position.
10. This assumption that breaking promises is rational may involve a misunderstanding of the nature of promise keeping, regarding promises as items subject to manipulation, rather than social norms. On this, see Chapter 5.
11. The assumption that each player knows that all others are rational is sometimes relaxed in favour of the assumption that each player believes that all others are rational.

CHAPTER 2

Rational Choice Models in Politics: I

Having examined the bases of the RCT model in the previous chapter, it is now possible to investigate in more detail how this model has been applied to the study of political phenomena. In this chapter the investigation will focus upon some of the early 'seminal texts' in the area, as these writings were primarily responsible for introducing the idea of studying politics through the use of the RCT model. This procedure has a number of benefits. Firstly, it permits a deeper investigation into how the assumptions germane to RCT have been applied in studying political phenomena, and thus facilitates an inquiry into how plausible these assumptions are where political phenomena are concerned. Secondly, it allows the status of the theories to be examined: what is the claimed nature of these theories, and how do they relate to the study of political phenomena? Thirdly, it indicates some of the problems confronting explanations using RCT in politics, and thus provides a framework whereby, in the following chapters, subsequent modifications to the ideas can be appreciated.

Mueller has noted that 'the classic contributions of Arrow, Downs, Buchanan and Tullock, and Olson attracted the attention of many political scientists' (Mueller, 1993: 46) and the contributions investigated in this section are by Downs, Olson, Niskanen, and Buchanan and Tullock, whilst Arrow's contribution is considered in Chapter 3.[1] The work of Niskanen is also included here because it focuses on the problem of bureaucratic provision, and has been widely influential in terms of policy issues.

DOWNS AND THE ECONOMIC THEORY OF DEMOCRACY

Anthony Downs's book *An Economic Theory of Democracy* was first published in 1957 as an investigation into both governmental and individual voter decision-making. Downs explicitly states that his intent is to investigate political processes through extending the 'economic model' of decision-making, and hence to provide 'a generalised yet realistic behaviour rule for a rational government similar to the rules traditionally used for rational consumers and producers' (Downs, 1957: 3).

This statement of intent introduces two issues that warrant further investigation. Firstly, there is a question concerning the claim that the model of the political process that is being offered is 'realistic'. Does this claim signify that the model is built upon well established empirical evidence, or does it indicate something different? In short, what requires investigating is the exact status of the model that Downs is providing. Secondly, although economic theories can specify the behaviour required of rational consumers and producers, it is not immediately clear what is being indicated by the claim that Downs is interested in providing a behavioural rule for 'rational government'. How would or could a 'rational government' differ from any other form of government?

Regarding the first question, Downs is clear that the model he is offering is not normative, but positive. That is, the model is not con- cerned to establish what actions governments *ought to* take (e.g. to maintain full employment), but rather with setting out what actions governments *will* undertake, and hence 'we try to describe what will happen under certain conditions' (Downs, 1957: 14). This is a some- what confident assertion, especially when taken with the recognition that Downs admits that his model is not based upon any description of actual behaviour. Hence he acknowledges that:

> The statements in our analysis are true of the model world, not the real world . . . Thus when we make unqualified remarks about how men think, or what the government does . . . we are not referring to real men . . . but to their model counterparts in the rational world of our study. (Downs, 1957: 34)

The model is identified as providing a 'realistic behaviour rule', even though it is not based upon the observation of how individuals 'really behave' in the political world. Indeed, Downs is quite happy to assert that 'theoretical models should be tested primarily by the accuracy of their predictions rather than by the reality of their assumptions' (Downs, 1957: 21). This instrumentalist view of theories, which claims that theories are merely instruments for making predictions, and the truth or otherwise of their assumptions is irrelevant, is controversial. It assumes that theories can be evaluated solely in terms of their predictive ability and the truth or otherwise of the theories' assumptions is a completely irrelevant matter. On this account, if the predictions made by astrologers appear to be as accurate as the predictions made in physics, then astrology is as valid a source of knowledge as is theoretical physics.

However, if Downs's instrumentalist perspective is accepted, can we assume that the model can be rejected if its predictions turn out to be false? The claim that the theory predicts how actors will behave, coupled with the acknowledgement that the accuracy of prediction can serve as a criterion for deciding between good and bad theories, seems to offer a ready-made standard by which Downs's theory can be evaluated. If the theory correctly predicts the behaviour of actors, it seems plausible to accept it as a valid way of explaining political phenomena. However, if the predictions of the theory prove false, it should apparently be rejected, and alternative explanations of political phenomena sought in its place. Yet the status of the theory is not, in fact, so easily decided:

> The relevance of the model in this study to descriptive science is twofold. First, it proposes a single hypothesis to explain government decision-making and party behaviour in general. Since this hypothesis leads to testable corollaries, it can be submitted to empirical proof . . . Second, the model tells us what behaviour we can expect if men act rationally in politics. (Downs, 1957: 33)

The different implications of these two claims provides a somewhat succinct illustration as to why there might be considerable disquiet concerning the application of RCT models to political phenomena. The first claim is that the model will provide an explanation as to how certain political decisions and behaviour come about. In this case the model can be 'submitted to empirical proof': it is either correct or incorrect in the light of evidence in providing such an explanation. If the model proves to be incorrect, then presumably it should be abandoned. However, say that the model predicts that behaviour of type x will occur, yet when an empirical study is carried out, this study reveals that behaviour of type y, not type x, does in fact occur. Can we thus assume that the theory is not substantiated empirically, and thus should be discarded? The answer to this question is no, because the second claim now comes neatly to the rescue. If the theory predicts behaviour of type x and empirically we discover behaviour of type y, this does not indicate there is anything wrong with the theory, only that what we are confronted with is irrational behaviour.

It would thus seem that whatever political behaviour is empirically observed to occur reinforces the claimed strengths of the model. If the behaviour of political actors confirms the predictions of the theory, all well and good, the theory is indeed of obvious benefit. However, if the observed behaviour confounds the predictions of the theory, this merely illustrates that such behaviour is irrational. Hence 'the model is not an attempt to describe reality accurately . . . in particular [it] ignores all forms of irrationality and subconscious behaviour even though they play a vital role in real-world politics' (Downs, 1957: 34).

Of course, by definition, any 'model' abstracts from reality. However, it might be wondered how useful a theory can be which ignores forms of behaviour that Downs himself recognizes as playing a 'vital role' in real–world politics. Downs's model describes how actors will behave *if* they behave rationally and the model provides an account of how actors ought to behave (to behave rationally). Given the positive connotations of the concept of rationality, and negative connotations of the concept of irrationality, it is difficult to avoid the conclusion that the model is indicating how political actors ought to behave in general. Hence the 'behavioural rule' for a rational government, noted earlier, will be a rule indicating how governments ought to behave, in order to behave rationally.

Downs's classification of the status of his own theory is thus somewhat ambiguous. Whilst it is true that the theory is not offering normative claims of the firm 'governments ought to do *x*', it is not simply offering an explanation of observed behaviour. Rather, Downs is offering an account of how political actors ought to act if they are acting rationally. Yet if the model does provide predictions of actor behaviour, and these predictions are likely to turn out to be false, as actors do not act rationally in the way the theory suggests, what are the uses of the model? Downs claims it enables political researchers to discover 1) where and when in politics actors behave rationally, 2) where and when actors behave irrationally, 3) how this irrational behaviour deviates from rational behaviour (Downs, 1957: 33).

The claimed ability to sharply distinguish between rational and irrational behaviour suggests that a fairly stringent account of 'rational behaviour' is being utilized. Recall from the previous chapter the distinction between individuals doing the best that they can and individuals doing the best that they *believe* that they can in relevant situations. With this second, weaker, claim there can be no automatic assumption that different individuals will gather the same information prior to acting, and hence two individuals, guided by different information, may act differently.

Downs's model thus seems to assume a strong rationality claim, which is open to the objection that it entails an 'exaggerated belief in the ability of the human mind to determine in all situations the uniquely rational course of action' (Elster, 2000: 39).[2] As Downs's argument appears to imply that it is possible to identify uniquely rational courses of action, and hence identify deviations from this, it thus seems appropriate to now investigate the second question indicated previously. Downs is interested in 'rational government': however, what, according to Downs, is the 'rational behaviour' that is applicable here?

Downs and the Question of Rationality

As noted, Downs claims to explicitly follow the assumptions of economic theory in his analysis of political processes, and hence his analysis of rationality appeals to 'economic rationality'. Downs offers five conditions that must be met for any individual behaviour to be regarded as rational (Downs, 1957: 6). It is worthwhile looking at these conditions in some detail, as they allow the outline of rationality provided in the previous chapter to be extended.

Downs's first condition is that the individual can always make a decision when confronted with a range of alternatives. The assumption here is that individuals will not behave in the manner of Buridan's ass, which, situated between two bales of hay, could not decide which to choose, and starved to death as a result. Hence the assumption is that, in any situation, an individual will be able to make a choice between alternatives. Buridan's ass would thus choose *either* bale of hay, rather than neither bale of hay.

The second condition states that all individuals can rank all alternatives confronting them so that each is either preferred to, indifferent to, or inferior to each other. This assumption of completeness entails that alternatives are comparable in some way. The reason for introducing this assumption is to prevent the possibility of alternatives being regarded as incommensurate or non-comparable. Whatever the justifications for this assumption in economic theory, it does raise questions in the context of political phenomena. For example, assume an individual faced with a policy choice between spending more money on the transport system, in order to make it safer, and spending more on the education system, in the hope of bringing improvements in this sector. The individual here may claim that there is no basis on which to compare the options, hence a choice cannot be made. The individual is thus claiming the absence of any common criterion or criteria that could be used in order to compare the policy on transport with the policy on education.

In the case of voting, it could be that two parties are competing for the votes of individuals by offering two different policies. One of these policies might call for money to be spent in order to reduce poverty and deprivation amongst those less well off, the other for money to be spent to reduce hospital mortality rates amongst the elderly. A voter may view each policy proposal as not likely to provide immediate benefit to themselves, but as both being equally laudable, though for different reasons. The voter may thus conclude that there is no common criterion which would allow them to be compared, and refuses to nominate a preference for either one. The voter is unable to decide on any preference. Downs's second condition thus entails that decisions can always be made, and preferences ranked, hence assuming that the alternatives confronting individuals are regarded by them as being commensurable, or comparable in some way.

Downs's third condition of rational action is that preferences are transitive. It has already been noted that there does not seem to be anything with non-transitivity over time: because an individual prefers

A>B>C today, it is not immediately clear why it is irrational for the individual to prefer C>A tomorrow. However, again, one of the issues at stake here concerns the nature of the political process. It has been noted that Downs is concerned with the relationship between governments and voters, and, at this point, it is worth asking whether parties seeking election are merely attempting to *reflect* voters' preferences, or to actively *shape and change* these preferences. The party might, for instance, attempt to persuade voters of the benefits of a certain policy. If the latter is the case, then individual preferences may well change, especially over the election period. In this case, the assumption of transitivity over time seems highly dubious.

The fourth condition is that individuals will always choose from amongst the possible alternatives the one ranked higher in their preference ordering. Hence if *a* is preferred to *b* then given a choice between *a* and *b* the individual will choose *a*. Hence, as noted in the previous chapter, individuals are assumed to be utility maximizers. Although this condition may initially appear fairly straightforward – after all, who in their right mind would select an option they preferred less than the option they rejected? – in the case of politics the issues involved may again not in fact be as clear. As an illustration of why this might be so, take the case of how, over the last few years, pollsters in the United Kingdom have systematically corrected for an underrepresentation of the claimed preference to vote for the Conservative Party at a general election. The perceived need for this correction has arisen because a wide discrepancy was detected between how individuals stated to pollsters that they would vote and how they actually voted in elections. The end result was that opinion polls systematically underrepresented the Conservative vote actually registered in elections.

After considerable debate, the pollsters concluded that individuals who preferred the Conservative Party to other parties, and subsequently voted for the Conservative Party, were ashamed of this preference, and hence did not indicate it to pollsters. Of course, in the end these individuals did prefer A and subsequently voted for A even though they indicated to pollsters they would vote for B. However, the point is that preferences may not automatically be revealed in choices because individuals may have *preferences over preferences* (Hahn, 1982). An individual may prefer A to B but be ashamed of this preference structure: they may thus prefer it if they preferred B to A. If an individual does prefer A to B yet would rather that they preferred B to A then which choice they take may well depend upon the context within which the choice is made. If they are ashamed of preferring A to B and are in a situation where voting A makes them feel this shame acutely, they may well vote B.

The final condition is that individuals always make the same decision when confronted with the same alternatives, which is implied if an individual strictly prefers one alternative to another. The arguments advanced in the previous point already indicate some of the problems inherent to this condition. Further, considerations of time are introduced, it seems open to the same objections that have been raised regarding the transitive preferences assumption. Essentially, in the case of voting behaviour Downs is assuming that 'citizens' political tastes are fixed' (Downs, 1957: 47), where 'we assume that every citizen has a fixed conception of the good society and has already related it to his knowledge of party policies in a consistent manner' (Downs, 1957: 47). As explored in the case of preferences above, this assumption seems to entail that political parties attempting to secure office will not be able to influence or alter voters' conceptions of a good society. It also seems to imply that voters' conceptions of what the good life consists in do not alter over their lifetime, a heroic assumption to say the least.

Downs's model thus permits an appreciation of the fact that the assumptions made in RCT models may be more questionable when political phenomena, not economic phenomena, form the subject of study. Having indicated Downs's view of the status of his model, and the rationality conditions relevant to the model, the model itself warrants further investigation.

Downs's Model of the Political Process

Downs's model assumes that governments are democratic and bound by certain constitutional limits. In so far as they are democratic, governments are formed from parties chosen to govern through periodic, competitive elections, where each eligible citizen has one vote. The constitutional limits on governments are such that governing parties cannot unduly interfere with other parties and must respect free speech. Political parties hence attempt to gain control of the 'governmental apparatus' through winning periodic elections. Political parties and citizens are viewed as mutually exclusive, where the former attempt to gain office through securing the votes of the latter. Individuals are rational in the form detailed above and self-interested, not altruistic. Individual behaviour is thus concerned with securing 'selfish ends' (Downs, 1957: 27). Parties are primarily motivated by the desire to win elections and, in order to do so, they formulate specific policies.

This claim that parties are primarily interested in winning elections in order to gain control of the 'governmental apparatus' bears more than a passing relationship to the account of democracy offered by Schumpeter, who was, perhaps not coincidently, primarily an economist. According to Schumpeter, 'the democratic method is that institutional arrangement for arriving at political decisions in which individuals acquire the power to govern by means of a competitive struggle for the people's vote' (Schumpeter, 1976: 269). Hence for both Downs and Schumpeter political parties are not interested in, say, attempting to promote 'the common good', but simply in gaining office, and policies are advanced accordingly.

In Downs's model voters, given the self-interested assumption, seek their own greatest benefit, or to maximize their utility. Voters thus receive benefits from governments, not all of which they might appreciate, although only those they are aware of enter into the voting decision. Assuming only two parties are involved, then individuals vote for the party that they expect to provide them with the greatest benefits over the forthcoming election period (Downs refers to this expected benefit as an expected 'higher utility income'). The difference between the benefits expected from each party is referred to as the 'expected party differential'. So how do rational voters arrive at expectations concerning the benefits they expect to accrue to themselves from each of the parties competing in the election? Downs's logic here seems somewhat puzzling.

He argues that, in the case of the party already in government, voters will assume continuity in policy issues, and thus the past will be viewed as a guide to the future, and hence the past performance of the government will be taken to provide a reliable guide to their performance after the forthcoming election. However, as the opposition party has no such 'track record' to evaluate, this leaves the problem as to how the expected benefits of this party are to be assessed, so that a comparison between the parties can be drawn. Downs rejects the idea that voters would look to the expected future performance of the current opposition party, because 'it would be irrational to compare the current performance of one party with the expected future performance of another' (Downs, 1957: 40). Downs's appeal here to the idea of rationality is potentially confusing. He does not justify this behaviour as being 'irrational' in the sense that it conflicts with the rationality assumptions detailed in the preceding section. In defining this behaviour as 'irrational', Downs merely seems to be implying that it would not be sensible. However, given this apparent lack of 'rationality', Downs claims that 'voters must weigh the performance that the opposition party would have produced' (Downs, 1957: 40) if they had been in power.

Downs's model thus advances claims that are not based on any empirical evidence, but resolve around claims concerning 'rationality'. Yet even a cursory examination of the arguments questions this appeal to rationality. Firstly, it seems quite plausible to suggest conditions under which a voter would arrive at a misleading result if following Downs's procedures. For example, say a voter believes that the party in government has performed well, and that the relevant period of office coincided with a period of economic growth. However, the individual expects an economic downturn, believes that the party in government will continue with its past policies, and also believes that these policies will be unsuitable during the forthcoming recession. Why would it be rational for the voter to allow their favourable impression of the party's past record to influence their decision about the future?

It is also far from clear why it is 'rational' for a voter to take note of the expected past performance of an opposition party. Voters are viewed as essentially re-running the previous election, working out how they should have voted at that election, and extrapolating this into the future. Even if Downs eschews the need to refer to any empirical evidence, the claimed decision-making processes seem so dubious it is difficult to understand how the term 'rational' is applicable.

Downs's model appears to assume, in keeping with economic models prevalent at the time of writing, that individuals form expectations based upon what has happened: they are essentially 'backward looking'. However, not only does this assumption remain unsupported by any appeal to rationality, it also seems, as noted above, an 'irrational way' for individuals to form expectations. The arguments also appear to place a considerable burden on an individual's information-processing capacity: is it feasible to suggest that individuals can establish what effects a set of policy proposals would have resulted in today if they had been put into operation, say, four years earlier?

It is now possible to return to the question of the behavioural rule that, according to Downs, any rational government will observe. Governments are viewed as seeking to maximize political support in order to secure a majority vote. As voter preferences are regarded as 'given', and can be discovered by governments, a rational government is one that adopts policies supported by the majority. Downs introduces a caveat, whereby a party may win an election if it caters to minorities with strongly held views. Hence in Downs's model, unlike the usual economic models, there is an acknowledgement of the importance of the intensity with which preferences are held. However, if the majority also holds strong views on the various issues, then a party must reflect these views in order to secure election and hence 'a passionate majority always determines policy' (Downs, 1957: 64).

Thus, in order to decide on issues involving government expenditure, governments conduct a 'hypothetical poll' (Downs, 1957: 73) in order to determine how the 'utility incomes' of voters will be affected by any proposed expenditure and the financing required in order to accomplish it. Governments hence calculate differences between vote-gain made possible by the expenditure and vote-loss occurring through the need to finance the expenditure. In keeping with the 'equi-marginal' principle noted in the previous chapter,[3] Downs argues that 'expenditures are increased until the vote-gain of the marginal dollar spent equals the vote-loss of the marginal dollar financed' (Downs, 1957: 52).

So far, Downs's model has assumed certainty – for example, that political parties can discover voter preferences across a range of issues, and that voters are aware of party policies on the various issues. The acknowledgement of the relevance of uncertainty in political processes leads Downs to discuss the relationship between uncertainty and information. As the previous chapter suggested that the attempt to incorporate information acquisition is one of the least persuasive aspects of RCT generally, it is worth exploring Downs's ideas here.

Uncertainty is viewed by Downs as lack of certainty concerning events, be they past, present, future or hypothetical events. Uncertainty can be 'reduced by information, which can be obtained only by the expenditure of scarce resources' (Downs, 1957: 77). Hence the model incorporates the idea, questioned in the previous chapter, that there is nothing problematic about information, and 'more' necessarily equals 'better'. For Downs, more information may not lead an individual to decide to alter their initial decision, but instead may lead to an increase in confidence that the initial decision was indeed the correct one to make.

With the introduction of uncertainty, then 'the clear path from taste structure to voting decision becomes obscured by lack of knowledge' (Downs, 1957: 83). Whilst some individuals remain convinced that they can calculate the most beneficial party for themselves, and vote accordingly, others are unsure about how the different parties will perform if elected, hence unsure what party they prefer. Political leaders can thus influence voters and persuade them that the policies their parties are advocating would be beneficial to the voter. Note that Downs is not doubting that voters still know what their own visions of the good life are: they are merely uncertain about the means of attaining these visions, and hence which party would better bring them about.

Voter uncertainty also reveals why party ideologies are important, as 'it is much cheaper to keep informed about ideologies than about issues' (Downs, 1957: 99). Thus voters may not be willing to devote scarce resources to discovering the difference between parties on issues relevant to them, but may economize on resources by voting for the party whose ideology appears most favourable to them. Similarly, given uncertainty, political parties cannot discover each individual voter's preferences, and hence become reliant on intermediaries, such as lobbyists and interest group representatives, in order to gain some idea as to voter preferences. Hence party policies tend to be developed that benefit a few, rather than the majority: the government cannot ascertain the preferences of the majority, and hence uses the votes of a few as a form of surrogacy for the majority view (Downs, 1957: 93).

However, once this uncertainty, and consequent need to engage in costly information collection, is introduced into the model, then the somewhat paradoxical conclusion of Downs's analysis of voting behaviour starts to become apparent. Given uncertainty, a voter needs to acquire information on the differences between party positions on policy issues. However, acquiring this information may incur financial costs (buying papers, policy documents, etc.) and certainly incurs costs in time taken in pursuit of and digestion of information. Yet is it rational for an individual to engage in information acquisition? With uncertainty, the voter gains information about policies in order to make an assessment of the 'party differential' – what the voter will gain if one party rather than another or others is elected. Prior to acquiring the relevant information, a voter might well estimate that this party differential will be significant – if the voter makes the wrong choice, the costs incurred by being governed by the wrong party could be considerable. Thus the voter may well feel it is worth the costs of acquiring information, as this will result in greater benefits being accrued when the correct voting choice has been made. However, this scenario only applies if the individual is the only voter:

> But in fact there are a multitude of voters. Therefore the party which eventually wins will probably be elected no matter how he casts his vote, as long as others vote independently of him. Thus the cost of making a mistake cannot be measured by his party differential, since this mistake may not alter the outcome. (Downs, 1957: 244)

Each individual voter needs to engage in costly information acquisition in order to establish their own party differential, and hence resolve how they should vote in the forthcoming election. However, given the fact that many others will also be voting in the election, then the chances of any one vote significantly affecting the result is minuscule. Thus each individual is required to engage in costly information acquisition when the outcome of their informed voting on the result of the election will be, in all likelihood, minute. Hence 'it seems probable that for a great many citizens in a democracy, rational behaviour excludes any investment whatever in political information *per se*' (Downs, 1957: 245).

Clearly some differentials are relevant here. For example, if the potential voter thinks that the contest between parties will be closely fought, and the result could depend upon a few votes either way, then engaging in information acquisition may well be considered rational. Thus in closely fought contests, an individual voter may well think that their individual vote could swing the result of the election, and is thus significant. Yet even here there seems some ambiguity concerning how individuals will behave. For example, how does an individual know whether or not the contest will be close unless they have already engaged in acquiring costly information about the likely outcome? Yet why engage in this activity if, in all likelihood, the contest will not be close, and the act of voting will thus not affect the result?

The basic logic of Downs's argument is such that it may not only be engaging in information acquisition but the act of voting itself that constitutes irrational behaviour for potential voters. If the act of voting is costless, then the only individuals who will rationally abstain from voting are those who are indifferent about who wins the election.[4] However, the act of voting is not costless, as it takes 'time to register, to discover what parties are running, to deliberate, to go to the polls, and to mark the ballot' (Downs, 1957: 265). Hence the rational voter is left in a similar position with regards to voting as they found themselves in regarding information: why engage in the costly activity of voting if the chances of your vote influencing the final outcome are minuscule?

The argument becomes more complex if the idea of interlocking expectations, discussed in connection with game theory in the previous chapter, is introduced into the model. Each individual thinks it is not rational for them to vote, given the costs of voting and likelihood their individual vote will have negligible effect on the outcome. However, each individual believes that other voters are equally rational, and hence will also arrive at the conclusion that voting is not rational. Yet if each individual believes that no other individual will vote, then their own vote will be decisive in selecting the winning party, as it will be the only vote cast. Hence if each individual believes that other individuals, acting rationally, will not vote, then it is rational for each to vote.

Consequently, either each decides that their vote is not worth casting, given the number of others also voting, or each decides others will also think this way, and hence they should vote. But:

> Both of these outcomes are self-defeating. When no one votes, democracy collapses. Yet if everyone who is not indifferent votes, in the next election each will abstain, since his ballot had so little effect previously (i.e. when everyone voted). Thus if we assume all men think alike, democracy seems unable to function rationally. (Downs, 1957: 267)

Note here the significant divergence between what Downs originally claimed that his model would provide and the results actually achieved. Initially Downs claimed that his model would denote where and when in politics actors behave rationally, where and when actors behave irrationally, and how this irrational behaviour deviates from rational behaviour (Downs, 1957: 33). However, the prediction that his model arrives at are indeterminate: it could be that no individual votes (as all individuals believe that their votes will not have any effect on the election result). Alternatively, it could be that all individuals vote, as each individual believes that no other individual will vote, and hence their individual vote will be decisive. Hence the predictions of the model fall anywhere between no-one voting and everyone voting, with no apparent way of establishing which of these numerous scenarios might prevail.

This indicates the paradoxical nature of Downs's model. On the one hand Downs was one of the first writers to attempt to explain political phenomena on the basis of a model of the individual derived from neoclassical economics. Hence his book has been highly influential in terms of the application of economics to politics. However, on the other hand the predictions of the model seem either indeterminate or false from the outset. The model predicts a likely outcome is that rational individuals will, in the main, not engage in voting. However, hundreds of thousands of people in Western democracies do turn out to vote. Hence either these individuals are displaying mass irrationality at a collective level, or the model itself is mistaken, and hence ought to be rejected as empirically inadequate

Of course, it could be suggested that the model does offer an insight into the tendency, over time, for voter turnout in Western democracies to have decreased. Thus it might be the case that individual voters have become more rational (in the manner of the model) and hence have increasingly decided that voting is irrational. This and associated issues will be explored further in Chapter 5. However, for now, the discussion of Downs can be concluded by briefly noting his explanation as to why individuals do in fact vote, in contradiction to the predictions of his model.

Essentially, Downs argues that rational individuals will be motivated by 'a sense of social responsibility' and thus some (but not all) individuals will vote because they value the benefits of democracy as a political system. Of course, it cannot be the case that all individuals are so motivated, otherwise the 'free rider' problem discussed above reappears. If each thinks all others will vote out of a sense of social responsibility, then each individual does not need to vote, as the voting of all others will serve to preserve the democratic system.

Needless to say there is a certain 'ad hoc' nature to Downs's response. If individuals are self-interested, why should they suddenly be prepared to act out of a sense of social responsibility? Once such motivations are introduced, then it seems that any outcomes from RCT can be regarded as equally valid. Further, as Downs recognizes, it is not immediately clear why individuals would not be prepared to engage in acquiring information, yet would be prepared to engage in voting, as similar arguments were used in each case. Downs's response is that the benefits of preserving democracy are greater than the benefits of being informed, and the costs of voting less than the costs of information acquisition. However, it is far from clear that the benefits of democracy and those of having access to information can be sharply separated. If few individuals attempt to acquire information, then why are factors such as a free press or freedom of speech to be valued? It would seem just as rational for individuals to take social responsibility for the values of responsible information provision as for the values of democracy.

Interestingly, Downs came to amend these earlier views. Where he had initially viewed preferences as 'given' he later acknowledged that 'in reality, the social values classified by economists as "given" preferences or tastes are extremely important variables in every society . . . changes in them greatly affect economic and political behaviour and institutions' (Downs, 1991: 145). This recognition of the importance of social values susceptible to change led him to question his earlier analysis of voting behaviour, as:

> No study of democracy and how it works can be either accurate or comprehensive unless it analyses the role of social values . . . I believe an absolutely critical ingredient in successful democracies consists in the values in the hearts and minds of the citizenry that support democratic institutions and behaviour patterns. (Downs, 1991: 145)

Hence the activity of voting is no longer to be understood in terms of individuals assessing the costs and benefits of this activity. Rather, the activity of voting is an act that can only be understood in terms of the 'social values' that it embodies.

OLSON AND THE LOGIC OF COLLECTIVE ACTION

Olson's book *The Logic of Collective Action,* first published in 1965, is primarily concerned to investigate the interrelationship between individual rational action and rational action at the collective, or group, level. Initially it seems plausible to assume that a group comprised of self-interested individuals with a common interest will attempt to further this common interest. Hence it would appear that rational individuals belonging to such groups would attempt to achieve the desired objective, assuming they would be better off if the object were achieved. Therefore, for example, members of a union who have a common interest in securing higher wages would all attempt to secure this objective. However, Olson argues that unless groups are either small or individual members are coerced in some manner, 'rational, self-interested individuals will not act to achieve their common or group interests' (Olson, 1965: 2).

Individuals in a group may thus all believe they would be better off if a certain objective were achieved, yet assuming they are rational these individual members of the group will not attempt to achieve the objective. Hence what is considered to be rational action at the individual level does not secure a rational outcome at the group level. Olson's argument, if correct, clearly possesses considerable relevance in understanding political processes, as it suggests that even if individuals realize they share a common interest with other individuals, and form a group to promote this interest, it is rational for each individual to refrain from undertaking actions to promote this interest.

It would thus appear that groupings such as pressure groups, workers, farmers and capitalists will encounter great difficulty in attempting to secure benefits for their members even though all their members agree on the desirability of such benefits. Essentially, Olson is advancing a form of the 'free rider' argument encountered in the previous chapter. Why should any individual give up their time and money in order to secure a group benefit when that individual will receive the benefits accrued by the group anyway? Olson implicitly rejects the argument advanced by Downs in the case of democracies – that rational individuals, recognizing that other rational individuals have no incentive to vote, may vote in order to preserve democratic institutions – as he denies that any individual will be motivated to work for the group interest because they recognize others will not be so motivated. Rather, given a large group, each individual will believe that their contribution will not be significant, and thus barely missed by the others. Thus each individual believes that their non-participation will not unduly affect the working of the group, and hence the benefits will still be secured, at no cost to the individual. However, as all individuals reason in this manner, the group will fail.

Olson explicitly draws the analogy between problems of collective action and state provision of services, discussed in the previous chapter. Hence for 'public goods', which are goods which cannot be withheld from any member of the group if consumed by one member of the group, states must levy taxes in order that they will be provided. Everyone in a community may believe that a system of street lighting must be provided, and indicate their willingness to pay for it. However, if such a system were provided, everyone would benefit from it even if they had not paid for its provision. Individuals who have not paid cannot be excluded: the lights cannot be turned off when a non-payer is gaining their benefit. Yet although each is prepared to pay, each reasons that their individual contribution will be so small that the street lighting will be provided even if they do not pay. Therefore payment for street lighting must be coerced, through taxation, from all benefiting individuals.

As noted above, Olson believes that the problems of collective action are more prevalent in large groups, and small groups may be exempt from such problems. Given his analysis, it does seem that this could plausibly be the case. For example, in a small group each individual will be aware that withdrawing from collective action would place a high burden on the remaining group members, hence is likely to have a significant effect. However, with a large group, an individual may believe that their contribution will be so insignificant that their absence would not cause any major problems.

Olson argues that the differences between small and large groups are more significant than this, and hence large groups are highly unlikely to secure a collective good. He thus identifies three factors which cumulatively will prevent large groups from furthering their common interests:

1) The larger the group, the smaller the fraction of the group benefit received by any one individual. Hence the rewards for group action become less adequate the larger the group.
2) The larger the group, the smaller the share of total benefit received by any individual, and the less likelihood that the individual will feel the need to contribute.
3) The larger the group, the greater the costs of group organization, and hence the more costs that must be incurred by individuals before any of the collective good can be obtained.

Consequently it is more likely that small groups will successfully provide themselves with collective goods. Indeed, as the share of the collective good for each individual is higher in smaller groups, it might well be the case that an individual in a small group is willing to pay all the costs in order to obtain the good, even when knowing that this action will result in others also gaining benefits whilst not accruing costs. Yet even with small groups, Olson argues that the level of collective good obtained will not be optimal. That is, the amount of the good provided will not be as high as the common interest of the group would benefit from. An individual may be prepared to incur the costs of receiving the good at the level of provision that this individual feels worth the sacrifice. However, this is by no means the same as the level of provision optimal for the group as a whole. Further, the assumption that the individual will also receive benefits because of the actions of others in the group also serves to reduce individual incentives to incur expenses. Given these various factors, Olson states that:

> The larger a group is, the farther it will fall short of obtaining an optimal supply of any collective good, and the less likely that it will act to obtain even a minimal amount of such a good. In short, the larger the group, the less it will further its common interests. (Olson, 1965: 36)

Olson is quite aware that larger groups may well possess certain advantages over small groups – for example, they would have greater political strength (Olson, 1965: 68). However, such advantages do not outweigh the disadvantages of individuals being increasingly unwilling to bear the costs of advancing group interests the larger the size of the group. So given these problems, how can groups with large memberships ensure that their members are prepared to incur expenses in order to advance group interests? The answer according to Olson is selective incentives, by which individuals who do join a group and do contribute to the attainment of the group's interests are treated differently from those who do not. Such selective incentives may be either negative or positive.

As an example of negative incentives, Olson cites the examples of compulsory memberships ('closed shops'), and the use of picket lines and violence in the case of trade or worker unions. If a union negotiates an improvement in conditions for workers in a certain factory, then all workers in that factory benefit independently of whether they are union members or not. Hence compulsory union membership ensures that all beneficiaries of union action must contribute to the costs of such action. Similarly, individuals who refuse to go on strike with the majority of workers in order to secure improved benefits do not incur the costs of striking, may well make the strike ineffective, yet will receive any benefits brought about by the strike action. Hence picket lines and subsequent possible violence are coercive means by which attempts are made to ensure costs are borne by all individuals who may benefit. Olson thus concludes that 'the large labour union . . . must be coercive, if it attempts to fulfil its basic function and still survive' (Olson, 1965: 96). However, selective incentives may also be positive. For example, workers' unions may provide free access to legal advice and representation if required. Professional unions may provide journals, subsidized conferences, defence against expensive litigation, etc.

Olson extends his analysis by arguing that the analysis of group behaviour offered by Marx is 'inconsistent'. This is because Marx assumes that individual behaviour, under capitalism at least, is rational and utilitarian, yet also believes that individuals belong to classes 'defined in terms of their economic interests, which they will use all methods, including violence, to further' (Olson, 1965: 103). Olson's point is, of course, that if individuals are rational and self-interested, then they will not engage in such collective action, even if they believe that the objectives to be attained by such action are worth achieving. Hence 'class-oriented action will not occur if the individuals that make up a class act rationally' (Olson, 1965: 105).

It has been pointed out that Olson's arguments about large groups being able to attain collective goods only through providing certain incentives fails to explain why such groups come into being in the first place (McLean, 1987: 67). If we assume the transition from a small group where contribution will occur (although probably at a lower rate than optimal) to a large group where incentives can be offered, an explanation is needed as to why individuals will contribute when the group has increased from being small, but is not yet large enough to be able to offer selective incentives. Further, as explored in Chapter 6, experimental evidence indicates that individuals are prepared to contribute to the provision of collective benefits to a significantly greater degree than Olson's theory predicts. Hence, as with the theory expounded by Downs, empirical evidence does not seem to provide the required support for the theory.

Olson's work, more so than that of Downs, reveals a basic, yet troublesome, assumption common in all RCT. This assumption is that it is the individual, not groups or characteristics of societies such as social norms, that forms the basic unit of analysis. Although the relevant debates will be explored in more detail in the next and subsequent chapters, it is worth noting some of the issues here. Olson's analysis does not consider, for example, that individuals may contribute to groups out of a sense of solidarity with the other members of the group. Not does it seriously consider the idea that individuals may feel a sense of commitment to the group and its objectives, and this sense of commitment motivates the individual to engage in group action. It might also be the case that individuals engage in collective action because their sense of identity, of being who they are, is caught up with group membership and action.

Again, the wider problem seems to be the assumption that political phenomena can be successfully investigated in terms of one method of analysis. As Barry has noted, Britain has traditionally been characterized by higher union membership than is the case in the United States. However, it is difficult to appreciate how this difference can be explained solely in terms of differences in selective incentives (Barry, 1978: 29). In this case, it would seem that historical differences, societal norms, and issues of different institutional arrangements between societies all come into consideration.

NISKANEN'S ANALYSIS OF BUREAUCRACY

Niskanen's book *Bureaucracy: servant or master?* is a short and succinct attempt to analyse bureaucracies with the aid of an economic model, an analysis which has proved to be highly influential. One such area of influence has been in connection with the claim that certain goods should not be provided by governments and the bureaucracies thereby required, but by provision through the market. Niskanen's analysis commences by noting that, in recent decades, bureaucracies have 'become the primary form of organisation supplying education services and the case of the poor and have rapidly expanded their role in supplying health and transportation services' (Niskanen, 1973: 1). Although written from an American perspective, he notes that the percentage of net national product organized by governmental bureaucracies has grown considerably in the last few decades in both the USA and the UK. Hence, writing in 1973, he notes that government bureaucracies organize 'a growing and substantial, but not yet dominant, proportion of the economic activity of the United States and Britain' (Niskanen, 1973: 2).

He questions whether the bureaucratic outcomes are desirable and efficiently organized and, crucially, whether the services supplied by bureaucracies could be better provided by other forms of organization. Bureaucracies are defined as non-profit organizations financed at least partly by a periodic appropriation or grant. Given the concern as to whether bureaucratic provision is preferable to provision by other forms of organization, Niskanen is keen to note that the difference between government and private collective organizations concerns the different costs involved in transferring membership from one organization to another. The cost of transferring membership between private organizations is lower than the cost involved in transferring from governmental organizations, as the latter would involve moving – from one state to another, or from one country to another. Hence although bureaucracies may be characterized as providing services that augment those supplied by markets, there is no necessity that such services must be supplied by governments, and one cost imposed on consumers by governmental supply is the cost of finding an alternative supplier, which would involve physically moving location. It is worth noting here that Niskanen does not provide any detailed analysis as to why services may have become provided by bureaus rather than by markets, nor why the previous decades have witnessed an increase in the amount of economic activity organized through governmental bureaucracies.

A bureaucrat is identified as an individual who is employed full-time in the bureaucracy and has a 'separate, identifiable budget' (hence is a senior official) (Niskanen, 1973: 11). The environment of the bureaucracy is characterized by its relationship to three groups: the organization providing the appropriation or grant ('the sponsor'), the suppliers of labour and the material factors of production, and the customers for the services. The most significant of these relationships is that with the sponsor, which takes the form of a 'bilateral monopoly'. That is, the sponsor, normally a governmental department, is dependent upon a particular bureaucracy to provide a given service, whilst the bureaucracy is usually totally dependent upon the sponsor for funding.

Whereas an organization operating under market conditions, such as a firm, offers units of its output at a price, a bureaucracy offers a total output in exchange for its budget. In Niskanen's view bureaucracies hence have considerable bargaining power: the sponsor wants the services provided that the bureaucracy does provide yet has no significant alternative provider it can rely upon. However, although the bureaucracy is providing an output, the relationship between bureaucracy and sponsor is such that discussions occur in terms of level of activity rather than quantity of output. For example, the sponsor and bureaucracy involved in educational provision are concerned with the number of students catered for, rather than educational services provided. Hence according to the analysis the relationship between output and activity level is obscured in the absence of testing. Consequently, for example, sponsor and bureaucracy are concerned with the number of infantry divisions provided rather than military capability as such and it is only in times of conflict that the relationship between these two can become visible to both parties. A further issue is that the output supplied by the bureaucracy is not directly related to the output demanded by the electorate. Rather, the sponsor mediates between the bureaucracy and the electorate regarding the output supplied by the bureaucracy.

Central to Niskanen's argument is the claim that the relationship between the bureaucracy and the sponsor is such that the role of the latter is essentially passive. The key to this assumption concerns asymmetric information, which is information possessed by one party in a transaction that is unavailable to the other party to the transaction. Although issues surrounding the idea of asymmetric information are explored in more detail in the next chapter, certain aspects relevant to the idea need to be noted in order to assess Niskanen's arguments.

In Niskanen's model asymmetric information is relevant because the bureaucracy is seen as possessing more information than the sponsor concerning costs and production processes regarding the services provided, and have a greater incentive to collect (and obscure) relevant information. It is thus assumed that the sponsor 'knows the budget it is prepared to grant for a given quantity of services but does not have the incentive or the opportunity to know the minimum budget necessary to supply it' (Niskanen, 1973: 17). Hence the sponsor knows what they want supplied by the bureaucracy, and knows the budget they are prepared to pay, but is ignorant as to whether the same service could be supplied for a lower budget.

However, assuming that the sponsor is ignorant concerning the minimum budget necessary to supply the required services, why should this cause any problems? In common with the general economic approach to politics, it is assumed that the bureaucrat is an individual maximizer: the question is, what does the bureaucrat maximize? In the case of a private firm under market conditions, it is assumed that managers maximize profits. This claim is regarded as flowing both from assumptions about rational behaviour and from considerations of survival: firms that do not maximize profits will become replaced by those firms that do. However, bureaucrats are not concerned with generating profits, so the goal of their maximizing behaviour is not obvious.

Niskanen argues that, on both rationality and survival criteria, bureaucrats will maximize their budgets. Maximizing the budget is seen as rational because bureaucrats are motivated by, amongst other things, salary, public reputation, power and patronage, which are seen as being increased the larger the budget that the bureaucrat is responsible for. Maximizing the budget is also beneficial to the bureaucrat on survival grounds, for two main reasons. Firstly, the larger the budget, the more the potential rewards for those employees under the bureaucrat's authority. Hence these subordinates are more likely to co-operate with, rather than undermine, the bureaucrat the larger the budget. Secondly, the sponsoring agent does not have the time, the information or the staff to identify new programmes that may be required, and is thus dependent upon the bureaucrat for identifying such programmes.

Hence the sponsor expects the bureaucrat to demand an increase in yearly budget, indicating that new programmes have been identified.

However, even given this, why is there an assumption that bureaucrats are trying to maximize their budgets rather than, say, the public interest? Niskanen argues that the bureaucrat can not possess sufficient information to discover what the public actually wants, and hence there will be diverse ideas within bureaucracies concerning what constitutes 'the public interest'. Given that discovering 'the public interest' is impossible, bureaucrats will adopt goals that are on a lower level, yet feasible to accomplish. So sponsors are ignorant concerning the minimum budget required in providing the required level of service, and the bureaucrat exploits this ignorance by maximizing the budget available to them. Consequently Niskanen states that:

> The one most important general conclusion of my model . . . is that (bureaucracies) are too large. For given demand and cost decisions, they supply a quantity of services larger than would maximise the net benefits of the service. (Niskanen, 1973: 31)

Given this result, Niskanen advocates various alternatives to the then current manner of bureaucratic provision. The first set of alternatives involves altering the structure of bureaucracies and incentives of bureaucrats. For example, competition between different bureaucracies responsible for supplying services could be encouraged, or bureaucrats could be 'rewarded' for acting in ways other than simply attempting to maximize their budgets. Secondly, the manner of sponsor regulation of bureaucracies could be altered.[5] The third set of alternatives entails the introduction of forms of provision through markets, rather than bureaucracies. Niskanen argues that:

> The increasing dissatisfaction with the performance of the bureaucracy in supplying some public services and the demonstrated success of private institutions should be sufficient basis for more experiment in the supply of public services by profit-seeking firms and non-profit institutions. (Niskanen, 1973: 58)

Niskanen offers as examples where private firms may successfully provide services: postal services, fire protection services, air traffic control, and certain police services. He is not arguing that all services currently provided by bureaucracies could be better provided by private firms, and suggests organizing supply though private firms could provide some form of 'yardstick' whereby the performance of bureaucracies could be compared (Niskanen, 1973: 58). However, Niskanen is clearly sympathetic to the idea that private firms are most likely to be more efficient than bureaucracies:

> All bureaus are too large. For given demand and cost conditions, both the budget and output of a monopoly bureau may be up to twice that of a competitive industry facing the same conditions. (Niskanen, 1973: 33)

This appears to be rather a sweeping claim to make, and it is quite unclear how the claim can be supported, given the assumption that the problem in the sponsor/provider relationship is asymmetric information. A certain sleight-of-hand seems to be involved in this comparison. If a central component of the argument for 'bureaucratic inefficiency' is the existence of asymmetrical information, and bureaucrats are aware of certain relevant information not available to sponsors, why should this be any different if private sector companies are involved? Although Niskanen does acknowledge that lack of perfect information may raise problems for common economic assumptions about private sector firms (Niskanen, 1973: 22), he fails to explore these problems further.

The claim appears to be that competition between private sector firms will somehow reduce problems raised by informational asymmetries, presumably because such firms will compete on price, and hence offer a 'truer reflection' of the actual costs of output provision. However, once issues and problems raised by asymmetric information are introduced, then the mainstream economic assumptions that guide Niskanen's basic analysis can start falling away at a rather alarming rate. It is worth noting some of these issues here, before exploring further issues in the next chapter.

One problem asymmetric information raises for Niskanen's assumption of the benefits of 'market competition' can be illustrated through adopting an analysis provided by Williamson (1986). Take a number of firms competing for a contract extending over, say, five years. It may be that, at the outset, each firm is 'equal' in the sense that each firm has an equal chance of winning the contract. However, if after five years the firms are again invited to tender for the contract: are they now still on an equal footing?

Williamson argues that this is not necessarily the case. At the initial bidding process, each firm is in an equal position, but they are not all equal after the five-year period. This is because, given informational asymmetry, the (say) sponsor and bureau have, in the intervening five years, become more knowledgeable about each other, and developed products accordingly. Hence the bureau will, in the five-year period, have invested in services specific to the requirements of the sponsor, whilst the sponsor will recognize that the bureau has developed these specific services. Consequently, when the bidding process is reopened after five years, the bureau and sponsor will, to a certain extent, have become 'locked in': the bureau will have developed 'sponsor specific' services, and the bureau will acknowledge this. Hence bureau and sponsor will have incentives to remain in the relationship they have already established. Intuitively, this seems to make sense: presumably the services provided by an education bureau are different from those provided by a defence bureau, and the special services involved are not transferable.[6]

A further issue that Niskanen does not consider is that, given asymmetric information, price differences may be taken to reflect differences in quality rather than monopoly exploitation. Niskanen's model implicitly assumes, in common with a number of economic models, that workers, like other economic goods, are all the same, or homogeneous, and hence all workers are essentially equivalents. Consequently if two workers present themselves at different wage rates, one high and one low, then, as these workers are identical, it is rational to employ the worker offering themselves at the lower rate. Hence introducing competition allows the firm offering the more 'efficient' – i.e. cheaper – workforce to be employed.

However, this assumption of homogeneity seems questionable in a number of markets, of which the labour market is a prime example. Say it is assumed that some workers are committed and conscientious, whilst others will be less reliable and trustworthy. As employers will not initially be able to differentiate between these two sets of workers, it may well be the case that the conscientious worker will only offer themselves for employment at a higher wage rate than the untrustworthy worker. In this case the higher wage demanded is a form of signalling: it indicates the quality of the worker to the employer, given that it is difficult for a poor worker to continue to misrepresent themselves as a good worker, as they will be dismissed if discovered.

Consequently, say the sponsoring department is provided with two quotes to provide a certain service, one from a private sector firm, one from a public bureaucracy, and assume the firm offers this service at a lower price than the bureaucracy. Now, in Niskanen's analysis, the sponsor does not possess adequate information concerning the relationship between the service provided and the optimal level of cost for providing this service. Hence the services provided by the two firms appear identical, though one is offered at a lower cost. However, given informational problems, it may be quite rational for the sponsor to select the higher bid, as they believe this higher bid reflects the fact that the service provided will be better than the service provided by the lower bidder *in a situation where the sponsor is incapable, for informational reasons, of differentiating between the competing services.*

For example, the higher bid may reflect a higher wage bill, which in turn reflects the fact that this potential provider will be hiring higher quality staff (more experienced, higher qualified, etc.), who cost more. The fact that higher quality staff are being hired may be reflective of the fact that a better service will be provided, even although this is not immediately obvious in comparing bids. The problem is that once non–homogeneous goods and subsequent informational asymmetries are admitted, and Niskanen's model does at least admit the latter, then a number of the assumptions of conventional economic analysis become questionable. Because a provider seems to offer a similar service at a cheaper rate, hence more 'efficiently', it cannot therefore be concluded this should be the preferred option, as the sponsor does not possess enough information to know that similar services are, in fact, being provided. Rationality may dictate that the higher priced service is more likely to offer the sponsor the required service.

The force of Niskanen's analysis thus derives from a rather hybrid model of economics. On the one hand the analysis assumes well behaved demand, supply and cost curves, homogeneous goods, and hence that 'cheaper' is equitable to 'more efficient', although these well behaved curves are ultimately only derivable given certain highly specific assumptions. However, on the other hand, Niskanen fails to consider that these assumptions become highly questionable once informational asymmetries are admitted.

At the empirical level, Niskanen himself maintains that 'there are now dozens of studies that support the inefficiency hypothesis' (Niskanen, 2001: 267). However, this conclusion is questioned by Boyne (1998), and Horn states that 'the limited evidence that is available does not seem to be consistent with Niskanen's conclusion that bureaus can act as budget maximisers' (Horn, 1995: 90). Niskanen later modified his basic model in response to criticisms and suggestions (see Niskanen, 2001). Whereas initially he had assumed that bureaucrats will attempt to maximize their budgets, resulting in both the budget itself and the output provided being larger than the optimal, he now accepts that bureaucrats will attempt to maximize their discretionary budgets – that is, the difference between the total budget and the minimum cost of providing the output expected by the sponsor. In this case, where the bureau's budget will still be larger than the optimal, the output produced will now be too small.

BUCHANAN, TULLOCK AND CONSTITUTIONS

Buchanan and Tullock's *The Calculus of Consent*, published in 1962, investigated the form of political institutions that individuals may select in order to advance their individual and collective interests. Although based upon an RCT model of individual behaviour, the analysis does not necessarily assume self-interested behaviour (Buchanan & Tullock, 1962: 3). Collective action is action undertaken by individuals when they choose to accomplish their objectives collectively, rather than individually. Individuals hence may want to explore the possibility that they would benefit from organizing an activity collectively. For example, individuals may organize collectively in order to reduce the external costs that the actions of others may impose, say through collectively providing a police force in order to combat crime. Alternatively, individuals may wish to secure additional or external benefits through collective action – for example, through providing collective protection against fire. Individuals are thus seen to be arriving at decisions concerning what kinds of decision-making institutions they wish to participate in, depending upon the decision to be made, where these institutions may comprise choice in the market, voluntary co-operation, or collective choices exercised through governments (Levacic, 1990).

However, there is a cost to collective decision-making, as individuals clearly need to reach an agreement with others on the provision of the collective good. There are also 'external costs', which are the costs any individual expects to have to endure as the result of the actions of others over whom the individual has no control. Buchanan and Tullock refer to the sum of these costs (costs of reaching agreement and external costs) as 'social interdependence costs' and assume that individuals will want to minimize such costs.

Given that individuals are attempting to minimize these 'social interdependence costs', how will decision-making proceed? At one extreme individuals may prefer that decision-making only occurs if a unanimous, or near unanimous, decision can be reached. In terms of the costs of reaching agreement are concerned, a unanimous decision, to which all must agree, is obviously costly. It would take considerable time, effort and organizational effort to secure a unanimous agreement. Hence an individual may be prepared to incur the high costs associated with reaching an agreement in situations where the expected external costs of any decision are high.

Say, for example, individuals are deciding whether a collective agency such as a government can modify or restrict individual human or property rights. In this case, individuals will envisage that collective action may impose severe costs on themselves, and hence will be unwilling to agree to such an arrangement unless they envisage that these costs will not be severe. However, the only way this can be guaranteed is through a unanimous decision, as any one individual will not agree to allow others to impose costs on them. Hence when an individual expects the external costs of collective action to be high, they will seek a unanimous agreement. Conversely, in some cases, for example the provision of a police force, or a fire service, individuals may regard these as imposing more costs if supplied through private organizations, rather than collectively. Here, the expected external costs are not as high as previously, and individuals will be unwilling to engage in the costly search for a unanimous agreement.

It was noted that the costs incurred in reaching a unanimous decision may be considerable, involving the costs of organization incurred when a considerable number of individuals are involved. However, if unanimous or near unanimous decisions are required, the costs of bargaining also increase. Say a proposed collective action requires the consent of 30 per cent of the affected population in order to proceed. In this case, all individuals are somewhat anonymous, in the sense that if any individual withdraws their consent, they can be easily replaced with another. However, if a unanimous, or near unanimous, agreement is required, then the agreement of each individual is crucial. Individuals may thus be prepared to invest in strategic bargaining, in order to gain additional rewards in exchange for their agreement. This introduces again a problem investigated in more detail in subsequent chapters: individuals may misrepresent their preferences in order to secure additional benefits. Hence it may be that all individuals would agree to the collective decision X: however, an individual may conceal this from the group, in order to secure additional benefits through bargaining.

Buchanan and Tullock thus argue that no one decision-making rule is valid for all collective decision-making. They argue it is rational for individuals to agree to a constitution, which lays down different decision-making rules for different forms of collective decisions. The analysis also indicates when individuals may decide to adopt forms of direct democracy, where decisions are made by the agreement of all, and where democracy may involve the election of representatives to arrive at these decisions (Sass, 2001). Decision-making through elected representatives involves additional costs ('agency costs') as these representatives, as utility maximizers, must be monitored and con-strained. However, as the costs of reaching an agreement increase with the size of the group, then it seems plausible to assume that direct democratic procedures will be chosen where groups are small, elected representatives where groups are large.

Although Buchanan and Tullock's model reveals a preference for unanimity rule in some cases, it reveals no particular preference for majority rule. However, the analysis can be taken as drawing attention to the problem, under majority rule, of majorities imposing con-siderable costs on minorities who have not agreed to this imposition. Say a political party is elected under majority rule that advances two policies: increasing taxation to fund an increase in health care provision, and redistributing money from the poor to the rich (or from rich to poor). Whereas the former policy may be acceptable for majority decision-making, the latter is not, as the individuals involved would not agree to this form of decision-making.

Buchanan and Tullock's book thus represents an attempt to answer the question noted in the previous chapter: what form of institutions would individuals agree upon in order to constrain their choices? On certain issues, Buchanan and Tullock argue that individuals would only agree to choices being constrained through the exercise of a unanimous decision, whereas in other cases a simple majority decision-making procedure might be quite acceptable. However, as well as exploring this question of a pre-constitutional stage, where individuals select the type of constitution they would like to determine choices, Buchanan and Tullock's book also explored issues that became significant in later RCT model-based investigations into politics. One of these issues, indicated above, concerned the strategic misrepresentation of votes. Another issue concerned the practice of 'logrolling'.

In order to illustrate the significance of this practice, Buchanan and Tullock (1962: chapter 9) provide the example of a township of 100 farms which is intersected by a number of main highways maintained by the state. Assume that these highways are fed by local roads, each of which is depended upon by four or five farmers. If a farmer wishes to have his specific road repaired, then this proposal is put to the vote of all the 100 farmers. If the proposal secures a simple majority, then the road will be repaired with all 100 farmers sharing the costs.

Buchanan and Tullock conclude that, on this simple scheme, no road would be repaired, as a simple majority of farmers could not be secured willing to bear the costs of repairing a road benefiting only four or five of their number. However, although all 100 farmers who vote must share the cost of repairing the roads, the approval of only a simple majority, or 51 votes, secures the repairs. Hence if 51 farmers can collude and form a coalition, whereby each votes for any proposal where only theirs and any of the other 51 farmers' roads are repaired, then the roads supplying these 51 farmers, and only these 51, will be built, but the cost will be borne by all the farmers.

This example illustrates the process of logrolling, whereby the welfare of an individual is improved if they accept a decision contrary to their desires, but where their preferences are weak, in exchange for a decision in their favour but where their desires are stronger. In essence, individuals will agree to support a policy which they mildly disapprove of in exchange for securing support from others for a policy which they are strongly in favour of.

Buchanan and Tullock argue that this process works for any government action which benefits specific individuals or groups in a discriminatory fashion yet is financed from general taxation. In this case, members of an effective coalition will receive a differentially larger share of the benefits expected to result from collective action and/or will bear a differentially smaller share of the cost of such action. The argument is thus illustrating how a collective decision reached on the basis of a simple majority rule may well have redistributive elements. Consequently, one of the arguments in support of the unanimity rule is to avoid this redistributive element through individuals accepting that only decisions supported unanimously will be enacted.

Buchanan and Tullock favour unanimity voting for certain decisions, although, as noted, this procedure faces a number of problems. Firstly, the time required in order to reach unanimity might be such that no decision can, in effect, be made. This problem is likely to be considerable if the relevant communities are composed of individuals with very different, divergent tastes. In this case, it simply might not be possible to reach a unanimous agreement, even if all affected individuals believe that such an agreement is desirable.

Secondly, the possibility of strategic voting with unanimous voting procedures may result in 'the mirror image of the "incentive problem" in the voluntary provision of a public good' (Mueller, 2003: 72). This 'incentive problem' exists because each believes that the good will be supplied without any cost incurring to themselves, given the small loss incurred by their withdrawing from contributing. In the case of a unanimity agreement concerning, say, a public good, each individual may understate their preferences, hence hoping to free ride, in which case the public good may again not be provided.

A further issue that the analysis does not directly address concerns the *scope* of the decisions that can, or ought to be, open to democratic decision-making. For example, say a government proposed a law altering property rights in such a way that individuals were now permitted to sell themselves into slavery. It could be that such a proposal would receive a unanimous endorsement. However, it could be argued against this that certain rights are *inalienable*, and even if everyone affected endorses the relinquishing of the right, the right simply cannot be relinquished.

Alternatively, it could be that individuals today would overwhelmingly agree on policy proposals which result in benefits in the short term, and where the costs of the policies are to be met by future generations who, as they are yet unborn, do not have any say on the proposals. For example, individuals may agree to endorse a sizable increase in nuclear power provision, acknowledging that the costs of dealing with the disposal of the spent nuclear waste will have to be borne by future generations.

CONCLUSION

The respective works of Downs, Olson, Niskanen, and Buchanan and Tullock were all highly influential in terms of introducing rational choice perspectives into investigations of political phenomena. Although all the works discussed raise interesting issues, many of which will resurface in later chapters, they also indicate some of the problems inherent in models in politics based on RCT. One problem concerns the status and empirical validity of the models. Although, as in the case of Downs, the theories may indicate how rational individuals, where 'rationality' is defined in terms of RCT, will behave, if individuals do not behave in the manner claimed, does this indicate mass irrationality, or problems with the theory? Similarly, if the predictions generated by the theories are palpably false, does the fault lie with the theories themselves, or the world they are claiming to model?

Another problem consists in the search for one model of behaviour to account for diverse forms of political phenomena. Apart from

Downs's problematic reference to 'civic duty', there is scant exploration of the idea that individuals may not simply act in the manner that the theories depict. Other factors may be at least, if not more, significant in explaining political actions than ideas of 'utility maximization'. Moreover, the models investigated can appear to exclude other considerations in a rather arbitrary manner. For example, Downs defends his idea as to how individuals arrive at their assessment of 'party differentials' by appealing to an idea of rationality that does not seem to be adequately supported. Niskanen's model of bureaucracy relies on the idea of asymmetric information, yet appears to restrict any consideration of the effects of this phenomenon to one instance, and rely on more conventional forms of economic analysis in order to explain the significance of such asymmetries. Given the various issues raised in the preceding discussions, the next chapter will explore in more detail the assumptions of RCT, and question to what extent they can be defended.

Notes

1. Arrow's contribution is considered later as it is more technical.
2. Elster is explicitly criticizing Weber's account of rationality. For a critical perspective on Elster's interpretation of Weber on rationality, see Parsons, 2003.
3. Chapter 1, note 5.
4. Strictly speaking, if voting is costless, it is not clear why indifference would involve not voting, as Downs assumes. If an individual 'is really indifferent . . . the loss from choosing one alternative rather than another is exactly zero. The person can choose either alternative and regret nothing in either case' (Sen, 1986a: 68). Hence with costless voting, an indifferent voter would vote for either alternative with no incurred loss.
5. I shall ignore commenting on this set of alternatives, as it refers to political processes in the USA.
6. In the 1980s I was engaged in investigating certain aspects of the enthusiasm shown by the then British government to bring private sector management consultants in to assess the efficiency of public sector organizations. In the National Health Service a frequent complaint was that the first six months or so of this 'consultation' involved the managers in the health service explaining to the consultants how the system worked.

CHAPTER 3

Further Assumptions, Issues and Models

In the first chapter the basic ideas behind RCT were examined, whilst the second chapter explored how this theory has been used to explore political phenomena. This chapter will explore in more detail the assumptions of the model, and explore further some of the issues that these assumptions raise. Having conducted this investigation, two further prominent examples of the early use of RCT in investigating political phenomena will be examined. The first of these is provided by Schelling, who was one of the first authors to systematically apply game theory in politics, specifically in connection with issues in international relations. As game theory has so far only briefly been considered, it seems appropriate to leave the investigation until after the more extensive discussion of game theory conducted in this chapter. The second example is provided by the work of Arrow. As this work is more formalized than the works considered in the previous chapter, it again seems suitable to defer the investigation until the axioms and assumption of RCT have been investigated in more detail.[1]

AXIOMS AND ASSUMPTIONS OF RCT

The first issue to consider is the preference relation. Although certain aspects of this relation have already been introduced, they warrant closer examination. Suppose an individual is comparing two alternatives, x and y, where the symbols x and y can represent any alternative. Let us assume that x is a left-wing political party, whilst y is a right-wing political party. An individual may prefer x to y, or may prefer y to x, or may be unwilling to make any judgement, as neither seems better, in which case the individual is indifferent between the alternatives. These options can be symbolized thus:

$x > y$, where an individual strictly prefers x to y;
$y > x$, where an individual strictly prefers y to x,
$y \sim x$, where an individual is indifferent between x and y.

If an individual strictly prefers x to y, then the individual will not choose y if x is available. It is worth noting that these relations can also be expressed in the following form:

xP_iy, where individual $_i$ strictly prefers x to y,
xI_iy, where individual $_i$ is indifferent between x and y.

The first thing to note is that the above formulations assume that preferences are *asymmetric* (Kreps, 1990: 19). This means that an individual cannot prefer both x to y and y to x. As indicated in Chapter 1, preferences are 'well behaved': there is no pair of alternatives where $x > y$ and $y > x$ for an individual. It has already been suggested that this assumption may be unreasonable if reference is made to an individual's decision-making over time: an individual may prefer x to y at one point of time, yet y to x at another point of time. Also note that in the above $x > y$ was defined as x is strictly preferred to y. This is because an individual may *weakly* prefer x to y, in which case $x \geq y$: in the case of $x \geq y$, then either $x > y$ or $x \sim y$.

The main assumptions, or axioms, of RCT can initially be offered for conditions of choice under certainty, and consist in the following (Hargreaves Heap *et al.*, 1992: 6; Sugden, 1981):

1) Reflexivity. For any x, $x \geq x$. This requires that any alternative is always as good as itself. This assumption can be seen as 'common sense' and is implied by the asymmetry of preferences, detailed above. (This axiom is sometimes defined in terms of irreflexivity: for no x is $x > x$.)
2) Completeness. As noted during the discussion of Downs, the assumption here is that any two alternatives can always be compared and ranked. Thus for every pair x and y, then either $x \geq y$ or $y \geq x$ or both. Hence for any pair the individual prefers y to x, or x to y, or is indifferent between them. The fact that an individual is indifferent between two alternatives hence does not imply that the individual is incapable of comparing the alternatives, merely that no preference either way is expressed. As noted in Chapter 2, what the axiom does rule out is the idea that alternatives may be regarded as incomparable.
3) Transitivity. If $x \geq y$ and $y \geq z$, then $x \geq z$. This assumption has already been introduced.
4) Continuity. The assumption here is that, for any two alternatives, it will always be possible to accept an amount of the second alternative in order to compensate for the loss of a small amount of the first alternative.

The necessity for the axiom of continuity may not be immediately apparent, and warrants further exploration. If axioms 1–3 are satisfied, then the individual has a preference ordering. However, as noted, it is assumed that individuals are utility maximizers, and hence that preferences can be represented by a utility function. Understanding the idea behind axiom 4 requires a closer look at this idea. In everyday usage, the idea of something having 'utility' commonly means usefulness. At one time economists used to speak of some mysterious measure, referred to as 'utils', which allowed the utility of various alternatives to be measured. However, as noted previously, in contemporary RCT, following economic theory, 'utility' refers to an individual's preferences. Hence if $U(x) > U(y)$ is true, then $x > y$ is true, or the individual prefers the alternative with the higher utility. 'Utility' thus summarizes an individual's ranking of alternatives, and the higher the utility, the more the individual prefers the end state in question (Sugden, 1981). Hence an individual who obeys the axioms given above can be represented as maximizing their utility. The term 'utility maximization' thus indicates that an individual's judgements about how to achieve wellbeing are complete – every pair of alternatives is ranked and ordered transitively (Mandler, 2001).

The continuity axiom is thus introduced in order to ensure that the preference order can be represented by a utility function of the required form, and it does this by stipulating that preferences must be con-tinuous, or that points that are geometrically close are also close in terms of preferences. The requirement for this axiom might become clearer if we note what this axiom rules out: the possibility of lexi-cographic preferences, which are preferences which do not permit trade-offs. The medal table in the Olympic Games provides an illustra-tion of a lexicographic ordering (Hargreaves Heap *et al.*, 1992: 330). If country A has one gold, no silver and no bronze medals, whilst country B has no gold, seventeen silver, and thirty-nine bronze medals, then country A will be given a higher ranking than country B, as there is no way that country B can 'trade-off' its silver and bronze medals for gold.

In economic theory, the possibility of lexicographic preferences is not accorded any great importance.[2] However, in the case of the RCT model as applied in political studies, the situation is considerably more contentious. For example, an individual may regard it as important to their self-esteem that they are regarded as a person of integrity. This individual may be unwilling to 'trade-off' this reputation even if they can benefit considerably if they were willing to countenance such a trade-off. In this case the individual will not behave in the manner predicted in RCT models. For example, two individuals valuing integrity who promise to co-operate in a prisoners' dilemma will co-operate, even if they perceive this as threatening their narrowly perceived 'self-interest'.

This introduces another common assumption made when RCT models are used in economics which may be of a more dubious nature when political phenomena are under investigation. Hence Kahneman and Varey note that 'there is a distinct tendency in economics and decision theory to view material assets as the main carriers of utility' (Kahneman & Varey, 1991: 130). The tendency to focus on material assets is closely related to the assumption that individuals are self-interested. To appreciate how economic and political explanations may differ because of lexicographic preferences, take the idea of an individual – say a shopkeeper – having a reputation for honesty.

In economic terms, cultivating a reputation for honesty would almost certainly be explained in terms of trading-off short-term material gains for long-term gains. Hence, although the shopkeeper might be tempted to be dishonest, thus securing immediate gains, they recognize, or come to learn that, securing a reputation for honesty is better in the long term. Cultivating a reputation is thus similar to forgoing immediate gains in a prisoners' dilemma.

The discussion of the prisoners' dilemma in Chapter 1 presented it as a 'one-off' game: individuals made a choice between competing strategies. However, assume that the game is played repeatedly over time – an iterated game. In this case, individuals might come to learn that co-operation is the best option. Similarly, the shopkeeper cultivating a reputation for honesty can be viewed as choosing 'co-operate' rather than defect as this strategy pays off in the long term. Here, the cultivation of a reputation for honesty in explained as a consequence of long-term material self-interest overcoming short-term self-interest.

However, another possible explanation might be that the shopkeeper has a reputation for honesty because they are an honest individual, and the reason they are such an individual is because it is crucial to their self-understanding, or sense of who they are, sense of identity. Such an individual might find it inconceivable to even contemplate dishonesty, no matter what the potential gains might appear to be. In this case the individual is unwilling to 'trade-off' their preference for honesty against anything else: the preference is lexicographically ordered.

Although economists invariably adopt the former of these explanations for the shopkeeper's honesty, it is not at all clear why, when studying political phenomena, the second form of explanation must be automatically ruled out. An individual acting politically might be an honest individual simply because that is what they understand themselves to be: it constitutes part of their identity. George Washington allegedly claiming that he could not tell a lie would seem to indicate a lexicographic ordering of preferences.

Even if lexicographic preferences are not admitted, there is, as Mandler further notes, a certain ambiguity entailed in stating that an individual strictly prefers x to y. On the one hand the claim implies that the individual systematically chooses x over y. On the other hand it implies that the individual judges themselves to be better off with x than with y. However, what criterion is being used by the individual to establish that they are better off with x than y: what ordering principle is applicable to preferences? It is one thing to say that strictly preferring x to y indicates that y will never be chosen if x is available, quite another to say that, therefore, the individual thinks they will be better off with *x* than *y* (also Sen, 1986a). Hence as Sen has noted, the claim that an individual has a 'preference ordering' is taken to represent a multitude of diverse claims:

> A person is given one preference ordering, and as and when the need arises this is supposed to represent his interests, represent his welfare, summarise his ideas of what should be done, and describe his actual choices and behaviour. Can one preference ordering do all these things? (Sen, 1982: 99)

STABILITY AND INDEPENDENCE OF PREFERENCES

Previous discussions have suggested that it seems implausible to treat preferences as being constant, especially when an individual is considered over his or her lifetime. Individuals change, and it appears quite acceptable for an individual to, say, prefer jazz to classical music when they are young, yet reverse this preference when they get older. However, it could be argued that there is still a constant preference at work, connected with musical appreciation. Hence Becker states that:

> That preferences are assumed to be stable does not refer to market goods and services but to underlying objects of choice ... such as health, prestige, sensual pleasure, benevolence, and envy. (Becker, 1976: 5)

If an individual suddenly ceases spending some of their income on attending classical music concerts in order to spend this income on purchasing mind-altering drugs, it can be argued that their preferences have not changed, because both sorts of activity involve the attempt to satisfy sensual pleasures. This may seem somewhat implausible, stretching the idea of a 'constant preference' beyond any degree of usefulness.

A further assumption that tends to be made is that preferences are independent: the preferences of any one person are not dependent on the preferences of any other person. However, in the economic sphere, it is clear that, in certain cases, preferences may be interdependent, not independent. For example, in the area of fashion, an individual may purchase a certain good precisely because others are buying it (the 'bandwagon effect').[3] Alternatively, individuals may not buy an item because others have it, or may only buy an item if its price is too high for many others to buy it (snob and 'Veblen effects'). A good example of a market where interdependent preferences seem significant is the labour market: individuals tend to assess the value of any proposed wage or salary changes in terms of what other groups are receiving.[4]

The problem for economics is that interdependent preferences can potentially create havoc for their standard assumption that demand decreases if price increases (Leibenstein, 1950). For example, once a bandwagon has started rolling, individuals may purchase the relevant good in increasing numbers, even if the price of the good increases. Similarly, if individuals value exclusive goods that can only be purchased at a high price, then demand may decrease if price decreases. Hence in the majority of cases in economics, it tends to be assumed that preferences are independent.

However, this assumption again seems more troublesome in the case of political phenomena. For example, in elections it might be suggested that undecided voters prefer to be 'on the winning side', and hence tend to vote for the party or candidate that they believe is likely to win the election. If this is the case then how this individual votes is dependent upon how he or she thinks that the majority of other individuals will vote. Indeed, in the case of the two groups of politicians and voters, it could well be the case that the preferences of each group are, to some extent at least, dependent upon the preferences of the other group ('I prefer this policy option because I am a loyal party supporter, and this is the policy adopted by my party').

RISK AND UNCERTAINTY

As the discussion of Downs in the previous chapter indicated, there is an important distinction between cases where individuals know their alternatives 'for sure', or to cases of decision-making under conditions of certainty, and cases where this does not apply, or decision-making under risk or uncertainty. In the case of most decisions, decision-making does not occur under conditions of certainty. For example, if an individual has to choose between taking or not taking an umbrella with them when going for a walk, their choice will be influenced by their assessment as to the likelihood of it raining. In this case, individuals are characterized as making decisions under conditions of risk or uncertainty and are viewed as maximizing their *expected* utility.

Under decisions of risk or uncertainty, individuals are viewed as attributing probabilities to outcomes. Hence the decision concerning the umbrella will depend upon the individual's assessment as to the probability of rain occurring. In order to appreciate how individuals are viewed as making rational decisions under these circumstances, the following example provided by Audi (1990: 418) is instructive. Imagine a surgeon has been requested by a patient to decide whether surgery or non-surgery is the best way to treat the patient's illness. The surgeon thinks there is a .60 probability of surgery curing the patient, which the surgeon values at 100. However, there is a .40 probability that the patient will die, valued at −75. On the other hand, non-surgery is regarded as having a .50 probability of resulting in a cure, a .20 probability of resulting in death, and a .30 probability of partial remission, valued at 30. (Note probabilities for each option must equal 1.) These possible outcomes are illustrated in Figure 3.1.

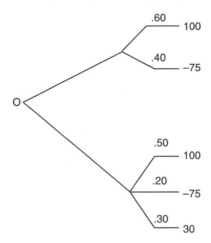

Figure 3.1

Given the values and probabilities assigned to each outcome, what decision should the surgeon arrive at? The option of surgery is (.60 x 100) + (.40 x −75), which gives 30. The option of non–surgery is (.50 x 100) + (.20 x −75) + (.30 x 30), which gives 44. Hence as the expected utility of non–surgery is higher than that of surgery, the rational action is non–surgery. A rational action here is thus an action which scores at least as high as any of the alternatives.

Several points are worth noting. Firstly, it is assumed that values can be assigned to outcomes, and thus a cardinal ordering is being used. Whereas in decision-making under certainty all that mattered was that the individual regarded $x > y$, in decisions under uncertainty or risk it is assumed that the individual knows by how much they prefer x to y. Secondly, although this is decision-making under uncertainty, it is assumed that individuals know *with certainty* what all the potential consequences of their actions will be. Hence in the example above, the surgeon knows that surgery will result in two potential consequences, non–surgery in three potential consequences. These consequences are characterized as 'states of nature'. Thirdly, individuals know how each possible state of nature will affect their utility. Fourthly, individuals can formulate a probability distribution, or 'bet' on the likelihood of each state of nature obtaining.

Again, the informational requirements assumed here are severe. Individuals are assumed to know all possible consequences of action, be able to rank the desirability of these various consequences, and be able to assign probabilities to the likelihood of any consequence coming to pass. However, how is this probability distribution arrived at? At the beginning of this section it was noted that the discussion is concerned with decisions made under conditions of risk or uncertainty. Economists tend to differentiate between decisions under risk and uncertainty by distinguishing between objective and subjective probabilities. For decision-making under risk, probabilities are taken to be objective, or everybody would assign the same probability to the same state of the world. For some decisions, this seems quite reasonable: for example, the probability of a fair coin coming up heads and not tails is 0.5. However, in the case of other decisions, it is not at all clear that objective probabilities are relevant. Two entrepreneurs attempting to predict market conditions a year into the future might arrive at very different conclusions – one might think there is a high probability of high demand for a certain product, the other might think there is a low probability that this state will obtain. Similarly, in the medical decision discussed above, two doctors might assign different probabilities to outcomes.

Decision-making under uncertainty thus characterizes situations where probabilities are assigned subjectively. Different individuals will assign different probabilities to the same states of the world: essentially, any individual's probability assignment is as good as that of anyone else. Intuitively, it might appear that, given this distinction, most decisions are made under conditions of uncertainty, not risk. For example, questions such as how many goals will team x score on Saturday, will it be raining next Tuesday, or which political party will be in power in ten years' time would be expected to elicit different responses from different people.

However, it is worth noting that economists frequently tend to assume that individuals exposed to the same information will arrive at the same subjective probability assumptions (the 'common prior' assumption, or Harsanyi doctrine). From the perspective of political studies, where emphasis is frequently placed on the importance of the issues raised in *interpreting* information, this may well seem an odd assumption. Would we really expect two meteorologists, even if exposed to the same information, to arrive at the same probabilities concerning the possibility of rain next Tuesday? However, the assumption is widely held among economists, although as one notes 'I leave others to defend this assumption . . . I cannot do so' (Kreps, 1990: 111).

This raises significant issues concerning the rationality of beliefs and differences between persons. If one individual believes that the probability of state a obtaining is y, yet another individual, exposed to the same information, believes that the probability of state a obtaining is y_i, it would appear that at least one of these individuals holds an irrational belief. Again, this indicates a certain potential incongruity between how economists incorporate RCT models and how they are frequently used in political studies, where the conditions pertaining to 'rational belief' may not be so stringent. Further, it assumes that differences between individuals are insignificant, as any one individual will formulate the same beliefs as any other individual, given access to the same information. Any idea that individuals may interpret information differently, depending upon their experience, culture or expertise, simply disappears.[5]

It is also worth noting that this difference between conditions of risk and conditions of uncertainty as formulated in a distinction between objective and subjective probabilities is characteristic of neoclassical economics, but is rejected by other economists and social scientists. According to this alternative formulation, situations of uncertainty are not characterized as situations where subjective probabilities are applied, but as situations where *no* probability can be formulated. The conventional, or neoclassical, view of uncertainty is characterized by the economist Kenneth Arrow as follows:

> Uncertainty means we do not have a complete description of the world which we fully believe to be true. Instead, we consider the world to be in one of a range of states. Each state of the world is a description which is complete for all relevant purposes. Our uncertainty consists in not knowing which state is the true one. (Arrow, 1974: 33)

As noted above, there is no 'uncertainty' as to the various alternatives, or states of the world, relevant to the decision-making process. The various states of the world are completely specified – the description of them is 'complete for all relevant purposes'. All that is uncertain is that the individual does not know which state of the world, or alternative, is or will become the 'true' state of the world. However, as the economist Shackle never tired of pointing out, this conception of 'uncertainty' leaves no place for the idea of *novelty*. In Shackle's view, uncertainty is more usefully characterized by the idea that we do not know what it is we do not know. The idea of novelty is important because part of the reason we do not know is because the relevant 'states of the world' have not yet been created.

For example, compare the world now to the world a century ago. Individuals a century ago would not have been in a position to assign probabilities to outcomes such as, in one hundred years' time, 'most households will have a computer' or 'most individuals will have mobile telephones'. How can we assign a probability to a state of the world obtaining where something occurs which we cannot even envisage? Similarly, Elster argues that 'genuine uncertainty' is relevant where complex, far-reaching technological decisions have to be made, arguing that 'assuming that we are facing a choice under uncertainty, does rational-choice theory tell us anything about what we ought to do? The answer is: very little' (Elster, 1986: 6).

However, remaining with the neoclassical definitions of risk and uncertainty, it should be noted that individuals can be differentiated into those who are risk takers, those who are risk averse, and those who are risk neutral. Imagine an individual is offered a lottery ticket for £10 which has .50 probability of winning £20, and thus has an expected return of £10. An individual who is risk neutral will be indifferent between buying and not buying the lottery ticket, whilst a risk loving person will buy the ticket (they may win £20). In contrast, an individual who is risk averse will refuse the ticket as they are unwilling to take the risk of losing. Typically, economic models assume that individuals are risk averse.

A final point is worth noting. As Arrow's definition of uncertainty noted above indicates, in incorporating uncertainty RCT models frequently assume that individuals have *already made* probability assessments about the various possible states of the world, not that they *would* make assessments if required. Thus Audi notes 'one may be cognitively so constituted that if someone asked whether there was a brass band playing in one's backyard, one would immediately dissent. It does not follow that, prior to entertaining this proposition, one believed it false' (Audi, 1990: 419). Again, the theory tends to make significant demands concerning the cognitive abilities of individuals – that they have already made probability assessments, not that they would, if queried on the matter.

AN ECONOMIC OF POLITICS?

One of the concerns frequently raised against RCT is that its advocates are, implicitly or explicitly, adopting a form of intellectual imperialism: they believe that economics offers the prime example of 'good social science practice', and hence all the social sciences should adopt procedures drawn from economics. However, leaving aside the question as to whether economic procedures can or should be applied in explanations of political phenomena, it is worth querying this assumption of a 'successful economic model'.

Firstly, it simply is not the case that RCT forms the basis of all explanations in economics. A number of economists are either agnostic, hostile to or regard as irrelevant the adoption of RCT in economic theories.[6] RCT forms the basis of what is commonly referred to as neoclassical microeconomics, but this form of economics by no means exhausts the whole of economics. It is thus more accurate to describe RCT as the application of a neoclassical microeconomic model of human behaviour to political phenomena, rather than speaking of an 'economic approach' *per se*.

Secondly, it is illusory to think that all economists committed to the use of RCT explanations in economics regard its adoption as a whole-hearted success story. Thus even economists who adopt RCT sometimes question the relevance of the theory. As explored later, it has been argued, despite the claims made in its name, the theory has not been successful at explaining economic phenomena. Further, the theory has not been successful at predicting what individuals, acting economically, will actually do. Hence economists themselves may question the claimed 'success story' of RCT in explaining economic phenomena. As Mandler notes (2001) it is somewhat ironic that the increasing penetration of RCT forms of explanations in political studies coincides with a growing unease, on the part of a number of economists, about the validity of the model in economic explanations.

Thirdly, even if all economists did view the use of RCT as remarkably successful in providing explanations in economics, there is no obvious reason why it should be equally successful in providing explanations in politics. The assumption behind the incorporation of RCT in politics is that the factors relevant to an individual deciding whether to vote in an election are analogous to the factors relevant in deciding whether to purchase a good. It may be the same individual who makes decisions in the market place as the individual who makes decisions in the political sphere. However, it cannot thus be assumed that these decisions are therefore analogous, and can both be explained in similar terms.

The view that RCT has provided a successful basis for explanations in economics which can thus be applied to explanations in politics thus contains a number of contentious assumptions. Firstly, it assumes that there is only one form of explanation in economics, which is false. Secondly, it assumes that economic explanations based on RCT have been successful, which is contentious. Thirdly, it assumes that economic and political phenomena are explicable in a similar manner. RCT may provide elegant explanations, and interesting conclusions, but does it actually help us to understand political phenomena?

RATIONAL CHOICE AND PUBLIC CHOICE

One problem in defining what RCT consists in becomes apparent when reference is made to the considerable amount of literature that is included under the title of 'public choice'. For example, Mueller defines public choice as 'the application of economics to political science' (Mueller, 2003: 1) and McLean states that 'public choice applies economists' methods to politics' (McLean, 1987: 9). These definitions raise the obvious question as to how RCT is distinct from public choice, as both are defined in terms of the application of economic methods to the study of political phenomena.

In attempting to answer this question, Friedman (1996) draws upon the distinction between 'thick' and 'thin' understandings of the rationality assumption. Friedman claims that RCT adopts a 'thin' understanding, which makes no assumptions about the underlying motivations of actors. Hence political actors may be selfish, altruistic, benevolent, or seek spiritual rather than material goods. The only assumption made is that individuals attempt to satisfy their preferences, but no assumption is made concerning the nature of these preferences. In contrast, public choice theories adopt a 'thick' understanding of rationality, which assumes that individuals are necessarily concerned to advance their own material self-interest. Hence on this account public choice theory comprises a subset of RCT – it is RCT with additional assumptions about actor motivation.

Unfortunately, it seems difficult to differentiate between RCT and public choice theories in such a clear-cut manner. For example, social choice theory, discussed later in this chapter, is normally discussed in the public choice literature, yet makes no assumptions about self-interested behaviour. Further, many advocates of the use of RCT models in politics do assume that actors are self-interested. For example, as noted in the first chapter, Elster argues that 'the assumption that agents are selfishly motivated does . . . have a methodological privilege' (Elster, 1985a: 9), whilst Pettit notes that 'rational choice theorists . . . appeal mainly to self-interested desires' (Pettit, 1996: 63). Elster justifies this assumption through arguing that non-selfish behaviour is actually parasitic upon selfish behaviour: there would be no pleasure in giving if there was no pleasure in having. Hence although no definitive demarcation between these approaches seems possible, the following may serve as useful 'broad sweep' generalizations.

Firstly, in terms of subject matter: the public choice literature tends to be concerned with various issues relevant to governmental decision-making. These issues may include decision-making under majority rule, with regard to bureaucratic structures, between and within political parties, and in the general context of aggregating individual preferences. In contrast RCT theories may be applied to more diverse subjects, such as peasant revolutions, class conflict and relationships between international actors. Hence it is possible to speak of 'Rational Choice Marxism', because a number of the issues that Marx dealt with may be open to rational choice explanations. However, the idea of 'Public Choice Marxism' seems rather strange, as Marx was not immediately concerned with the issues that engage public choice theorists. This again makes public choice a subset of RCT, but tends to define public choice in terms of the issues that animate it.

Differentiating the public choice literature in terms of its subject matter would appear to be in keeping with Buchanan's definition of public choice theory as the theory of government failure (Buchanan, 1989: 25). Buchanan is making the point that, for decades, welfare economic has investigated cases of market failure, arguing that such failures require governmental intervention in order to resolve them. The assumption in this literature was that governments would act as 'benevolent despots', acting in 'the public interest', and questions as to whether governments themselves could fail in this regard, or whether individuals in government agencies might have their own interests and agendas, were effectively ignored.

Secondly, the public choice literature tends to be keener to deploy various 'useful techniques' drawn from the economists' mathematical tool-kit. The literature thus tends to be resplendent with various geo-metrical and algebraic formulations. Hence one writer concerned with social choice theory noted that 'social choice theory is a natural subject for an economist with a background in mathematics' (Craven, 1992: ix). However, with a few notable exceptions (e.g. the work of Roemer), the RCT literature tends to be less formalized.

In the end, any differentiation between the rational choice and public choice literatures seems somewhat arbitrary. Hence, according to the position articulated here, the models provided by Downs, Niskanen and Buchanan investigated in the previous chapter would tend to be classified as public choice, whilst the model advanced by Olson would be classified as rational choice. Yet all four models are referred to in both sets of literature.

THE STATUS OF THE THEORY

The previous discussion of Downs raised the issue as to the status of models that incorporate RCT. According to some advocates, RCT is a descriptive theory that offers an account of how individuals actually make choices. Recall that, in the Becker quote in the first chapter, it was claimed that the theory is equally applicable to 'brilliant or stupid persons'. However, in the strong form, which claims that individuals do the best that they can, the theory assumes that individuals are capable of performing complex mathematical feats, when most individuals clearly are not so capable, hence it does not seem to describe actual behaviour.

Alternatively, it might be argued that the weak form of RCT, which assumes only that individuals do the best that they believe that they can, does offer a descriptive theory. Thus Pettit claims that:

> Rational choice theory . . . is focused on actual people in the actual world, not on ideally rational people. And it is directed to try to explain and predict the behaviour of those people, not to articulate lessons in what is normatively rational for them. (Pettit, 1996: 22)

However, as explored in the following chapters, individuals frequently do not make choices in the way RCT assumes that they do, whether the theory is advanced in its strong or weak form. It is thus highly dubious that the theory does describe how individuals actually make choices.

It has thus been argued that the theory is not descriptive, but normative. That is, it offers an account as to how individuals ought to make
choices, in order to be rational. Thus if an individual's behaviour does
not conform to the model, the individual is behaving irrationally. This
appears to be the assumption that Downs makes in developing his
model. Yet there are also a number of situations where it is far from
clear that individuals do the best for themselves by following the RCT
model. It is thus also dubious that the model offers a theory of choice
that individuals ought to follow in all situations. Hence the status of the
model is not at all obvious.

As an example of the latter, take the 'centipede game' in Figure 3.2.
There are two players, A and B, and a series of monetary payments. At
each decision node, the players must decide whether to end the game
or to carry on. Hence at the first decision node, if either player decides
to end the game at this point, then player A receives no units of money,
whilst player B receives one unit. If neither player decides to end the
game at any node, it proceeds to the end, where player B receives
100 units of money, player A 101 units. Intuitively, it would seem rather
silly for any player to end the game at the first node, where A receives 0
units and B receives 1 unit, when considerably more money can be
earned by each player if the game continues.

Figure 3.2

However, if each player is interacting as RCT dictates, then the first
node is exactly where the game will end, as the common knowledge of
rationality assumption (CKR), introduced in the first chapter when
discussing the prisoners' dilemma, ensures this. To appreciate why, take
the last node where A receives 101 units and B 100. Now B would be
better off stopping the game at the node immediately preceding this
end state, as B would then receive 102, rather than 100 if the game
carried on. However, given CKR, then A knows this, and realizes that, if
B stops the game at this node, A will receive 97. Yet if A stops the game
at the previous node, A will receive 98 rather than 97. Hence it is
rational for A to stop the game at the previous node. Again, B knows
this, and so on. The end result is thus that B stops the game at the first
node, at least receiving 1. This problem is known as the problem of
'backward induction', and arises because of the CKR assumption
coupled with a finite game where the pay-offs are equally known to
each player.

The prisoners' dilemma game as explained above was a 'one-off
game' – each individual made one choice, and the game was not

repeated. However, as explored in the case of the reputation for honesty, if the game were repeated over time, surely individuals would come to realize that their actions were self-defeating: they are not achieving the better (if not the best) result for themselves achievable by co-operating? This may be so, but only if the individuals do not know how long this extended play will go on for, otherwise the 'backward induction' logic comes into play. Say both players know that the game will be repeated one hundred times: should they co-operate on the first move, knowing that if they do not, they will end up with their third best scenario, whilst co-operation would at least bring them their second best scenario. Unfortunately, each will realize that, in the final game, whatever occurred before, it will be rational for each to defect. Consequently, by the remorseless logic of backward induction, each will decide it is rational to defect in the penultimate game, and so on, so each will defect in the first game.[7]

METHODOLOGICAL INDIVIDUALISM AND A SCIENCE OF POLITICS

Although the issues of methodological individualism and the scientific study of politics are not necessarily related, they will both be explored in this section. The investigation of RCT so far has referred solely to individuals and their preferences, beliefs and actions. RCT thus embodies a commitment to methodological individualism (MI): a doctrine that builds upon the intuition that the ultimate constituents of the social world are individuals and social events are brought about by people (Watkins, 1973). Although various forms of MI have been advocated, in the case of RCT it is best identified as an explanatory thesis which claims that all explanations of the structure and change of the phenomena that form the object of social science investigation are to be conducted solely in terms of the intentions, beliefs, goals and actions of various individuals (Elster, 1986).

MI is thus a form of reductionism: it claims that all explanations in politics, or the social sciences generally, can be reduced to claims about individuals. The main thrust of the MI thesis can be appreciated through noting the forms of explanations that MI is opposed to. Advocates of MI argue against claims such as the state, which is not an individual but a supra-individual entity, has the 'function' of acting in the interests of the bourgeoisie, or that the structures of capitalism are such that individuals are determined to act in certain ways. Proponents of MI thus reject what is termed 'collectivism', understood as the doctrine that there are supra-individual entities that are prior to the individual in the explanatory order. This 'collectivism' or 'methodological holism' (Watkins, 1973) is closely associated with structural or

67

functional forms of explanation, where political phenomena are explained in terms of a 'function' they serve.

For example, Bowles and Gintis (1976) argue that the educational system exists and persists because it promotes the interests of the capitalist class. Hence a certain social phenomena – the educational system – is explained in terms of a certain 'function' that it serves – promoting capitalist interests. The main objection against this form of explanation is that it fails to offer any account as to how the relevant phenomena came into being, only why they persist, and hence fail to identify the factors relevant to a satisfactory explanation (Elster, 1985a). For example, it would seem that the explanation for the education system consists in indicating that it came into existence because of something it would perform in the *future* – promoting capitalism.

Although not all advocates of MI are necessarily proponents of RCT, an adherence to RCT forms of explanation does entail a commitment to MI. The issues surrounding the debate between MI and alternative forms of explanation are complex. However, an indication of the problems facing the MI aspect of RCT can be appreciated through noting the sort of explanations frequently offered in the main 'model' for RCT – neoclassical economic theory. As any introductory textbook indicates, economists claim that firms maximize profits. However, a firm is not an individual, but is comprised of a number of different individuals. This has led the economist Kenneth Arrow to note that, although neoclassical economics does appear to agree that all explanations must refer to the actions of individuals, 'every economic model one can think of includes irreducible social principles and concepts' (Arrow, 1994: 2). Arrow is not only referring to the frequent reference to households, firms, corporations, etc., in economic models, but argues that a term such as 'technical information' is irreducibly social, hence not necessarily explicable in individualistic terms.

Many explanations in politics appear to rely on claims about complex social entities, not individuals. This issue is important, because many of the areas investigated by advocates of RCT appear to involve such social entities as political parties, bureaucracies, labour organizations, and so on. MI may remain plausible here, if explanations about entities such as bureaucracies and political parties, say, can be reduced to explanations concerning individuals and their intentions. The question of the MI basis of RCT models will be periodically addressed in the course of the investigations into RCT explanations of political phenomena pursued in the following chapters.

The claim by advocates of MI that functional forms of explanation do not provide adequate explanations invariably means that function explanations do not indicate the relevant *causal mechanisms*. The following chapters will investigate in more detail what the identification of such causal mechanisms may entail. For now, it is useful to note that the claim that such mechanisms need identifying is closely related to the claim that RCT has placed investigations in politics on a more 'scientific' basis than was previously the case, as the following quote illustrates:

> The political science that a college student at the end of World War II might have encountered was primarily *descriptive* and *judgemental*. It was much less orientated toward *explanation* and *analysis*. The transformation of the study of politics from storytelling and anecdote swapping . . . to explanation and analysis constitutes a significant movement along a scientific trajectory . . . Political science isn't rocket science, but this emphasis on explanation and analysis moves it closer in form to the physical and natural sciences than was the case in an earlier era. (Shepsle & Boncheck, 1997: 7–8)

The introduction of RCT in political studies is thus seen as inherently progressive. Whilst previously political studies were primarily concerned with 'storytelling', it is now able to provide, through incorporating RCT models, explanation and analysis of political phenomena. Advocates of RCT are frequently enamoured by the perceived success story of the natural sciences, and believe that the social sciences can become more 'progressive' if they adopt the methods of the natural sciences. RCT is thus seen as placing the study of political phenomena on a scientific basis that was previously lacking.

One of the hallmarks of natural science often cited by commentators is that scientific knowledge is empirically accurate. Although what exactly this entails is open to dispute, a rough generalization can be taken to be 'the more predictive success, the better' (Kincaid, 1996: 50). Hence if RCT is providing a scientific basis for political studies, it would seem plausible to assume that the theory has been rather good at generating predictions concerning political phenomena. However, as the investigation of Downs's theory revealed, and following chapters explore in more detail, the predictive success of RCT has been, at best, ambiguous, at worst a downright failure.

Given the claimed scientific status of RCT it might initially seem that any such failure is damning. RCT claims to be scientific, one of the defining features of science is frequently taken to be the ability to formulate correct empirical predictions, yet RCT models often fail this empirical test. However, advocates of RCT remain undaunted by this problem:

> The criteria for evaluating rational choice models are rather different from those used to judge more conventional empirical approaches. For the latter, we tend to explore the robustness of their empirical generalisations about the real world. For rational choice models we tend to make judgements on the basis of what we think about their assumptions and their internal logic. (Laver, 1997: 6)

Questioning assumptions and internal logic seems undoubtedly sound procedure regarding any theory in the social sciences. However, it is not clear why this questioning means issues about the empirical soundness of the theory should be apparently set to one side. A certain scepticism seems warranted regarding the claimed scientific status of RCT, as the models it produces do not necessarily follow the procedures often used to distinguish between good and bad scientific practice.

A RETURN TO GAME THEORY

The first chapter introduced the prisoners' dilemma game, which is an example of a non–cooperative game which can either be played as a one-off game or repeatedly (an iterated game). However, there are other forms of games that have been used to illustrate features in political life. Imagine two countries in dispute about a piece of land, where each claim it for themselves. Each country has a choice between being aggressive ('hawk') or being acquiescent ('dove'). The pay-offs are represented in Figure 3.3. If both countries act as hawks, they fight. If they both act as doves, they divide the disputed land between them. If one acts as a hawk, and the other acts as a dove, then the hawk gets the disputed land. In this case each country is better off acting as a hawk if the other acts as a dove (thus gaining the disputed land), and better off acting as a dove if the other acts as a hawk (losing the land, but avoiding the fight). In this case there are two Nash equilibria (hawk, dove), (dove, hawk): each is better acting as a dove if they expect the

| | Country 1 | |
	Hawk	Dove
Hawk (Country 2)	−2, −2	2, 0
Dove (Country 2)	0, 2	1, 1

Figure 3.3

other to play hawk, and hawk if they expect the other to play dove (Hargreaves Heap & Varoufakis, 1995: 198).[8] In this game, no one player has a dominant strategy.

Of course what complicates this game is the fact that each player has an incentive to indicate that they would act as a hawk, even if they may not, in order to persuade the other player to act as a dove. The hawk/dove game hence provides an illustration of the posturing, brinkmanship, pretence and threats that surface in a number of conflict situations

The 'chicken game' has the same form as the hawk/dove game. In the chicken game, for example, two individuals decide to resolve a dispute between them by riding straight at each other, with the loser being deemed the one who turns away first. If neither turn away (both act as 'hawks'), they crash, risking serious injury. If both act as doves, they avoid injury, but neither can be deemed the winner. The pay-offs can thus be modelled along the lines of the chicken/hawk game. Other games can be represented as co-ordination games. For example, if you encounter someone walking towards you on a narrow bridge over a gorge, where you can both just pass, should you move to your left or your right? Pay-offs are represented in Figure 3.4. In Figure 3.4, if each go to either their left or their right, they will pass unhindered. However, if one chooses to go to their left whilst the other chooses right, they will collide, with potentially disastrous results. Here, both going left and both going right are Nash equilibria, although it is not at all clear which of these strategies should be chosen: the two walkers must somehow co-ordinate their actions. Co-ordination games have

Walker 1

	Left	Right
Left	0, 0	−2, −2
Right	−2, −2	0, 0

Walker 2

Figure 3.4

been used to indicate how conventions (discussed in Chapter 5) may evolve. For example, in Britain there is a convention to drive on the left hand side of the road, whereas in the United States the convention is to drive on the right. It does not matter which convention is chosen, as long as all drivers in the respective countries abide by the same convention. Hence the convention can be viewed as coming about to resolve co-ordination problems.

Schelling (1963) has conducted some experiments concerned with co-ordination problems, and found that individuals frequently can find ways of co-ordinating their behaviour around what he termed 'focal points'. For example, imagine you and your friend become parted from each other's company in New York, where would you go to try and meet up with your friend (assuming neither of you have mobile phones)? Most people answered the information booth at Grand Central Station. Similarly, you and a partner are asked to name heads or tails as the result of tossing a coin. If you both call the same, you win a prize. Most people call 'heads'.

Game theory has been used in order to explain a number of political phenomena. However, some of the examples offered above also reveal the weaknesses of the theory: if no dominant strategy clearly exists, then it is not possible to predict what the outcome of any situation will be, as multiple equilibrium positions exist. Yet there are various ways that predictions concerning outcomes can be made in game theory, even if each player does not have a dominant strategy. For example, take the following example, the Battle of the Bismarck Sea, which uses a situation that actually occurred during World War II.

Admiral Imamura has been ordered to transport troops across the Bismarck Sea, and has two options, the shorter Northern Route or the longer Southern Route. Admiral Kenney wants to bomb the troop ships, and the time for this is reduced if he sends his planes in the wrong direction, and then has to recall them. The pay-offs are shown in Figure 3.5.

IMAMURA

		North	South
KENNEY	North	2, −2	2, −2
	South	1, −1	3, −3

Figure 3.5

Figure 3.5 represents a 'zero sum game' as the advantages to one player for any move are equal to the disadvantages for the other: the players' preferences are mutually opposed. Neither player has a dominant strategy: Kenney would choose South if Imamura chose South, and North if Imamura chose North. In contrast, Imamura chooses North if Kenney chose South, and be indifferent between North and South if Kenney chose North. However, despite no player having a dominant strategy, Kenney seeks to maximize his bombing opportunities, and thus may adopt a *maximin* strategy: that is, he attempts to ensure the best of the worst possible outcomes (seeks to maximize his minimum pay-off) (Colman, 1995: 57–8). Kenney thus seeks to avoid the pay-off 1, resulting if he chooses South whilst Imamura chooses North. Hence, in adopting a maximin strategy, Kenney chooses North. In contrast, Imamura seeks to minimize the number of days' bombing, and thus adopts a *minimax* strategy, which seeks to minimize the maximum (negative) pay-off. Imamura thus avoids South, as it could result if three days' bombing if Kenney chooses South. Thus Imamura on a minimax strategy also chooses North.

Alternatively, this choice of strategies can be explained in terms of *weakly dominant strategies* (Rasmusen, 1989: 31). A weakly dominant strategy is a player's best response to any strategy the other players might pick in so far as whatever strategy they pick, hers is no smaller than with any other strategy, and greater in some combinations. For Imamura, North is a weakly dominant strategy, as the pay-off from choosing North is no lower than the pay-off from choosing South, yet greater if Kenney picks South. What move is it rational for Kenney to make? He does not have even a weakly dominant strategy. However, if he believes that Imamura will choose his weakly dominant strategy, then he will reason that Imamura will not pick South, and will pick North. Kenney now has a strongly dominant strategy, which is to pick North. Hence whether the decision process is carried out in terms of minimax/maximin or weakly dominant strategies, the prediction is that both Imamura and Kenney will both pick North, which was what actually happened.

The example above in terms of weakly dominant strategy predicts North/North, and this is known as an *iterated dominant strategy equilibrium*. What Kenney and Imamura do is delete a weakly dominated strategy, then recalculate until one strategy remains for each player. Each player is assumed to go through a process whereby dominated strategies are successively eliminated. To illustrate this further, take the game illustrated in Figure 3.6 (from Hargreaves Heap & Varoufakis, 1995: 47). Given the pay-offs above, how will the game proceed? Strategy C4 will never be played by player C, as one of her other strategies is always better. Hence if R plays R1, C will play C3, if R2, then C2, if R3 then C2, if R4, then C1. C4 is thus a dominated strategy and C will delete it as an option. Player R will realize this, and hence will delete option R4, as this option will only be played as a response to C4, which has been eliminated. Player C will then delete C1, as this will

	C1	C2	C3	C4
R1	5, 10	0, 11	1, 20	10, 10
R2	4, 0	1, 1	2, 0	20, 0
R3	3, 2	0, 4	4, 3	50, 1
R4	2, 93	0, 92	0, 91	100, 90

Figure 3.6

only be played as a response to R4, now eliminated. Player R will thus delete R1, as this would only be played if C1 was played, which is now eliminated. C will thus delete C3, as this would only be played against R1, now eliminated. C thus has only strategy C2 remaining, and hence R will play R2, which 'beats' R1. Hence (R2, C2) is the iterated dominant equilibrium in the game.

The games considered so far have all been games of complete information, where all players know the rules of the game. Hence the players know the pay-offs and strategies available to themselves and all other players. To say that all players have complete information does not imply they all thus have perfect information, as each may not know how the other will respond (e.g. the Battle of the Bismarck Sea above). However, it could be that the players have *asymmetric information*, or private information. The idea of asymmetric information was introduced in the previous chapter in the course of the discussion of Niskanen, where, in this case, one player knows something that the other player or players do not. Take the example shown in Figure 3.7 (from Hargreaves Heap *et al.*, 1992: 121). Here, Jane does not know Fred's pay-off for playing R, although Fred himself knows this pay-off. Jane's best response to Fred playing L is T, and to Fred playing R is to play B. She can also see that, if X is less than 2, Fred will choose L, and Fred will choose R if X is more than 2. How does Jane react? The assumption is that Jane will attach a subjective probability distribution to the range of possible values of X, thus forming an estimate of X. For example, Jane may think that X will fall in the range between 0 and

	Fred		
		L	R
Jane	T	2, 2	1, X
	B	1, 2	2, X

Figure 3.7

3 with equal probability, hence assigning an expected value of 1.5 to X, in which case she expects Fred to choose L, and hence she chooses T.

It is worth noting that, although this game involves asymmetric information, it does not involve any great deviation from a game of complete information. It is still being assumed that, even though Fred has private information, Jane knows that she has this information, and is able to assign a probability distribution concerning what this information provides. Hence if Fred chooses, against Jane's expectation, to play R, it is simply the case that Jane has assigned a wrong probability distribution to X. Even with asymmetric information, the game involves risk, not uncertainty.

However, it may be the case that Fred possesses information that Jane is completely unaware of. Indeed, Jane might be completely unaware of the possibility of Fred possessing any such private information. In this case Jane will not be able to assign any probability distribution, and hence may be genuinely *surprised* by the action that Fred takes. The claim that 'I did not know you could do that' captures a situation where one person knows something others do not, and consequently the (ignorant) others do not even think a certain action is possible. This is the form of situation that Shackle, as noted above, refers to as a situation exhibiting 'novelty'.

The idea of asymmetric information plays a key role in some of the RCT models investigated in the following sections, and hence deserves further investigation. However, before doing this, it is worth briefly noting some of the other terms that are frequently used in connection with game theory (though not necessarily solely in this context).

Tit-for-tat

Tit-for-tat refers to a possible strategy response in iterated (played more than once) non-cooperative games such as the prisoners' dilemma. Basically, a player adopting tit-for-tat chooses to co-operate on the first and subsequent moves in a game such as the prisoners' dilemma, switching to defect if the other player chooses defect. The tit-for-tat player then selects defect for all subsequent moves, unless the other player selects co-operate, in which case the tit-for-tat player returns to co-operation in the subsequent move. Hence the player chooses a strategy rule in the form 'I will play strategy S in the first round, and in subsequent rounds will do whatever player 2 did in the previous round'.

Reputation

This idea of 'reputation' was introduced in the previous chapter in connection with honesty, where, in repeated games, individuals may forgo immediate benefits in order to secure longer-term benefits. Hence a firm may make more profits in a 'one-off' sale though producing shoddy goods. However, if the firm produces over time, it might forgo producing shoddy goods in order to cultivate a reputation for producing quality goods. As explored further below, this sort of situation assumes asymmetric information. Buyers purchase the goods not knowing that they are shoddy. However, having purchased the goods and realizing them to be shoddy, buyers boycott the firm from thereon (Kreps, 1990: 531).

Random or Mixed Strategy

In this case the individual choice of strategies is random, selected by, say, the tossing of a coin. The intuition here is that it may be advantageous to be unpredictable. For example, a fast bowler in cricket may well be able to take a batsman's wicket by bowling the occasional, unexpected, slow ball (Hargreaves Heap & Varoufakis, 1995: 71). How does the bowler decide when to bowl the slow ball? If any system, or rule, is adopted, the batsman will soon learn what this rule is, and hence be expecting the slow ball. The best 'system' may thus be a random one: say throwing a dice before each over, and bowling the slow ball according to the number thrown up.

Undoubtedly, game theoretical models have become highly influential in economics, particularly microeconomics, over the last couple of decades. However, it is worth noting a few problems with these models. Firstly, as some of the above examples illustrate, the results of the models may well be indeterminate: a number of strategies may be possible for each player, and it cannot be predicted which strategies will be chosen. Hence it is frequently the case that the outcome of games cannot be predicted. Secondly, as with RCT in general, game theory models do not inquire into how or why individuals may have the preferences they do. As Berger and Offe note, 'the game starts only after the actors have been constituted, and their order of preferences has been formed as a result of processes that cannot themselves be considered as being part of the game' (Berger & Offe, 1982: 525). Thirdly, the models frequently tend to make heroic assumptions about the capacity of individuals to process information. In this sense they are similar to economic models that assume individuals will do the best they can, rather than the weaker assumption frequently adopted in RCT models in politics, which assume that individuals will do the best that they believe that they can.

Before leaving the subject of game theory, it is interesting to consider the problem that has become termed 'Newcomb's paradox', named after the physicist who first invented it (Nozick, 1990). Assume you become friendly with an individual who, the more you know them, the more you become impressed with this individual's apparently amazing powers of prediction. Not only does the individual seem to be able to correctly predict what you will do, they are always invariably correct when predicting what your friends will do. Indeed, the individual's powers of prediction are so astounding that you seriously believe they may have originated from another planet.

However, one day your amazing friend informs you that they must leave, and as a leaving present they have left you two boxes, A and B. You have to choose between two options: the first option involves you choosing to open both boxes, A and B, whereas the second option involves you choosing to open only box B. One of these boxes, box A, is transparent, and you can see that it contains £1,000 for certain. However, the other box, box B, is opaque, and your friend tells you that it contains either £0 or £1million. The twist here is that, if your friend has predicted that you will only open box B, then they will have put £1million in box B. However, if your friend has predicted that you will choose both boxes, then they will have put £0 in box B. Consequently, if you choose to open just box B, and your friend has correctly predicted this choice, then you will receive £1million. However, if you choose to open both boxes, and your friend has correctly predicted that this is what you will do, then box B is empty, and you only receive the £1,000 from box A. Should you open both boxes A and B or only box B?

The paradox arises because it seems possible to give equally compelling arguments for either choice. For example, as your friend has always predicted correctly, then, if you only open box B, the friend will have predicted this, and have placed £1million in the box. Similarly, if you open both boxes, then your friend will have predicted this also, and box B will be empty. Hence choose only to open box B. Alternatively, it could be argued that, as box B already contains either £0 or £1million, then nothing you can do after the money has already been placed can possibly affect the result. Hence you should open both boxes, as at least you will receive the £1,000 in box A. If box B contains nothing, then it would still have contained nothing even if you had chosen to open only box B.

Interestingly, two of the decision-making principles already discussed can point to different conclusions, depending upon which scenario you adopt (Colman, 1995: 304ff). According to the principle of expected utility maximization, you should make the choice which yields the maximum expected pay-off. If you choose both boxes, your friend will almost certainly have predicted this, and you receive £1,000. However, if you select to open just box B then, your friend having predicted this, you will receive £1million: hence only open box B. However, on the dominant strategy principle, then the dominant strategy might be to open both boxes: the pay-offs are represented in Figure 3.8.

		YOUR FRIEND	
		ONLY B WILL BE TAKEN	BOTH A & B WILL BE TAKEN
YOURSELF	JUST B TAKEN	£1MILLION	£0
	BOTH A & B TAKEN	£1 MILLION + £1,000	£1,000

Figure 3.8

ASYMMETRIC INFORMATION

This section of the chapter will investigate in more detail the subject of asymmetric information. Two particular conditions that may result from asymmetric information are *moral hazard* (hidden action) and *adverse selection*. Moral hazard refers to situations where one party to a transaction may undertake certain actions that affect a second party's valuation of the transaction, but cannot be monitored or enforced by the second party (Kreps, 1990: 577). For example, if you hire some workers to fit out your new kitchen, you would like to think that they would work hard, efficiently, and do a good job. If you thought they would not work in this manner, you would not be willing to pay them the sum of money you have agreed. However, barring observing their actions continually, you have no obvious way of monitoring the situation. This form of moral hazard is often known as the principal/agent problem, where one individual (the principal) hires another (the agent) to perform some task that the principal cannot adequately monitor. Niskanen's model of bureaucracy, discussed in Chapter 2, assumed this form of informational asymmetry between the sponsor and the provider.

Alternatively, take an insurance company that is either insuring a factory against the risk of fire or a driver against the risk of an accident. In the case of the fire insurance, the company would prefer it if the company took steps to avoid the possibility of fire – for example, by not storing potentially inflammable substances close to fire risks. With the car insurance, the company would prefer the car driver to drive carefully and conscientiously. However, in neither case can the insurance company continually monitor the compliance or otherwise of the other party with these preferences.

The 'solution' to these problems is for the first party to offer the second party an *incentive* to act in the way that the first party prefers. For example, you might initially only pay the workers some of the money for the kitchen conversion, reserving the remainder until you have had the work inspected and judged adequate. Alternatively, you might offer them more money if they complete the work, satisfactorily, in a certain time period. Similarly, the insurance company might require the company to pay the first 10 per cent of any damage caused by fire, and offer the motorist a discount ('no claims discount') if there is no claim against the insurance.

Adverse selection refers to a situation where a particular good may come in a variety of qualities, and one party to the transaction, but not the other, knows the quality in advance (Kreps, 1990: 626). Take the following example, drawn from Akerloff (1970 – see also Kreps, 1990: 625ff). Imagine you possess a used car which you know to be in a good condition, and which you wish to sell for £2,500. Suppose a buyer is prepared to pay up to £3,000 for a car like the one you are selling, one which is in good condition. It may seem that a trade would be readily established. However, the problem for you is that of convincing the buyer that you have a car in the required condition: after all, sellers of cars, whether good or poor, invariably claim that their cars are in good condition.

Suppose the buyer is willing to pay £3,000 for a car in good condition, and £2,000 for a car in a poor condition, and guesses that $\frac{2}{3}$ of the cars for sale are in a poor condition. As the buyer has no way of telling which cars are in good condition and which are in poor condition, the buyer puts the value of a car at £2,333.33. Hence the only cars sold are those in a bad condition (whose owners are prepared to accept £1,000 and leap at £2,333.33), and you cannot sell your car.

Insurance markets again offer pertinent examples of the problems raised by adverse selection. For example, say a firm offers health insurance to any applicant at a sum of £x. However, assuming that the firm does not undertake checks on the health of individuals, this action will result in both 'good' and 'bad' health risks receiving insurance. Consequently, if you are in good health, it might be worth you obtaining a medical certificate stating so, and presenting this to the company in an attempt to receive a refund.

However, if the firm refuses, it may be tempting for another firm which does require individual health assessments to enter the market and offer health insurance at a lower price to individuals who are in a good state of health. The upshot of this form of manoeuvring may be that any individuals in poor states of health, or those displaying certain risk factors, may not be able to secure health insurance at any price.

Whereas problems of moral hazard may be alleviated by providing incentives, adverse selection issues are alleviated through *signalling*. Hence if you know your car is in good condition, but the buyer does not, it is advantageous for you to provide a 'signal' indicating the quality of the car. You might, for example, have a full record of the service history of the car to provide to the potential buyer. Alternatively, you might ask a motoring organization to inspect the vehicle, and make a copy of this inspection certificate available to potential buyers.

Issues surrounding moral hazard and adverse selection can readily be identified in political studies: for example, how does a voter know that an individual will make a good President prior to voting them into office? How does a voter know that their chosen candidate will pursue the policies they were elected on? However, once informational asymmetries are admitted, then problems may well be raised concerning the possibility of formulating predictions, as the following example, drawn from Grossman and Stiglitz, illustrates (Grossman & Stiglitz, 1976: 1980).

Assume a certain asset in fixed supply is on sale, and there are two groups of potential buyers. One of these groups – the informed – are prepared to engage in the costly activity of information gathering, in order to obtain information about the potential returns available in holding the asset, whilst the other group is not prepared to engage in the costly activity of information gathering. Say the informed group, on collecting information, arrive at the conclusion that the returns for holding the asset seem good, and hence buy the asset, thus raising the price.

The uninformed group do not possess the relevant information. However, when the price of the asset starts to rise, they judge (correctly) that the price rise is a result of other individuals discovering that the asset is worth purchasing (the uninformed infer that the price increase indicates that the quality of the asset is 'good'). The uninformed individuals then also buy the asset, until presumably the price of the asset rises until it correctly reflects the information about its likely return. At this point, the price fully reflects the information available. However, if the price of the asset fully reflects the information available, then there is no longer any incentive for the informed group of individuals to collect information. As no information is being collected, then no information is now being reflected in the price of the asset, and the price of the asset falls until the informed individuals judge it is now worth engaging in information collection.

Two morals can be drawn from this cautionary tale. Firstly, given asymmetric information, there may not be any determinate solutions to problems. Hence in the above there is no determinate price, but a range of prices is possible. Secondly, despite the claim that RCT represents the incorporation of economics into politics, it frequently, as indicated previously, adopts rather outmoded methods of economic analysis. These two factors may well be interrelated. This is because advocates of RCT in politics frequently justify the use of the model through referring to its scientific, predictive, abilities. However, a number of studies in recent economic theories, especially those connected with informational asymmetries, challenge the ability of models to arrive at determinate results (Stiglitz, 1987).

This chapter has investigated in more detail the axioms and assumptions relevant to RCT models, and explored further certain aspects of game theory. It would thus now seem appropriate to investigate the work of two authors who adopt game theoretical and formal theories in analysing political phenomena. The first author investigated is Schelling, who utilizes game theory, whilst the second author, Arrow, presents a formal model of problems in democratic decision-making.

SCHELLING: STRATEGY AND CONFLICT

Schelling's book *The Strategy of Conflict* is an attempt to use game theory in order to investigate certain issues that arise, although not exclusively, in the area of international relations. Schelling thus investigated areas such as bargaining, limited war, mutual deterrence and surprise attack. Schelling's field of study was the 'strategy of conflict' (1963: 3) and, as an investigation into strategy, the interest lay with the exploitation of potential force, rather than the application of force. Schelling's main concern in investigating the exploitation of potential force was to investigate the various 'bargaining games' that could be involved.

Although the analysis studies these bargaining games based on 'the assumption of rational behaviour' (Schelling, 1963: 4), Schelling is somewhat critical of (then) contemporary game theory.[9] For example, he regards game theory to be operating at too high a level of abstraction to be immediately relevant to a number of issues (Schelling, 1963: 10), and criticizes the tendency for game theory to focus upon non-cooperative, zero sum games such as the prisoners' dilemma. The criticisms of the tendency for game theorists to focus on non-cooperative games is advanced because Schelling believes that many conflict situations are based upon mutual common interests, as well as conflicts of interest. For example, in the case of deterrence, then:

> Even in international affairs, deterrence is as relevant to relations between friends as between potential enemies ... The deterrence concept requires that there be both conflict and common interest between the parties involved: it is as inapplicable to a situation of pure and complete antagonism of interest as it is to the case of pure and complete common interest. (Schelling, 1963: 11)

Consequently, whereas a non-cooperative game such as the prisoners' dilemma represent one extreme, and a co-operative or co-ordination game, such as two motorists negotiating a narrow road, represents the other extreme, Schelling argues that many situations in international affairs are best viewed as lying somewhere between these extremes, involving elements of both conflict and co-operation.

It was noted earlier in this chapter that Schelling had drawn attention to the significance of 'focal points' in order to illustrate how individuals may co-ordinate their actions tacitly, or in the absence of communication. For example, two individuals who become separated in New York will both tend to think of meeting at the information booth at Grand Central Station as a good place to regain contact with the other. Schelling notes that what is important in these examples of focal points is the attempt by the individuals involved to co-ordinate expectations in the absence of communication. Hence I go to Grand Central Station because I expect you also to go there, and you go because you also expect me to go there. Consequently:

> Tacit coordination of expectations ... is a real possibility and in some contexts a remarkably reliable one. The 'coordination' of expectations is analogous to the 'coordination' of behaviour when communication is cut off; and, in fact, they both involve nothing more nor less than intuitively perceived mutual expectations. (Schelling, 1963: 71)

The example of two individuals co-ordinating expectations through choosing a 'focal point' such as Grand Central Station assumes that the individuals involved have a common interest: they both want to meet up. However, Schelling further argues that focal points can be significant in situations where individuals have divergent interests. For example, one experiment he conducted consisted in two individuals having to co-ordinate their expectations through selecting 'heads' or 'tails', where both receive a prize if they choose the same, neither receive a prize if they choose differently. In a common interest game, as discussed earlier, the tendency is for both individuals to call 'heads'.

However, Schelling offers a similar example where, in this case, if both choose 'heads' individual A receives $3 and individual B $2, whereas if both call 'tails' individual A receives $2, individual B $3. Again, both individuals receive nothing if their calls are different. Clearly, individual A would rather the two players co-ordinate their actions on 'heads', individual B on 'tails', and hence they have divergent interests. However, Schelling discovered that, even in this case of divergent interests, individuals tended overall to call 'heads'. Consequently, even given divergent interests, 'heads' remains a focal point.

Schelling argues that this 'tacit bargaining' is important in a number of areas in international affairs. For example, both sides to war tend to accept there are certain limits to the war, even in the absence of communication: gas was not used in World War II (Schelling, 1963: 75). However, he also argues that focal points are important in areas where communication is involved, such as negotiations, not just in cases of tacit bargaining.

Focal points indicate the significance of interlocking expectations, where choices depend upon expectations concerning the behaviour of others. Hence:

> The best choice for each depends upon what he expects the other to do, knowing that each is similarly guided, so that each is aware that each must try to guess what the second guesses the first will guess the second to guess and so on, in the familiar spiral of reciprocal expectations. (Schelling, 1963: 87)

The case of interlocking expectations has already been encountered in the case of standard game theory, as investigated in the first chapter and earlier in the present chapter. Hence recall that common knowledge of rationality entails that each expects the other to act rationally, and expects the other to expect themselves to act rationally, and so on. Further, a dominant strategy was defined in terms of the best response to what each expects the other to do. So how does Schelling's account of interdependent expectations differ from that prevalent in standard game theory? Schelling argues that strategies 'have symbolic . . . characteristics that transcend the mathematical structure of the game' (Schelling, 1963: 96). Hence the interlocking expectations that Schelling is interested in permit individuals to co-ordinate actions even where, from a purely mathematical perspective, the game does not possess any clear strategies and corresponding solutions.

The extreme computational feats demanded of individuals in RCT models, especially in its strong form, have been questioned on a number of occasions in the previous chapters. Schelling is making the point that individuals can arrive at solutions to potential and actual conflicts without performing these feats. Indeed, adopting mathematical solutions to conflict situations may well serve as a form of a 'focal point'. For example, if two mathematicians are attempting to co-ordinate their expectations, and each knows that the other is a mathematician, they may well appeal to mathematical 'focal points' in order to achieve co-ordination. However, in other cases, 'there is no presumption that mathematical game theory is essential to the process of reaching agreement, hence no basis for assuming that mathematics is a main source of inspiration in the convergence process' (Schelling, 1963: 114).

As Schelling acknowledges (Schelling, 1963: 91, 106), the interlocking expectations that concern him bear more similarities to those found in norms and traditions, rather than mathematical game models. The significance of interlocking expectations in the case of norms is explored in more detail in Chapter 5. Suffice for now to take an example of a norm, say, not smoking in certain designated areas. Part of the reason that individuals do not smoke in non-smoking areas is because they expect others to expect them not to smoke there, and the part of the reason that others expect you not to smoke is because they expect you to expect that they expect you not to smoke, and so on.

Schelling further questions the assumption of symmetry that, as noted, is frequently made in game theoretical models: the assumption that each player knows not only their own pay-offs, but those of the other players as well. However, he objects that in many 'exciting cases' (Schelling, 1963: 117) an individual cannot assume that the opponents' values are symmetrical to their own. Hence in many situations, especially those involving differences in cultures, it may not be possible for an individual to assess what value the other would attach to certain outcomes.

One area explored by Schelling concerns the relationship between threats, promises and commitment in bargaining situations. To illustrate some of the issues involved here, take the game illustrated in Figure 3.9 (Schelling, 1963: 126). As before, the first set of figures in each partition represent the pay-offs to player 2, the second set of figures the pay-offs to player 1. Assume that player 1 makes the first 'move', then he would choose strategy 1, leaving player 2 the choice between receiving 1 (strategy 1) or 0 (strategy 2). The assumption is hence that if player 1 chooses strategy 1, player 2 will also choose strategy 1. However, what if player 2 issues a threat that, unless player 1 selects strategy 2, and insist in playing strategy 1, then player 2 will choose strategy 2, resulting in a zero pay-off for both?

Now if player 1 does choose strategy 1, it would clearly not be in the interests of player 2 to choose strategy 2, and both players know this. However, if player 1 believes that player 2 is *committed* to play 2 if they play 1, that is if player 1 believes that the threat is credible, then player 1 might choose to play strategy 2: a pay-off of 1 is better than zero. Schelling suggests that this way of modelling threats offers insights when investigating phenomena such as 'deterrence, atomic blackmail,

		PLAYER 1	
		1	2
PLAYER 2	1	1 2	2 1
	2	0 0	0 0

Figure 3.9

the balance of terror' (Schelling, 1963: 119). To illustrate how this could be so, take the example of nuclear deterrence between the two superpowers, the USA and the Soviet Union, during the cold war period.

The argument would be, somewhat crudely, that country A would not make a move that would advantage country A, and comparatively disadvantage country B, because country B would then threaten (nuclear) retaliation, and both countries would lose out. However, there is something rather puzzling about this logic, which can be appreciated in terms of the figure above. The assumption here is that player 1 would rather play strategy 1. However, the threat of player 2 choosing strategy 2 in response, if credible, would lead player 1 to choose strategy 2. However, if player 1 did choose strategy 1, then it would be irrational for player 2 to select strategy 2: why would player 2 choose a pay-off of zero if a pay-off of 1 is available through playing strategy 1 in response?

Hence the threat can only work if player 1 thinks that player 2 would act irrationally, and choose the zero pay-off. However, whilst player 1 must assume that player 2 would act irrationally, player 2 must assume that player 1 would act rationally. That is, given the threat of player 2 choosing strategy 2 if player 1 chooses strategy 1, player 1 will choose strategy 2. Hence player 1 must assume that player 2 would act irrationally, and player 2 must assume that player 1 would act rationally. The model hence assumes both rational and irrational behaviour. Hence the use of models similar to that of Schelling have been criticized as 'models' of deterrence theory as follows:

> The only way to explain the 'remarkable stability' of the Cold War period is to assume, simultaneously, that the players are at once rational and irrational. The players are rational when they are being deterred – presumably because they fear the cost of initiating a conflict – but they must also be presumed to be irrational when they are deterring an opponent and threatening to retaliate – presumably because they do not fear the cost of conflict. (Zagare, 2004: 116)

Hence in the Schelling model above, player 1 illustrates the rational component of the argument – accepting 1,2 rather than 2,1 in order to avoid 0,0. However, player 1's strategies assume irrationality – accepting 0,0 rather than 1,2 in order to try and achieve 2,1.

It could be argued that the question of the usefulness of game theory in understanding issues such as deterrence may not be quite as bleak as Zagare's comment, above, indicates. For instance, it may be possible to provide a model where each player assumes that the other player is irrational.[10] In this case, for example, each player may assign a probability to the outcome whereby the other player adopts a strategy that appears to be irrational. However, it is far from clear that even this adaptation would alleviate the problems of Schelling's model, as the model requires one player to *convince* the other that they would behave irrationally, when they have not, until now, necessarily done anything to warrant this level of conviction.

ARROW'S IMPOSSIBILITY THEOREM

Kenneth Arrow's book *Social Choice and Individual Values*, first published in 1951, was another major work in the field of rational/public choice, leading to a number of wide-ranging discussions on the subject of social choice theory. Although Arrow's theorem is frequently regarded, along with the works of Downs, Olson, and Buchanan and Tullock, as one of the pioneering works in the area, it displays a higher level of formalism than the works by the other authors. It thus seems appropriate to discuss the theorem at this stage, rather than in the previous chapter.

It is worth noting that the term 'social choice theory' can refer to either a particular *field* of study of a particular *approach* or series of approaches (Sen, 1986b: 213). This 'dual aspect' recalls the discussion of the difference between the public choice and rational choice literature discussed earlier in the chapter, where, say, public choice could be defined either in terms of an approach (assumes self-interested behaviour) or a field (concerned with governmental decision-making, etc.).

Arrow himself states that 'social choice theory was intended to provide a rational framework for decisions that, for whatever reason, have to be made collectively' (Arrow, 1977: 3). Hence the main question asked in social choice theory is of the form: how can the different views, interests, preferences or judgements of different individuals or groups in a society become aggregated into collective interests, preferences, etc. (Cain, 2001: 83; Sen, 1986b)? The areas covered in social choice theory include the following (Cain, 2001):

1) Issues in social welfare measurement. For example, how can different possible states of society be compared and evaluated based on individual preferences? The interest here lies in constructing a social welfare function (SWF) which provides a rule enabling this comparison and evaluation.
2) Problems in democratic decision-making such as whether decisions should be made through majority voting procedures.
3) Problems of institutional design, such as which decisions should be made privately, which publicly or collectively and, if the latter, how made?
4) Issues in constitutional decision-making, such as deciding how much emphasis should be placed on individual rights, and what principles of distributive justice should obtain in society.

The potential subject area of social choice theory is thus vast, even excluding issues in measuring social welfare, discussion of which tend to be restricted to the discipline of welfare economics. Social choice theory also tends to be the most mathematically based of the views so far investigated – recall the comment earlier in this chapter that social choice theory seemed a 'natural field' for a mathematically trained economist.

Although the potential scope of social theory is very broad, in the present context it can be viewed as significant because it questions the possibility of arriving at decisions through democratic processes. Arrow's theorem can be seen as radically questioning the form of democratic decision-making currently prevalent in Western democracies and elsewhere. If democratic decision-making is viewed as a process whereby the preferences of individuals are aggregated in order to provide collective outcomes, then Arrow's theorem indicates how this process may be impossible.[11] An appreciation of the issues raised by Arrow can be given through noting the paradox of voting first detailed by Condorcet. Imagine three individuals have to decide between the following three possibilities:

1) Maintaining the current level of general taxation (a);
2) Increasing general taxes, resulting in an increase in spending on education (b);
3) Increasing general taxes, resulting in an increase in spending on health care (c).

The first individual ranks these possibilities $a > b > c$, the second individual ranks them $c > a > b$, the third $b > c > a$. As the leader of a political party you want to adopt a policy reflecting these preferences: which policy should you adopt? The result of a vote expressing these preferences will indicate that two individuals (the first and second) vote $a > b$, two individuals (the first and third) vote $b > c$, whilst two individuals (the second and third) vote $c > a$. Although the individual preferences are transitive, the collective preferences are intransitive. As party leader, you are incapable of adopting any of the three policies on the basis of claiming it commands majority support. The end result is a cycle, where each option can be viewed as preferred to the others. Arrow's theorem can thus be seen as applicable to situations where a decision is to be made amongst various alternatives where the decision is reliant upon the values of the individuals involved. Hence the question:

> If a decision is required amongst competing alternatives, and if the decision is to depend on the values of the individuals in certain specified ways, are there choice procedures that satisfy these specified dependencies? (Fishburn, 2001: 1)

Arrow argues that the only collective choice mechanism that is always transitive is dictatorial – a somewhat worrying result. The power of Arrow's theorem derives from the fact that, unlike some of other arguments investigated, the assumptions the theorem makes appear to be quite innocuous, hence readily acceptable. Arrow's argument applies if there are at least three distinct states (as in the Condorcet result above) and two distinct individuals and assumes the following conditions (Arrow, 1977):

1) Unanimity (Pareto criterion). If all enfranchized citizens agree $S_1 \geq S_2$, then S_1 is selected over S_2 by the collective choice rule.
2) Transitivity. If $S_1 > S_2$ and $S_2 > S_3$, then $S_1 > S_3$.
3) Unrestricted Domain. Given any three alternatives, all preference orderings are possible. Hence any of the following alternative rankings are possible.

Best	S_1	S_1	S_3	S_2	S_2	S_3
Middle	S_2	S_3	S_1	S_1	S_3	S_2
Worst	S_3	S_2	S_2	S_3	S_1	S_1

4) Independence of Irrelevant Alternatives. The pair wise comparison of rankings does not depend on the position of other 'irrelevant'

alternatives. Hence if S_1 is socially preferred to S_2 then other alternatives are irrelevant.
5) No Dictator. If person one is a dictator and prefers S_1 to S_2, then society prefers S_1 to S_2. Hence there is no individual for whom their preferences become societies' preferences irrespective of anybody else.

Arrow proved that all collective choice rules that satisfy conditions 1–4 violate condition 5. Hence, assuming all orderings of preferences are allowed (unrestricted domain), and given the problem of cycles detailed above, the only means of arriving at a decision is through dictatorial imposition.

How serious are the issues raised by Arrow's impossibility theorem? The theorem claims that there is no perfect way of aggregating individual preferences into a collective decision. Indeed, it seems that it is impossible to derive any voting system, such as majority rule, which is not highly likely to result in lapses into dictatorship (Dryzek, 2000: 35). Arrow's theorem thus appears to challenge the viability of any form of democratic decision-making. It seems that, in order to avoid this conclusion, it is necessary to relax some of the assumptions. As dictatorship seems rather unpalatable, and unanimity is seen as a perfectly reasonable condition, attention has tended to focus on the other three conditions. For example, as indicated previously, the transitivity assumption may be unduly restrictive at the individual level, and even more so if extended to the collective level.

One problem with intransitivity at the collective level is that ways of arriving at decisions may seem to be arbitrary. For example, given the results in the Condorcet example, one way of arriving at a decision would be for you, as party leader, to select the relevant policy by simply flipping a coin, or drawing straws. Such a procedure may seem quite arbitrary: however, as Mueller notes (2003: 588), arbitrary decisions are frequently seen as 'fair'. For example, in sporting contests, winners emerge, and are regarded as fair winners, even though the initial draw indicating who plays against whom may be entirely arbitrary.

It has also been argued that full transitivity can be weakened and, for example, quasi-transitive preferences allowed. With this, transitivity of the preference relation is maintained (strong preferences), but not of indifference (weak preferences). Hence say for individual one bP_icP_ia whilst for individual two aP_ibP_ic it can still be claimed that bPc, whereas aIc and aIb (Craven, 1992). Similarly, a group may prefer x to y, be indifferent between y and z, yet not prefer x to z. Whereas Arrow's theorem is concerned with constructing a social welfare function, allowing quasi-transitivity produces a social decision function. However, after reviewing various proposals concerning the relaxation of the transitivity assumption, and the results of these relaxations, Mueller concludes that 'there appears to be little lost by sticking to the full transitivity requirement' (Mueller, 2003: 587).

Secondly, the unrestricted domain, which allows all feasible options, may be more 'liberal' than is actually required for decision-making in communities. For example, communities may share similar norms, beliefs or views, which automatically preclude certain options. Alternatively, it seems plausible to argue that certain domains should be restricted from consideration because they ought not to be subject to a collective rule. Thus, as noted during the discussion of Buchanan and Tullock in the previous chapter, certain rights such as individual property rights might well be regarded as inalienable, and hence preferences regarding such rights would be inadmissible in the collective decision procedure.

Thirdly, the condition of the independence of irrelevant alternatives may well be too restrictive, especially in the case of political phenomena. Arrow defends this condition thus:

> Given the set of alternatives available for society to choose among, it could be expected that ideally, one could observe all preferences among the available alternatives, but there would be no way to observe preferences among alternatives not feasible to society. (quoted in Mueller, 2003: 590)

However, because preferences amongst alternatives that are not feasible cannot be observed, this does not entail that they play no part in the choice situation. For example, say a party activist has to choose between two candidates, A and B, where the majority winner is elected leader of the party. The activist may initially feel inclined to prefer A to B, on the grounds that B's views appear to be too left wing. However, the activist recalls that another candidate, C, almost entered the contest, and this candidate C has strong left-wing convictions. On reflection, the activist arrives at the conclusion that, compared to C's views, the views of B are not really that left wing, hence votes for B. Thus, although electing C is not feasible, this possibility does influence the choice between A and B.

This problem would seem to be compounded if sequential decision-making is considered. For example, faced with a choice between right-wing candidate A and left-wing candidate B, the individual voter prefers B. However, the individual also knows that there is a further stage to the election process and that, if A loses at the first stage, then at the next stage a candidate even further to the right, C, might enter the contest. As the voter despises the policies of C, they vote for A in the first round.

Although these two examples refer to the individual voter, they remain applicable to collective decision-making. The first example highlights certain features relevant to the problem of 'framing', discussed later in Chapter 5, whilst the second example refers to individuals voting strategically, or misrepresenting their true preferences.

This issue was raised in the previous chapter in connection with Buchanan and Tullock's arguments.

It was precisely because of the possibility of collective decisions being arrived at through strategic voting that Arrow introduced the independence axiom:

> An important objective of Arrow in imposing the independence of irrelevant alternatives axiom was to eliminate the possibility of individuals being made better off under a collective decision procedure if they did not state their true preferences as inputs into the collective decision process. (Mueller, 2003: 592)[12]

In summarizing the somewhat paradoxical status of the implications of Arrow's impossibility theorem, Tullock has observed that:

> One of the real problems raised by Arrow's book was why the real world democracies seem to function fairly well in spite of the logical impossibility of rationally aggregating preferences. (Tullock, 1988: 68)

However, there have been more fundamental criticisms of Arrow's theorem. For example, Buchanan (1954) has questioned the whole idea of assuming that the claim that 'S_1 is socially preferred to S_2' can be given any meaningful sense.[13] It is one thing to claim that an individual prefers X to Y. However, to assume that societies can be so depicted is based on a false analogy with individuals. Further, the analysis assumes a 'benevolent despot' who merely aggregates information on preferences, although the assumption other models investigated previously is that any such individual will themselves be engaged in maximizing behaviour.

As noted, Arrow's theorem has generated a considerable body of research. At a theoretical level it reveals potentially fateful problems for democratic decision-making, revealing the logical impossibility of aggregating individual preferences. However, as Tullock, above, notes, contemporary democracies do not appear to have become unworkable because of the problems that Arrow raises. Hence the theory might illustrate a case of 'theoretically a problem, but in practice not a problem'.

Moreover, it could also be argued that Arrow's theorem reveals a further limitation in the attempt to explain political processes in terms of models drawn from economics. For instance, it could be disputed to what extent preferences over political issues are comparable to preferences over economic goods. Hence if I prefer apples to bananas, then I am unlikely to offer any reason for this preference, other than the fact that I like apples better than bananas. However, if I say that I prefer a redistributive policy over a non-redistributive policy, then I will no doubt hold reasons as to *why* I prefer one policy over another. In the case of preferences over political matters, people hold preferences for reasons, and these reasons may be questioned, challenged and revised. According to this argument, political preferences are subject to processes of deliberation, and thus not analogous to preferences over economic goods (Dryzek, 2000).

CONCLUSIONS

This chapter has built upon the previous two chapters through investigating in more detail the assumptions and axioms of RCT models. Although these models appear to be based upon a limited number of axioms, further investigation reveals that other assumptions are frequently incorporated into the models. For example, models tend to assume that individual preferences are independent, that decision-making under uncertainty can be modelled, and that unique solutions to problems can be discovered.

However, if instances of asymmetric information, uncertainty and surprise are introduced, then the claimed scientific status of RCT models appears to be somewhat threatened. This is because it is by no means clear that determinate solutions to problems can be resolved, hence threatening the claimed predictive power of the models. The situation is similar in the case of game theory. Although ideas like Schelling's 'focal points', and the possibility of players using probability calculations and not merely adopting dominant strategies does permit some flexibility in terms of attempting determinate solutions, in many games there is no unique equilibrium point, and any number of 'results' may be forthcoming.

The models of Schelling and Arrow reveal how aspects of international relations and majority decision-making can be modelled through using game-theoretical and collective decision rules respectively. Arrow's model appears to question the viability of majority decision-making, although this questioning may be more apparent than real. This is especially so if the model reveals certain limitations involved in assuming that political decisions are analogous to economic decisions.

In the case of Schelling, the problem of modelling irrational behaviour appears to be an issue. Although it may be possible to provide models where each assumes a probability of other players making irrational moves, it is not clear how any one individual can convince other players that they will, for sure, act irrationally.

Notes

1. An axiom is frequently regarded as a 'robust' assumption.
2. However, the economist Carl Menger, one of the 'founding fathers' of marginal utility theory, did assume a lexicographic ordering.

3. Anyone who has ever purchased Christmas presents for children will have been lucky if they have not experienced the difficulties in trying to find any shop that still has stocks of the toy that your child must have because all of their friends want them.
4. Keynes (1973) famously rejected the possibility of a general wage cut being capable of remedying unemployment, as each group of workers was concerned with their *relative* wages vis-à-vis other groups.
5. Contemporary macroeconomics models with microeconomic foundations frequently incorporate a 'representative individual'. The assumption here is that, if expectations are formed rationally, all individuals would form the same expectations, hence any one individual can be used to represent all individuals. This assumes, of course, that all individuals are utilizing the same macroeconomic model.
6. This would include the majority of Post Keynesian, Austrian, Institutional, or Sraffian inspired economists. Also, as the following chapter illustrates, attempts to incorporate RCT into Marxian economics may also be problematic.
7. Hardin (1997) disputes that this 'remorseless logic' will occur.
8. Strictly speaking, there are only two pure strategy Nash equilibria.
9. Schelling's book is based on a series of articles that he first published during the 1950s.
10. An introduction to 'modelling irrationality' is provided in Kreps, 1990, chapter 13.
11. There are, of course, alternative models of democratic decision-making.
12. It should also be noted that the independence of irrelevant alternatives condition demands that only ordinal, not cardinal, preferences are included. In other words, individuals cannot indicate the strength of their preferences over issues, and it is not possible to compare utilities between individuals.
13. It is worth considering that the term 'S_1 is socially preferred to S_2' is potentially ambiguous. Sen (1993) lists three possible interpretations of the term:

    1) As a way of evaluating outcomes. Hence to say that S_1 is socially preferred to S_2 indicates that S_1 is judged to be a better state of affairs for society than is S_2.
    2) As a form of normative choice. Hence decision-making in society should be so organized that S_2 must not be chosen when S_1 is available.
    3) As a form of descriptive choice. Here, decision systems are so organized that S_2 will be chosen when S_1 is available.

CHAPTER 4

Rational Choice Models in Politics: II

The two previous chapters have considered a variety of models that have been developed based on RCT in order to investigate political phenomena. This chapter is concerned with investigating some of the developments that have occurred in rational choice theory following on from these works. In many ways these developments represent an extension and deepening of the issues raised in the models investigated in the previous chapter.

However, it must be acknowledged that at present there is a vast literature concerned with various aspects of RCT. This is especially so in the case of the public choice literature, where a recent book surveying the literature runs to over 700 pages yet notes that this only covers 'a fraction of the literature' (Mueller, 2003: xvii). Given the extent of the relevant literature, all this chapter can hope to achieve is to indicate some of the main issues covered in recent writings based on RCT. In attempting to achieve this, the following investigations will focus mainly upon attempts to interpret classic texts in politics in terms of RCT models, investigations into rules and institutions, political entrepreneurs, spatial models of politics, and electoral systems.

RECENT INTERPRETATIONS OF 'CLASSIC' TEXTS

Hobbes

In *Leviathan* Hobbes envisages a state of nature, essentially a state of war, where the life of each is 'solitary, poor, nasty, brutish and short'. In this state of nature each individual has a right, given by nature, to self-preservation. There is also a fundamental law of nature that each should seek peace. However, as there is no authority capable of enforcing laws then, if peace is not achievable, each should seek 'the advantages of war'. The only way an individual can remove themselves from the state of nature is by forming a covenant, or contract, with others whereby each agrees to surrender their rights to a sovereign who is thereby authorized to enforce laws. Hence, left to their own devices, individuals will lead dismal lives, which can only be avoided through their agreeing to a sovereign who can enforce. The structure of Hobbes's argument is such that a number of commentators have identified it as an early 'paradigm' of a prisoners' dilemma (see, for example, Gauthier, 1986; Hampton, 1986; McLean, 1981). Hence:

> In Hobbes's story, each individual in the state of nature can behave peacefully or in a war-like fashion. Since peace allows everyone to go about their normal business with the result that they prosper and enjoy a more 'commodious' living (as Hobbes phrased it), choosing strategy 'peace' is like 'not confessing' . . . when everyone behaves in this manner it is much better than when they choose 'war' (confess). However, and in spite of wide ranging recognition that peace is better than war, the same prisoners' dilemma problem surfaces and leads to war. (Hargreaves Heap & Varoufakis, 1995: 148).

So does Hobbes's analysis of the move from a state of nature to civil society represent a prototype prisoners' dilemma? Recall the structure of a prisoners' dilemma, as in Figure 4.1. The suggestion is that C, C represents civil society, and D, D the state of nature. However, it is necessary to appreciate what, in Hobbes's argument, might be represented by C, D. Why would an individual be worse off by agreeing to enter civil society if the other did not? Plausibly, an individual would be worse off if they pursued peace, and the other pursued war, as they would be subject to arbitrary acts of violence by the other, whilst forgoing such acts themselves. However, this does not appear to be a realistic interpretation of Hobbes's argument.

1

		C	D
2	C	–3, –3	–10, 0
	D	0, –10	–8, –8

Figure 4.1

If an individual or group of individuals decide to authorize the sovereign, hence leaving the state of nature, whilst others choose to remain, then they are now subject to laws enforced by the sovereign. Consequently, individuals subject to laws are prohibited from, say, stealing from others. However, it is far from clear why this should imply that individuals who are subject to the sovereign should allow those who have chosen to remain in the state of nature total licence to wreak havoc upon them. The instruction is to seek peace and, if this is impossible, to seek the advantages of war. This situation is not the same as turning the other cheek whilst the other happily relieves you of all your belongings.

It is thus unclear why an individual who remains in a state of nature whilst others depart this state is thereby in a superior position than if all remain in a state of war. Similarly, it is difficult to appreciate why an individual who contracts to appoint a sovereign whilst others do not is thereby in a worse position than was the case in the state of nature. It would seem that an individual who defects when others co-operate is, at best, in the same situation as previously, whilst those who co-operate when others defect are, if anything, in an improved situation. At least, given that some others also co-operate, there are now less individuals (defectors) prepared to make the individuals' life a misery.

However, if individuals are thus never better off in a state of nature, why the reluctance on the part of individuals to appoint a sovereign? Two factors seem relevant in Hobbes's analysis. Firstly, as individuals surrender all of their rights to the sovereign, then the sovereign is essentially 'all powerful', and has neither duties nor obligations towards the individuals. The issue of trust therefore operates at a different level than it does in the prisoners' dilemma. In a PD, the issue is whether each can trust the other who is a potential party to the contract: can prisoner 1 trust prisoner 2? Of course, in non-cooperative game theory, it is irrational for one individual to trust another if the other individual can benefit by betraying the trust. In contrast, in Hobbes the question is can each party to the contract trust another who they appoint to enforce the contract? As the sovereign is not party to the contract, trust pertains to a situation where they all must trust another, not all trust each other.

In terms of the prisoners' dilemma above, an analogous situation would be as follows. Even if all agree to co-operate, what guarantee is there that the pay-offs will now be −3, −3 rather than −8, −8? The individuals in a PD may agree to confess, and subsequently find out that the officer of the law has misled them on the pay-offs, and they would, in fact, have received a better pay-off by defecting. Note that in the prisoners' dilemma, although each prisoner is conceived to act strategically, the law officer does not do so.

The second factor concerns the actual result of each individual agreeing to seek peace through joining into a covenant. All the individuals have known so far is a state of war: how do they even have any conception as to what a state of peace would consist in? Not only are they being asked to place their trust in the sovereign to bring about peace, they are being asked to enter into a peaceful society when they have no conception as to what this state would consist in. It would seem that, for each individual who is tempted to be a party to the covenant, the two states they are being asked to compare are *incommensurable*.

They have no way of comparing these states, as they have no clear conception as to what one of the states would consist in. There might be a law of nature urging them to seek peace: however, as they do not know what such a peaceful state would consist in, how would they know what pay-offs result in such a state?

Imagine your fairy godmother suddenly appeared, and offered you the chance of immortality in exchange for a fee of £100. Would you consider the loss of £100 to be worth the gain of immortality? It would seem that formulating an answer to this question is difficult because we have no idea what being immortal would entail. For example, what would our conception of time be like? Alternatively, would you accept £100 in order to change your gender? It would appear that the choice facing Hobbes's individuals in state of nature is similar to the problem of attempting to decide between goods that simply cannot be compared. It is as if the C, C box is represented by (??).

This suggests not only that Hobbes's argument cannot be readily represented as a prisoners' dilemma, but also reveals certain further assumptions that the prisoners' dilemma embodies. For example, if it is not rational for each prisoner to trust the other, why is it rational for each to trust, and hence take at face value, the promises made by the arresting officer? Further, the prisoners' dilemma, as with most of the arguments investigated so far, assume that individuals are capable of comparing the various states on offer, that the relevant states are commensurable. However, this may not be so, especially if the game envisages a leap into the unknown.

Marx

Recently, Elster has suggested that many of the insights in Marx's work can be identified as formulated in ways compatible with RCT models. Elster makes two specific claims here. Firstly, that 'Marx . . . was committed to methodological individualism, at least intermittently' (Elster, 1985a: 7). As the qualification recognizes, Elster is quite aware that a variety of Marx's explanations do not conform to a methodological individualist framework. For example, as Elster notes, Marx's explanations frequently appeal to the idea of 'capital' as being a primary actor. Hence in the *Grundrisse* Marx notes that 'As long as capital is weak, it still relies on the crutches of past modes of production, or of those which will pass with its rise. As soon as it feels strong, it throws away the crutches, and moves in accordance with its own laws' (quoted in Elster, 1985a: 7). Clearly, an explanation which refers to capital feeling strong and throwing away its crutches is not an explanation formulated in terms of individuals, their beliefs and desires.

Nonetheless, Elster argues that, for Marx, the methodological individualism framework does form the basis for 'much of his important work' and hence that Marx frequently offers an 'intentional explanation of individual action in terms of the underlying beliefs and desires' (Elster, 1985a: 4). It was noted in the previous chapter that it is possible to subscribe to a methodological individualist position without thereby being committed to RCT models. However, this brings in the second claim advanced by Elster – that Marx, at times at least, assumes maximizing behaviour (Elster, 1985a: 10ff). The claim that Marx would be somewhat sympathetic in certain instances to the assumption of maximizing behaviour,[1] coupled with the claim that his analysis at times embodies a commitment to methodological individualism, may well suggest that certain aspects of Marx's analysis of capitalism could be susceptible to characterizing in terms of some form of RCT model.

In order to assess this suggestion, it would seem appropriate to briefly consider Marx's analysis of group behaviour, as this was the area of Marx's work that Olson in particular criticized. Recall from Chapter 2 that Olson essentially argued that Marx underestimated the difficulties facing any attempt by individuals to organize into larger groups to advance communal interests, because of free rider problems. Elster approaches Marx's analysis of the collective action of classes under capitalism through noting the issues raised by Olson:

> One should seek for micro-foundation for collective action. To explain the collective action simply in terms of the benefits for the group is to beg all sorts of questions, and in particular the question why collective action fails to take place even when it would greatly benefit the agents. (Elster, 1985a: 359)

Elster hence examines certain significant aspects of Marx's account of class in the light of Olson's identification of problems of collective action, stating that 'I define . . . class consciousness as the ability to overcome the free-rider problem in realising collective action' (Elster, 1985a: 347). The question of collective action in Marx's work is hence viewed in terms of an RCT model where 'the gains and losses associated with collective action must, for the present purpose, be measured in terms of expected utility' (Elster, 1985a: 351). Initially Elster focuses on the material gains and losses for the individual who does not take into account any such gains and losses incurred by others. Elster's analysis identifies three relevant variables:

a) the gains from co-operation, or what the individual gains if all participate in the collective action;
b) the free rider gain, or what the individual gains if all except themselves participate;
c) the loss from unilateralism, or what an individual loses if they are the only one, or one of few, who participate in the action. (This loss is analogous to the 'sucker problem' discussed in the first chapter in connection with the prisoners' dilemma, and, in this case, may include costs of punishment.)

Marx's writings on questions relevant to class action on class consciousness are obviously complex and range over a considerable number of writings. However, taking the individual's decision to take part in a revolution in order to replace a capitalist economic system with a socialist/communist economic system, the relevant question becomes: can this decision be modelled as a collective action decision in the manner of Olson's RCT model? It seems possible that a number of reasons could be suggested as to why this modelling is implausible. The following investigation will initially focus on one reason, concerning the question of the relationship between the forces and relations of production in Marx.

According to Cohen, 'what makes a *successful* revolution possible is sufficiently developed productive forces' (Cohen, 1978: 203). This explains the possibility of a successful revolution independently of any reference to collective action problems, but as being reliant upon the development of the productive forces. In order to appreciate to what extent the arguments of Elster and Cohen are, or are not, compatible, it is necessary to briefly consider Marx on the question of the relationship between the forces and relations of production. The nature of this relationship in Marx's writings has been subject to numerous commentaries, and here is clearly not the place to review them. Fortunately, this can be avoided as Cohen performs an admirable service in clarifying this relationship, and the following relies on his account.

Cohen argues that Marx's forces of production are comprised of the means of production (instruments of production such as tools, machines, premises and instrumental materials, and additionally raw materials and spaces) and labour power (Cohen, 1978: 55). Somewhat crudely put, the development of societies throughout history is characterized by the increasing development of the forces of production. This development can occur either through the replacement of any given instruments of production by better ones (e.g. replacement of the water wheel by the steam engine) or by better utilization of existing instruments of production.

In contrast, the productive relations, comprising the economic structure of a society, are the 'relations of effective power over persons and productive forces' (Cohen, 1978: 63), which can, with some leniency, be usefully represented as relation of legal ownership. Hence, under capitalism, the worker owns all of his or her labour power, but none of the means of production he or she uses, as these are owned by the capitalist. Hence the capitalist hires the labour power offered by the worker, which is then applied to the means of production owned by the capitalist in order to produce commodities. In contrast, under feudalism, the serf owned both some of her or his labour power (they mainly worked for the lord, but were also allowed to work their own land) and some of the means of production (their own land).

Initially, the onset of new relations of production allows for the development of the productive forces. However, at some later point in history the relations of production now start to 'fetter', or impede, any further development of the forces of production. Hence whereas initially the onset of the feudal system facilitated the development of the productive forces, it then started to impede this development, until the overthrow of the feudal system of productive relations by capitalist productive relations, which then allowed further development of the productive forces. However, the same development occurs under capitalism, so that there is a 'growing incompatibility between the productive development of society and its . . . relations of production, which expresses itself in bitter contradictions, crises, spasms' (Marx, quoted in Cohen, 1978: 202).

Given this, then under what conditions would it be rational to join a revolution in order to overthrow capitalism and bring into fruition a socialist society? Well, as the Cohen quote earlier indicated, it all depends upon the development of the productive forces, and hence 'when capitalism's worst crisis occurs, productivity sufficient to establish a stable socialist society is available' (Cohen, 1978: 204). Consequently, unless capitalism is experiencing its 'worst crisis', then the forces of production are insufficiently developed in order to sustain a socialist society, and an individual would be rather foolish to join a revolution in order to attempt to bring about such a society.

However, what if an individual did believe that 'the time was ripe' for the establishment of socialism through revolutionary action: would they be tempted to 'free ride' upon the actions of others?[2] As noted, Elster identified three variables relevant to the gains and losses associated with collective action: gains from co-operation, free rider gains, and losses from unilateralism. Regarding the relationship between these variables, he states that 'Other things being equal, the probability of collective action increases with the first of these variables and decrease with the second and third' (Elster, 1985a: 352). So it would seem that collective action is possible if the perceived gains of the action outweigh the advantages of free rider and expected losses from unilateralism variables. However, Elster concludes that 'in general, collective action will be either individually unstable (large free-rider gains) or individually inaccessible (large losses of unilateralism) or both' (Elster, 1985a: 352).

What are the gains that can be achieved in overthrowing capitalism in favour of socialism? In his earlier writings, Marx argues that individuals under capitalism are in a state of alienation – from their 'species being', from others, from the products of their labour, and from nature itself. In his later writings Marx charts the various means through which workers under capitalism are exploited. Hence the transition from capitalism to socialism will witness an end to alienation and exploitation – in short, to an increase in freedom (Cohen, 1978: 204). Further, as the productive forces can now be further developed, the worker could envisage receiving real material gains – the productive forces grow, and exploitation is abolished. So would the perceived advantages of collective action – an end to alienation and exploitation and consequent increases in freedom and material rewards – be such to overcome the free rider and unilateralism issues?

It seems somewhat plausible to suggest that the advantages accrued to the individual through the overthrow of capitalism are such that they would not simply 'outweigh' the other two factors. Rather, they would render any consideration of the factors irrelevant. In short, the advantages achieved under socialism, *if recognized and potentially attainable*, are such that they would not be risked through trading them off against other considerations. In other words, the 'preference' for the form of freedom achievable under socialism, if recognized and attainable, would act as a lexicographic preference. Lexicographic preferences were discussed in the previous chapter: they are preferences that an individual would not consider trading-off against any other option.

Consequently, the goal of increased freedom and material gains would be regarded as so worthwhile that the individual would not even *consider* risking its potential achievement by not participating in the possibly required revolutionary action. Of course the main consideration here is an individual recognizing that alienation and/or exploitation can be overcome with the overthrow of capitalism and that the crisis in capitalism is such that a socialist society can be supported, and is thus feasible. Here, as Elster recognizes, leadership may well be necessary in order to educate and inform individuals (Elster, 1985a: 351). However, this leadership is primarily educational about what can be achieved and when, rather than attempting to persuade individuals not to free ride.

However, it could be suggested that there is a problem in Marx's account of revolutionary collective action that does bear some resemblance to the free rider problem, although not in the form detailed by Elster. In Marx's writings there appears to be a sense of inevitability concerning the transition between the different social and political forms, a strong suggestion that the old relations of production will *inevitably* be overthrown, and replaced with new ones, if they continue to 'fetter' the growth of the productive forces. In this case the dilemma for the potential revolutionary might take the form: why bother joining the revolution in order to overthrow capitalism if capitalism will inevitably disappear? The individual is now not free riding on the actions of others, but on a historical process: capitalism is historically doomed, and will perish, immaterially of whether I attempt to overthrow it or not.

This possibility is merely suggested, as it indicates a possible form of a 'free rider' problem different from that explored by Olson and Elster. In opposing this possibility, Cohen notes that 'the future socialist revolution [is] . . . inevitable, not despite what men may do, but because of what men, being rational, are bound, predictably, to do' (Cohen, 1978:

147, footnote 1). However, this would appear to confirm the view of Olson and Elster that Marx's analysis embodies, but does not address, a 'free rider' problem. If each knows that it can be predicted that others will create the revolution, why should each bother to participate, if they can free ride on the backs of others?

In conclusion, this brief review of Marx's position on the transition from capitalism to socialism, and the question of revolutionary collective action, indicates there may well be tensions within Marx's ideas. However, despite the insights into Marx's writings that might be possible through explaining some of his ideas in terms of a RCT model, it is doubtful that this is the case in the example of revolutionary action.[3] Whatever the merits of investigating problems of collective action in terms of the RCT 'free rider' problem, this problem does not seem to encapsulate the issues raised for the potential revolutionary in Marx's account. The Marxist revolutionary would seem to be animated by issues such as the following. Moral concerns such as: do capitalists inevitably exploit workers? If so, will the overthrow of capitalism bring an end to alienation and exploitation? Practical concerns such as: are the productive forces sufficiently developed in order to sustain socialism? Is this capitalist crisis *the* crisis that indicates this is so? Will capitalism evolve into socialism anyway, despite the intentional action of individuals? These sorts of questions seem somewhat different from the question: why bother, if I can free ride? The beliefs of the Marxist revolutionary thus concern beliefs about social groups (classes), historical forces and historical inevitability, rather than beliefs about the actions of other individuals. However, as Elster acknowledges (Elster, 1985a: 6), beliefs such as these are not reducible to beliefs about individuals, and hence are incompatible with the methodological individualism that animates RCT models.

The above discussion is not intended to imply that the use of RCT models cannot provide any insights into Marx's arguments. However, although some of Marx's arguments may be explicable in these terms, there is a major tendency for Marx's analysis of capitalism to appeal to functional forms of analysis, which are not compatible with the basic tenets of methodological individualism.[4] Further, in the case of revolutionary activity itself, the tendency in Elster's analysis to see this activity predominantly in terms of the problem of free riding is potentially more confusing than helpful.

THE EVOLUTION OF RULES AND INSTITUTIONS

Models based on RCT have been advanced in order to explain the evolution of rules and institutions. These explanations may have either a descriptive or a normative component: they may offer an explanation of how certain institutions or rules may have come into existence, or they may offer an explanation as to why certain rules or institutions ought to be developed. As an example of the former, how might individuals in a prisoners' dilemma situation voluntarily agree to the establishment of an institution that can compel co-operation? As an example of the latter, given the possibility of free riding where public goods are concerned, is it possible to devise rules or institutional structures whereby individuals will correctly indicate their willingness to pay for a public good?

Both of these examples illustrate how institutions or rules either have come into existence, or ought to come into existence, through voluntary agreement. These explanations thus indicate how individuals may have brought, or ought to bring, certain rules and institutions into existence intentionally. However, there are other forms of explanation that explain the evolution of institutions as *unintended consequences* of intentional actions. Although RCT models have, in the main, been more concerned with the intentional evolution of rules and institutions, it is worth indicating how the origin of an institution may be explicable as an unintentional outcome of action.

The economist Menger, who was one of the 'founding fathers' of neoclassical economics, offered the following explanation of the evolution of the institution of money (Menger, 1892). Assume originally a barter economy, without money, where individuals trade goods with each other. In this case, individuals are restricted to trading a good they do not want for a good that they do want with another person. Such trading conditions are clearly highly restrictive. For example, an individual willing to barter apples must complete the exchange before the fruit perishes, and is thus limited to obtaining whatever they can before the fruit perishes. However, assume that the apple trader is prepared to accept a non-perishable commodity which they themselves do not want to consume, but which they know that other traders will be prepared to trade for. This individual thus increases their prospect of ultimately receiving goods on more favourable terms. Others, realizing this, will also see the advantage in trading in exchange for this commodity. Hence the commodity becomes more liquid – it is acceptable to an increasing number of individuals. Eventually, the institution of money as a medium of exchange thus evolves simply because each individual recognizes the value to themselves of trading in this commodity. Hence an institution – money – is explained as the outcome of individual action, although none of the individuals entered trade with the intention of creating the institution of money.

This example does not refer to individual maximizing behaviour, which is not surprising as Menger himself did not subscribe to the various axioms of RCT models. However, Menger did subscribe to what is now termed the doctrine of methodological individualism, and hence the evolution of a certain institution – money – has been explained solely in terms of individuals and their actions. This form of explanation – a 'hidden hand' explanation – is quite common in economics. A certain institution, or process, or outcome, is explained as the unintentional outcome of intentional action. Although the idea of an unintentional outcome of intentional action might sound rather strange, it should be readily understandable. For example, if I arrive home and turn on the light switch, thus frightening the burglar into leaving the premises, I did not turn the switch on with the intention of frightening the burglar: this outcome was the unintended result of me (intentionally) switching the light on.

Menger's account thus explains how a certain institution evolves in an unplanned manner ('organically') because a certain form of behaviour is adopted by an individual in order to improve their position, and this behaviour is then adopted by others. Other authors have used RCT models in order to examine how certain institutional arrangements may affect behaviour: for example, North and Thomas (1973) and Olson (1982) have used RCT models in order to investigate economic growth. The investigations of North and Thomas focus on the question of how property rights are assigned, arguing that economic growth will not occur unless the existing underlying economic organization is efficient.

The assigning property rights has frequently been advanced as a solution to various problems of communal living, as the example of the 'tragedy of the commons' illustrates (Schmidtz, 1991). Assume you live in a community with others, where one of the main sources of food is provided by the communal fruit trees. One summer, imagining that the fruit will now be ripe and ready to pick, you walk to the communal fruit trees, only to discover that the best fruit has already been taken by others, and you are left with only a little of the fruit, and that is in a poor condition.

Determined not to repeat the experience, next year you go to the fruit trees earlier. Even though you know the fruit will not yet be ripe, at least you will get some. However, of course, everybody does the same, and you all end up eating unripe fruit. Yet if an individual or group of individuals erect fences around the trees, thus claiming them as private property, then others can be prevented from picking the fruit until it is ripe. Hence the tragedy of the commons is averted through assigning property rights.

North and Thomas illustrate their argument with the example of the invention by John Harrison of a clock to aid shipping navigation, where Harrison won a prize from the then British government for his invention. The invention, which benefited shipping generally, would not, they claim, have been so readily invented if the incentive of the prize money was absent. However, a more efficient solution would have entailed the assignment of property rights to intellectual property.

Individuals thus have an incentive to innovate, as they will directly benefit from any proceeds accruing when the innovation is taken up and used by members of the society.

North and Thomas thus argue that individuals must be encouraged by means of incentives to undertake socially desirable activities, pointing out that the main hindrance to such undertakings are caused by a discrepancy between social and private rates of return. This discrepancy means that some third party or parties will, without consent, receive some of the benefits or avoid some of the costs of these activities. This analysis thus incorporates a form of the 'free rider' argument. As individuals can receive the benefits accruing from inventions without incurring any of the costs incurred in the development of inventions, then each will be tempted to 'free ride'. However, as all are so tempted, then no one has an incentive to invent, and societies where this is prevalent will not experience the economic growth of societies where this is not possible. The assignment of property rights to intellectual products hence provides an incentive for individuals to engage in activities that have a collective benefit.

Olson's analysis of economic growth also focuses – perhaps not surprisingly, given his earlier book – on free rider problems, although in a somewhat different manner. Olson's inquiry is animated by the question as to why great empires decline and collapse, whilst there can be remarkable rises in the wealth and power of other countries previously regarded as peripheral actors on the world stage. Olson is particularly concerned by the fact that, since the ending of World War II, the United Kingdom has suffered from slower growth and higher inflation and unemployment than countries such as Japan and (then) Western Germany, despite the fact that the latter two countries suffered more severely from the effects of the war. Regarding growth, the data shown in Table 4.1 illustrate Olson's concern.

Olson's explanation for these discrepancies in growth rates draws upon the arguments he advanced in his earlier book. He argues that certain groups, for example consumers, tax payers, the unemployed and the poor, lack the selective incentives and/or numbers to organize

Country	% Annual increase in real gross domestic product per worker, 1960–1990
USA	1.36
West Germany	2.50
Japan	5.03
United Kingdom	1.98

(Adapted from Jones, 1998: 4)

Table 4.1

themselves effectively. Therefore, those groups that can organize effectively have an interest in pursuing policies that are advantageous to themselves because the costs of these policies fall disproportionately upon the unorganized. Whereas, as noted in Chapter 2, Olson previously tended to neglect exploring the difficulties faced by groups in attaining a level whereby selective incentives could be introduced in order to secure collective action, he now acknowledges that the difficulties entailed in establishing selective incentives means that groups will take a long time to emerge.

However, once such groups have emerged, they will tend to survive even when the collective good they were established in order to provide is no longer needed. Hence stable societies with unchanging boundaries will tend to accumulate more organizations for collective action over time (Olson, 1982: 41). Olson argues that the influence of these collective groups is not benign: they will reduce efficiency and aggregate income over time, and make political life more decisive. Hence, compared to West Germany and Japan, the United Kingdom suffers from a form of institutional sclerosis precisely because it has endured a longer period of relative stability compared to the other two countries.

Olson's book was published in 1982, and, in the light of his claims, it is worth noting the data in Table 4.2. Although the data in Table 4.2 is not directly comparable to that in Table 4.1, and is complicated because of the unification of Germany, the figures do not readily support Olson's argument. In the case of growth, measured in terms of GDP, then the United Kingdom and United States have shown a slight increase in growth rates between the periods 1980–1995 and 1995–2002. However, during the same periods Germany and Japan have witnessed a reduction in growth rates – quite a significant reduction in the case of Japan, although all four countries witnessed relative stability during these periods. Hence recent figures on growth rates in three of the countries that Olson uses to support his argument (Germany, Japan, UK) do not, in fact, appear to do so.

Country	1980–1995	1995–2002	Change between periods
Germany*	1.6	1.4	−0.3
Japan	2.9	0.6	−2.3
United Kingdom	2.1	2.2	0.1
United States	2.0	2.3	0.3

* West Germany before 1991, and omitting 1991.
(From De Serres, 2003)

Table 4.2: Average trend growth in GDP per capita

The arguments advanced by North and Thomas and Olson respectively may well have some explanatory justification. Nevertheless, in keeping with Elster's interpretation of Marx, they reveal an unfortunately too common trend identifiable in many practitioners of RCT: the tendency to explain complex social and political processes in terms of a single, or limited number, of factors. However, in the case of RCT models being used in institutional explanations, restricting the analysis to a limited number of features can lead to a severe problem. To appreciate why, take the following characterization of institutional explanations frequently found in the literature (Goodin, 1996).

Recall that, in Chapter 1, it was noted that RCT models may be used in order to explain how and why individuals select certain constraints on actions. As an example, Buchanan and Tullock's work, investigated in Chapter 2, suggested that, for certain decisions, individuals would adopt majority decision-making, whereas for other decisions they would adopt unanimity decision procedures. Individuals are thus viewed as selecting different institutional structures, which act as constraints (majority or unanimity procedures), depending upon the decision in question.

Institutions are thus identified as 'constraints' and, according to Goodin, such constraints are 'advantageous to individuals and groups in the pursuit of their own more particular projects' (Goodin, 1996: 20). Hence, for example, in the work of North and Thomas, investigated above, property rights can be viewed as institutional constraints that nevertheless provide advantages in developing intellectual ideas. Goodin continues his argument by noting that 'the same contextual factors that constrain individual and group actions also shape the desires, preferences, and motives of those individual and group agents' (Goodin, 1996: 20).

Here lies the problem. Institutions are explained in terms of the outcomes, or products, of individuals' desires or preferences and beliefs. However, the institutions that are to be explained as outcomes (the explanandum) may themselves shape the very desires and beliefs that are being used in the explanation (the explanans). In other words, the institutions are explained as outcomes of the very desires and beliefs that they themselves produce. The explanation becomes circular, hence not an explanation at all.

POLITICAL ENTREPRENEURS

The idea of individuals acting as entrepreneurs in order to overcome free rider problems was touched upon in Elster's interpretation of Marx earlier in this chapter, where Elster argued that leaders may need to educate and inform individuals. Popkin's analysis of rural society in

Vietnam offers an account as to how political entrepreneurs may facilitate the overcoming of free rider problems (Popkin, 1979). Popkin analyses the peasant comprising this form of society as a 'rational problem solver' (Popkin, 1979: ix) who possesses a sense of their own interest and who needs to bargain with others in order to achieve mutually acceptable outcomes. The analysis explicitly defers to the 'economic model', where choices are viewed as maximizing expected utility (Popkin, 1979: 31). This way of approaching the issues is compared to the 'moral economist' approach, which views social relations in pre-capitalist society as being 'more moral' than those in capitalist society, and hence the breakdown of this pre-capitalist society is harmful to peasant welfare. Consequently, according to this 'moral approach', peasant protest movements are a defensive reaction to capitalism, which seek to maintain the previous more moral society. Popkin argues that, according to this account, peasant revolts do not encounter collective action problems, as 'there is a community orientation whereby the free-rider and leadership problems are easily overcome by proper socialisation to norms placing a high value on voluntarism' (Popkin, 1979: 25).

In contrast to this viewpoint, Popkin argues that peasant revolts cannot be understood as attempts to restore the old order through collective class action. Rather, revolts tend to be concerned to tame, not overthrow, market relations, and issues are not identified in terms of threats to a class, but in terms of their risk to any individual participation, and hence 'whether a self-interested peasant will or will not contribute to a collective action depends on individual – not group – benefits' (Popkin, 1979: 251). However, given potential free rider problems, how do peasants become organized in order to attempt to achieve collective benefits? In this case group leadership becomes crucial:

> Any attempt to organise for group action must recognise the distribution between individual and group and must provide effective leadership, as well as sufficient incentives, to overcome individual resistance to collective action. (Popkin, 1979: 252)

Leaders are thus recognized as playing a crucial role in overcoming possible free rider problems. Popkin acknowledges individual peasants may have a desire to contribute to collective action for ethical or altruistic reasons, in which case the role of leadership is limited to persuading these individuals that their particular organization is the best way to achieve the collective objectives. Further, selective incentives are not necessarily needed in cases where individuals can be excluded from groups unless they participate, hence losing benefits. However, leadership is important, not only for providing selective incentives, but for co-ordinating contributions, manipulating information and breaking large groupings into more effective smaller groups.

Leaders are thus viewed as being 'political entrepreneurs', who encourage participation in collective action through concentrating on local goals which can attain immediate benefit. This idea of individuals acting as 'political entrepreneurs' in order to overcome potential free rider problems has formed the focus for a variety of recent work using RCT models (Laver, 1997). Such entrepreneurs are regarded as crucial in mobilizing others in such a way that the disincentives to action that form the focus of various RCT explanations can be overcome. Hence according to Laver:

> The possibility of contracting for the services of a political entrepreneur does more generally offer a potential way out of many troublesome collective action problems. The entrepreneur supplies 'political services' for a fee. These services may include enforcing agreements made by group members, imposing sanctions on free riders, or getting more deeply involved in the co-ordination and generation of collective action. (Laver, 1997: 70–1)

Laver recognizes that it would not be rational for individuals facing free rider problems to grant such political entrepreneurs any possibility for dictatorial rule, and hence entrepreneurs are granted '"enough" but not "too much" power' (Laver, 1997: 71). One condition germane to individuals not granting entrepreneurs 'too much' power concerns the size of the group involved. Laver hence argues that 'political entrepreneurs will only offer an attractive solution to collective action problems for groups that are large enough . . . to resist mass coercion' (Laver, 1997: 75). However, this introduces a dilemma: it is only large groups that can resist coercion that will find entrepreneurial services attractive, yet these are precisely the groups that, according to Olson, will find collective action more difficult to undertake. Hence the group finds an entrepreneur attractive because this individual will allow free rider problems to be overcome, yet the group must have already overcome the free rider problem in order to collectively appoint an entrepreneur.

Laver's solution to this dilemma is to appeal to the idea of 'political factions' and thus 'any faction or alliance of factions that can prevail over the remainder of the public regardless of their opposition will be able to deal with a political entrepreneur and make a contract for the provision of a political regime for the public as a whole' (Laver, 1997: 72). Thus, if some individuals – a political faction – can overcome the free rider problem amongst themselves, they can secure the services of an entrepreneur to enforce solutions to collective action problems on the general public. However, even if a faction, being smaller than the population at large, may find it easier to overcome free rider problems, the possibility of such problems still exists. So how does the faction overcome free rider problems within its members?

The solution to this problem appears to be that the incentive for faction membership is provided by the fact that members of the faction can thus impose their will on the majority. Thus 'there are likely to be a divergence of tastes within the public on matters that all consider to be important' (Laver, 1997: 72), and hence the winning faction may be able 'to coerce the remainder of the public if need be' or 'dominate the remainder of the public' (Laver, 1997: 73). However, even if the remainder of the public at large cannot agree on matters because their tastes diverge, it is difficult to appreciate why the majority here would agree to being 'coerced' or 'dominated' by a minority. Recall that the free rider problem was deemed to exist because individuals who wanted a collective good faced insufficient incentives in order to organize and secure the good. However, the solution offered to the problem here appears to be that the majority must accept policies fostered upon them by the minority even though the majority do not agree with them. This seems to be less a solution to free riding, more of an argument justifying the imposition of the values of a mobilized minority upon a disorganized majority.

SPATIAL MODELS OF POLITICS

The influence of Downs's book *An Economic Theory of Democracy* extended beyond studies of the rationality of voting, as it was also influential in the development of spatial models of politics, so called because the various policy positions of candidates or parties seeking election are conceived as points along a 'space'. These models thus attempt to formalize the view that policies can usually be represented along a continuum ranging from 'extreme left wing' to 'extreme right wing', with a variety of positions in between. The 'policy space' can comprise more than one policy, although each issue is represented as a specific dimension comprised of a series of alternatives. There are three main components to the model (Hinich & Munger, 1997: 5ff):

1) Voter choice. Voters choose candidates of policies 'closest' to the voters' ideal conception as to what governments should do. Voters are assumed to be utility maximisers.
2) Party platform selection. Political parties know how voters choose and therefore make proposals or choose candidates that will attract the most votes.
3) Under certain conditions parties in a two-party system will converge towards the centre of the distribution of voters.

One of the attractions of spatial theory for its advocates lies in the claim that it reinforces the presumed scientific status of RCT. Hence, according to Hinich and Munger, a strength of spatial theory is that it provides 'predictions about aggregate outcomes, given no more information that 1) individual goals and (2) the decision process'

(Hinich & Munger, 1997: 12). In order to appreciate how the theory appears capable of formulating predictions, consider the simple example provided by Hinich and Munger of a committee composed of three people who are choosing an entertainment budget for a club. Individual A prefers the budget to be $50, individual B prefers $75, whilst individual C prefers spending $250. These preferences can be represented spatially along a continuum, as shown in Figure 4.2. The assumption is that the further the budget deviates from $50 towards $250, the less individual A prefers it. Similarly, the further the budget deviates towards $50, the less C approves. So, given these different preferences concerning the budget, what will the outcome be? The prediction is that a budget of $75 will be selected, as this option beats any other proposal. This is because individuals A and B will vote for $75 in preference to any larger budget, whereas individuals B and C will vote for $75 in preference to any smaller budget. Hence, in pairwise majority rule elections, where a winner between two alternatives is chosen by a majority decision, the median, or middle, value beats or ties with all other alternatives. The budget of $75 may also be termed the Condorcet winner, named after the French mathematician the Marquis de Condorcet, which is the position that beats or ties with any other alternative in majority rule contests.

Figure 4.2: The Continuum

It would thus appear that this simple spatial model does allow predictions to be formed, predicting a budget of $75 to be the one that will be chosen by the committee. However, this is clearly a simplified model and, in order to investigate to what extent the form of analysis can be extended to predict the outcomes of other political issues, it is necessary to appreciate the assumptions that have been made. These assumptions include the following (Hinich & Munger, 1997, chapter 1):

1) Unidimensionality. There is only one issue – the budget, in the above example – and individuals prefer their own 'ideal budgets'. Further, it is assumed that alternatives can be ordered along a dimension, such that individuals can arrange policies along a continuum from 'less' to 'more'. All individuals are also assumed to share this perception of order, so that all individuals are voting from the same dimension.
2) Preferences are single-peaked. The closer a budget is to the individual's 'ideal budget', the more the individual prefers it.
3) Voting is sincere. The individual votes according to their preferences over alternatives.

4) Symmetry. Another assumption frequently, though not necessarily, made is that the declines in satisfaction are equal for equal departures from the ideal in either direction.

In assessing the suitability of these assumptions for investigations in politics, it is useful to note cases where the assumptions do not hold. The assumption that there is only one issue that is being decided obviously does not hold for many of the decisions arrived at in complex democracies. Initially, it might seem that the addition of more issues will not necessarily result in any problems, and each issue can be regarded separately. For example, if the committee above is also voting on a budget to pay for visiting speakers to come and give talks on a variety of subjects to the members of the club, it would seem that the voting procedure for this decision could be investigated independently of the voting procedure regarding the entertainment budget. However, this assumes that the preferences of all the voters are separable, which may not be the case.

Take individual A in the above example, who preferred that $50 be spent on entertainment, yet accepted a budget of $75. This individual's ideal budget for visiting speakers may have been $100. However, having agreed to more being spent on entertainment than she would ideally have liked, the individual now believes that less than $100 should be spent on visiting speakers, as she does not want the club to have to take out an overdraft. Hence her preferences on budget two (the visiting speaker) are dependent upon the outcome of voting in budget one (entertainment). The individual still holds a preference for an ideal budget of $100 for visiting speakers: however, given the context in which the voting occurs, her actual preference might not reflect her ideal preference.

The example illustrates an issue relevant to the complex area of 'agenda setting' in decision-making, as the outcome of the voting procedure may reflect the order in which issues surface on the agenda. Hence if the vote on the visiting speaker was taken before the vote on the entertainment budget, then individual A's indicated preference may then have reflected her ideal preference. The associated assumption of continuity, that alternatives can be arranged along a continuous dimension from 'less' to 'more', is also problematic. For example, alternatives regarding some issues, such as capital punishment, do not readily translate into a continuum: it is either 'yes' or 'no'. Similarly, voters may perceive issues in this stark manner: an individual vehemently opposed to blood sports may not be willing to counter any alternative other than an outright ban on the relevant practices.[5] It is also unclear that all relevant individuals can be viewed as selecting from the same perceived ordering, as the same alternatives may be presented in different ways, thus altering perceptions.[6] The second assumption, that preferences are 'single peaked', is also not necessarily supported. Suppose three individuals are choosing between three policy options regarding employee/employer relations. Option A is to give more power to the employees, option B is to maintain the status quo, whilst option C is to give more power to employers. Individual one prefers maintaining the status quo, followed by more power to employers, with more power to employees last. Individual two prefers more power to employees, followed by the status quo, with more power to employers last. However, individual three believes that the present state of affairs is resulting in a continual paralysis in industrial relations, and prefers more power to employers, followed by more power to employees, with the status quo last. These preferences can be represented spatially, as in Figure 4.3.

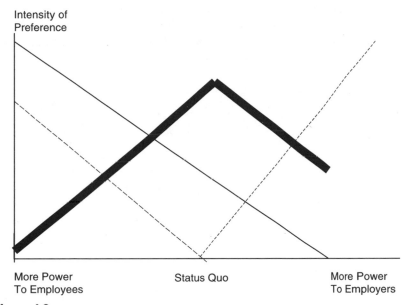

Figure 4.3

As Figure 4.3 reveals, the preferences of individuals one and two are both 'single peaked'. However, the preference profile of individual three is not single peaked, as the extremes are preferred to the 'middle ground'. Although the preference for the 'middle ground' of the status quo is closer to the preferred preference of more power to employers than the preference for more power to employees, the latter is preferred. In this case then a voting cycle results: a 2:1 majority in each case prefers A to B, B to C and C to A. Although the preferences of individual three do not seem unreasonable, they cannot be encompassed within the model.

The next assumption, which is that individuals vote according to their preferences, can also raise a number of problems. For example, a number of individuals in contemporary democratic elections engage in tactical voting, whereby they vote for the candidate most likely to beat their least favoured candidate, rather than for the candidate that they actually prefer. Concealing preferences, or voting in ways that do not accord with preferences, can be an important factor in coalition building. Thus if there are two issues on an agenda that require votes, then two or more individuals may form a coalition, whereby individual A misrepresents her preferences when voting on the first issue in order to support B's preferred option, in exchange for B misrepresenting his preferences on the second issue in order to support A's preferred option. Although both of these practices involve voters concealing their 'true preferences', the first practice tends to be termed strategic or tactical voting, the second sophisticated voting. Sophisticated voting of the form in the example above is an example of 'logrolling', whereby individuals have an incentive to engage in the exchange of votes. Take three voters, 1, 2, and 3, deciding between two issues, A and B, as in Figure 4.4 (from Stratmann, 1997).

ISSUES

VOTER	A	B
1	5	−1
2	−1	5
3	−1	−1

Figure 4.4

On a simply majority vote, if voters sincerely indicate their preferences, then both issues will fail, each defeated by two votes to one. However, there is a clear incentive for voter 2 to misrepresent their preference, thus ensuring that issue A passes, if voter 1 also misrepresents their preferences on issue B so that B passes. Voters 1 and 2 thus collude in order to secure a successful outcome for issues they strongly support in exchange for voting in favour of an issue that they mildly disapprove of. In this example, it seems that the practice of logrolling has resulted in a beneficial outcome: issues strongly supported by one individual, yet only mildly objected to by two individuals, are passed. However, as Stratmann points out, if the −1's are replaced by −3's, voters 1 and 2 still have an incentive to trade (they gain 5 through losing 3). However, the overall outcome is negative, not positive. There is thus considerable debate in the literature as to whether and, if so, when, logrolling achieves results that are beneficial overall.

The final assumption noted was that the preference function was symmetric. However, this may well not be so. For example, in the example of the committee vote on the entertainment budget, individual B favoured £75. However, it could be that this individual feels that $75, although an ideal position, is also the least that should be spent on entertainment. Hence this individual might be relatively relaxed about any budget increase over $75, yet strongly object to any budget offered below this sum. However, even if all individuals have an asymmetric preference function, the final result will remain the same: a budget of $75 will be passed.

What if the model is extended from the case of committee voting to voting for parties in elections? In this case the median again holds forth: the claim is that two candidates competing in an election will adopt the policy position favoured by the median voter. The argument replicates the earlier discussion of committee voting, and is illustrated in Figure 4.5 (Mueller, 2003: 231). In Figure 4.5, L is the position of the

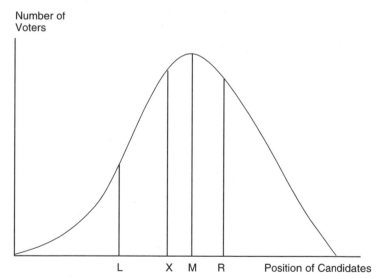

Figure 4.5

left-wing candidate, R the position of the right-wing candidate, X the midway position between L and R and M the median position. The assumption is that candidate L will receive all the votes to the left of the midway position X, whilst candidate R will receive all the votes to the right of X. Hence if candidate L moves his position further towards R, then X will also move towards R, and L will receive more votes. Both candidates hence receive more votes by moving towards the position of the median voter.

The assumptions made in this model are heroic, to say the least. It assumes that there is only one issue to be decided, that the candidates can be divided along one dimension on the issue, that the preference distribution is symmetric and has only one peak, that all individuals vote, and that there are only two candidates (Mueller, 2003: 232). The model also assumes that individuals only espouse policy positions in order to win votes (hence have no commitment to any particular policy issues), voters are fully informed about the candidates' policy positions, and candidates are fully informed about voter preferences (Ordeshook, 1997). Further, in common with economic models generally, it assumes that preferences are 'given' and are not formed or moulded by the election process itself.

It is worth noting that a number of models have been developed which relax some of these assumptions (see Ordeshook, 1997: 258). However, despite the restrictive nature of the assumptions, advocates claim that:

> A large experimental literature . . . demonstrates the robustness of spatial theory's primary results . . . we find at least one institutional arrangement – winner take–all elections in which the victorious candidate has a relatively free hand at implementing his or her campaign platform – that yields but a few political parties . . . all of whom compete with centrist policy platforms. (Ordeshook, 1997: 259)

Elections to the British parliament are conducted on a 'winner takes all' arrangement: does recent experience bear out this optimistic conclusion? For one thing, it would be necessary to omit consideration of results from Northern Ireland, where voting patterns are heavily influenced by religious considerations. However, the experience of the behaviour of British political parties during the 1980s and early 1990s does seem to conflict rather sharply with these predictions, as this period is commonly viewed as one of severe policy polarization, with the two main parties adopting extreme ideological positions.[7]

However, against this, and in support of the model, it could be argued that the Labour Party in Britain remained, and would have continued to remain, unelectable unless it shifted its position towards that of the median voter. Further investigation of the question as to what extent recent electoral experiences in Britain reflect the predictions of the spatial model is undoubtedly interesting, although warranting more investigation than can be offered here.

ELECTORAL SYSTEMS

As the previous discussion may have indicated, a considerable amount of research has been carried out on the advantages and disadvantages of various electoral systems. It is probably not surprising to note that, if preferences change, outcomes can change. However, anyone with a vague knowledge of different electoral systems is probably also aware that if preferences remain constant, outcomes might change if institutions change (Hinich & Munger, 1997: 17). The British electoral system, where the winner takes all, is frequently cited as an example of an institution where outcomes do not appear to directly reflect preferences. For example, in the 1997 general election the Labour Party received 43.3 per cent of the total votes cast, hence less than half of voters chose the Labour Party. However, on the basis of this vote, Labour won 63.6 per cent of the parliamentary seats, and was thus able to form a government with a clear majority over all other parties. Moreover, in the 1979 election the Conservative Party received more of a share of the vote (43.9 per cent) than Labour received in 1997, yet won only 53.4 per cent of parliamentary seats (Johnston, 2001).

As the British Liberal Democratic Party, who invariably receive a considerably lower percentage of parliamentary seats than their vote would suggest, continually lament: the voting system in use in the British electoral system does seem to run counter to the individual's intuitive sense of a fair result. The public/rational choice literature has thus explored the issue as to how different methods of summarizing the same underlying structure of preferences produce different choices (Riker, 1982: 41). Despite the problems that the above examples raise, it has been argued that, in cases where the choice is between exactly two alternatives, simple majority voting is the most desirable system of voting. This is because simple majority voting between two alternatives satisfies the following three conditions:

1) Monotonicity. This is where an increase in the value of some Di (a persons' preferences or values) implies an increment (or at least not a decrease) in the value of F(D) (the amalgamated preferences or values). Hence a change from favouring y to either indifference between x and y or to favouring x has the result of improving x. (Strong monotonicity is where, if a tie exists between two alternatives, and just one vote shifts position, the tie is broken.)
2) Anonymity. This is a situation where one vote cannot be distinguished from another.
3) Neutrality. This is where the method does not favour either alternative. In other words, the dice are not loaded in favour of one alternative or another. Hence a contrast to neutrality is provided in voting systems which favour the status quo. For example, in

the 1979 referendum on whether or not to establish a Scottish parliament, the issue was not settled by simple majority voting, as the parliament would only be established if over 40 per cent of those entitled to vote supported the establishment. The vote for establishment gained majority support, but failed to collect the required 40 per cent and thus the parliament was not established.

In order to appreciate how alternative voting systems may not comply with these three conditions, take the single transferable voting system, currently used for all election in the Republic of Ireland, and elections to the Australian Senate, amongst others. In this system the candidate with the least votes is eliminated, and these votes are then transferred to the voters' second preferences. However, compare the two votes shown in Tables 4.3 and 4.4 (from Riker, 1982, after Doran &

	D1			
Number of Votes	*First Choice*	*Second Choice*	*Third Choice*	*Fourth Choice*
9	W	Z	X	Y
6	X	Y	Z	W
2	Y	X	Z	W
4	Y	Z	X	W
5	Z	X	Y	W

Table 4.3

	D			
Number of Votes	*First Choice*	*Second Choice*	*Third Choice*	*Fourth Choice*
9	W	Z	X	Y
6	X	Y	Z	W
2	X	Y	Z	W
4	Y	Z	X	W
5	Z	X	Y	W

Table 4.4

Krovick, 1977). In Table 4.3, 9 votes are for $W > Z > X > Y$, 6 are for $X > Y > Z > W$, and so on. There are two seats being contested, four candidates, and twenty six voters. Typically, the quota (q) is given as follows:

$$\text{Quota} = \left(\frac{\text{voters}}{\text{seats} + 1} \right) + 1$$

Hence, in this example, the quota is $(26/3) + 1 = 9$ (rounded down). Thus a candidate has to secure 9 votes to be elected, and thus W is elected on the first ballot. To select the second candidate, as Z receives the least votes, they are eliminated, with these votes passing to X (the second choice). X is therefore elected as the second candidate, with eleven votes. However, compare this to Table 4.4. In Table 4.4, W is again elected on the first vote, Y is eliminated, and these four votes go to Z, which is elected as second candidate with 9 votes. Hence X is elected under D1, Z under D. However, all that has changed between D1 and D is that X has risen in two preference orderings. Hence even though the valuation of X has increased by two votes in D compared to D1, X wins in D1 but not in D.

The voting procedure here thus violates the monotonicity requirement, as the increased support for X in D does not lead to the selection of X. In simple majority rule, where the candidate who is ranked first by more than half of the voters is chosen, the monotonicity requirement is met. However, alternative voting procedures, besides simple majority and STV, are possible. As noted in the course of the discussion of Buchanan and Tullock in Chapter 2, one of the disadvantages of majority rule is that it allows logrolling and hence may have redistributional effects, and thus a unanimity principle may be viewed as preferable.

Given possibilities such as these with majority rule, attention has been directed to the importance of agenda setting and who controls the agenda. For example, take again a Condorcet result from three individuals voting as in Table 4.5. The individual preferences in Table 4.5 are transitive, but collective preferences are intransitive. However, assume that the winner is selected in a two–stage process. For example, say in the first stage X is voted for against Y. In this case, as two individuals prefer X to Y, then Y wins. If, at the next stage, the vote is between X and Z, then Z wins, and thus reflects the social choice. What is thus selected as the social choice depends upon the order in which the alternatives are presented, as Table 4.6 illustrates.

Individual A	Individual B	Individual C
X	Y	Z
Y	Z	X
Z	X	Y

Table 4.5

Stage	Agenda 1	Agenda 2	Agenda 3
1st Stage	x versus y: x wins	z versus x: z wins	z versus y: y wins
2nd Stage	x versus z: z wins	z versus y: y wins	y versus x: x wins
Social choice	Z chosen	Y chosen	X chosen

Table 4.6

Consequently, individual A would prefer agenda 3 (X chosen), individual B agenda 2 (Y chosen) and individual C agenda 1 (Z chosen) (Cain, 2001). Hence the significance of which individual ultimately controls the agenda.

Given the preferences in Table 4.5, then majority voting will not provide any winner. However, in Table 4.6 the same preferences give x, y and z as Condorcet winners with regard to agenda A, B and C respectively. According to the Condorcet criterion, the candidate who defeats all others in pair-wise elections using majority rule is selected (Mueller, 2003: 147). However, there may be times when this procedure may appear somewhat unfair. For example, take Table 4.7 (Mueller, 2003: 149). In Table 4.7 X is the Condorcet winner, as it is preferred by simple majority rule. However, whilst X is the preferred option for three people, it is the least preferred for the remaining two. In contrast, Y is the most preferred by two people, yet not the least preferred by the other two. There is thus a sense in which the selection of X involves three individuals imposing their preferred choice on the other two, and, overall, it might be though that Y should emerge as the preferred option. Such a result – i.e. Y – would be given by the procedure of the Bourda count. According to this procedure, the candidate given the lowest ranking is awarded one point, the second lowest two points, and so on. Hence in Table 4.7, given the Bourda count, candidate X would receive 11 points, candidate Y 12 points, and thus candidate Y would be selected.

There is a vast range of work within the public choice literature which explores the various issues and problems arising from different voting procedures, and the above discussion can thus only provide

V1	V2	V3	V4	V5
X	X	X	Y	Y
Y	Y	Y	Z	Z
Z	Z	Z	X	X

Table 4.7

a brief overview of some of the issues involved. However, before leaving this chapter it is useful to illustrate another issue that resembles Arrow's Impossibility Theorem – Sen's impossibility of a Paretian Liberal.

SEN AND LIBERALISM

Sen's problem arises if individuals have 'nosey preferences' – i.e. preferences over outcomes involving other individuals. In its initial formulation, Sen considered two individuals, a prude (A) and a lewd (B), and the act of reading a copy of Lawrence's *Lady Chatterley's Lover*. Sen's argument can be understood in terms of the three following social states:

a) neither reads the book;
b) the prude (A) reads the book and the lewd (B) does not;
c) the lewd (B) reads the book and the prude (A) does not.

The prude (A) is assumed to prefer that no-one reads the book, but would rather herself rather than the lewd read it (she is presumably worried about the further debilitating effect it might have on the lewd). Hence, for A:

$a > b > c.$

In contrast, the lewd (B) would prefer it if the prude read the book, either because she enjoys the thought of the prude's embarrassment, or because she thinks it would enlighten the prude. Further, the lewd would prefer it if she read the book than if no-one read it. Hence, for B:

$b > c > a.$

Sen assumes a 'liberal sphere' for each individual. That is, each has a recognized personal sphere where her preferences alone are significant (a condition of minimal individual liberty, or ML). Given this, then each can decide whether or not they themselves read the book. By this condition, then, the prude A has a>b. That is, they would prefer that no-one read the book rather than that they read it. By the same condition, the lewd B has c>a. That is, they would rather read it than no-one read it.

However, recall from the discussion of Arrow in the previous chapter that, in its weak form, the Pareto principle (P) states that if every individual prefers social state X to social state Y, then X must be socially preferred over Y. In the case here, both individuals rank b>c, and hence by the Pareto principle then social state b must ranked above c. Hence, the prude A has a>b, the lewd B has c>a, yet the Pareto principle gives b>c.

As was the case with Arrow's theorem, a cycle results: a>b (prude's preferences), b>c (Pareto), yet c>a (lewd's preferences). Again, in common with Arrow's theorem, the cycle results despite the fact that only a few, apparently reasonable, restrictions are involved.[8] However, possibly the most contentious area of Sen's argument concerns his condition of minimal individual liberty. To appreciate why, take two concerns that have been raised in the literature on Sen's argument.[9]

One concern is that, on Sen's view, rights are conditional. Thus prude preferring no-one to herself to lewd reading the book is conditional upon lewd not reading the book: if lewd does read the book, prude's preference becomes irrelevant. Yet rights are normally seen as unconditional, and not dependent upon what others do. If I have a right to life, this right is not conditional upon the actions of others. A further concern is that Sen defines choice over states of the world: each chooses what their preferred states of the world would be. However, it seems just as plausible to argue that rights are over actions, not social states. If I have a right to do x I may or may not choose to exercise this right. Hence both prude and lewd can have a right to read the book, but not rights over social states.

These two concerns could indicate that there is possibly a wider issue involved here. In the case of the prude it is assumed that she would prefer no-one to read the book to herself reading it, and prefers herself reading it to the lewd reading it. Sen argues that the preference of no-one over herself should be regarded as part of her 'personal sphere', and hence protected by ML. However, it is not immediately obvious as to why this preference ranking should lead to a 'personal sphere' entailing rights. The prude might prefer that neither read the book: however, to what extent can this be understood as a right which confers obligations on the lewd?

It thus seems that Sen assumes that at least one individual – the prude – is allowed illiberal preferences to be preserved in her 'personal space'. The prude does not want the lewd to read the book. However, this preference appears more dictatorial than 'nosey', and it is not clear how, or why, this preference should be defended in terms of rights issues.

CONCLUSION

The areas investigated in this chapter draw upon and extend the initial rational choice models investigated in Chapters 2 and 3. Initially, the chapter investigated the suggestion that Hobbes's derivation of the need for a sovereign, given an initial state of nature, can be understood in terms of a prisoners' dilemma. Although there are no doubt similarities between the two situations, there also appear to be a number of differences which question the claimed analogy. For example, the basic structure of a prisoners' dilemma considers the pay-offs to be known and strategies are only available to the prisoners, not the arresting officer.

Elster's analysis of Marx, although recognizing that Marx is by no means committed to rational choice theories of explanation, argued nevertheless that issues relevant to Marx's understanding of revolutionary action can be understood in terms of 'free rider' issues. However, although this analysis is undoubtedly of interest, Marx's analysis of societal change would appear to involve a variety of considerations that are not easily captured as 'free rider' problems. The chapter then investigated claims that property rights and political entrepreneurs can be understood, in part at least, as 'solutions' to such free rider problems.

In the case of spatial models of politics, investigations focused on issues such as the median voter theorem. Although a number of the ideas investigated claimed that this was one area where rational choice theory can offer robust predictions, the assumptions that frequently have to be made in order to generate such predictions are frequently severe. The subsequent investigation of electoral systems allowed issues in preference concealment, agenda setting and logrolling to be investigated. Finally, the chapter investigated Sen's argument that rights issues might conflict with the Pareto principle, an argument that can be viewed as a development of Arrow's theorem as investigated in Chapter 3.

Notes

1. Elster does suggest that Marx's explanations on occasion seem to assume satisficing, rather than maximizing, behaviour.
2. It is worth noting that Marx did not believe a revolution was inevitable: the transition to socialism could occur by peaceful means.
3. See the conflicting views in Carver and Thomas (1995).
4. For a useful discussion of Marx on these grounds, see Booth (1993).
5. This issue is not unlike the problem raised for assumptions of continuity raised by lexicographic preferences, as noted earlier.
6. On this issue, see the discussion of framing in Chapter 6.
7. For a qualified defence of the spatial model in this context, see McLean (1987).
8. More technically, the Impossibility of a Paretian Liberal claims that there is no social decision function (SDF) that satisfies an unrestricted domain (U), P (Pareto), and ML (minimal liberalism). P and ML have already been introduced, and a social decision function (SDF) is a complete and consistent (i.e. not involving

cycles) social preference defined over the set of collective social states for any set of individual preference orderings. This SDF has an unrestricted domain (U) if it works for any individual preference orderings.

9. The above draws on Mueller (2003: 643ff), which explores in more detail some of the issues raised by Sen's argument.

CHAPTER 5

Rational Choice and Politics: Empirical Evidence and Norms

Chapters 1 and 3 of this book investigated the basics of rational choice theory and indicated some of the general problems faced by the theory, whereas Chapters 2 and 4 were more concerned with issues and problems raised in connection with specific models adopting rational choice theory in order to formulate explanations or predictions in politics. One of the more contentious areas involving the use of RCT in politics concerns this claim that the models involved are scientific, hence can formulate predictions that are, or can be, confirmed by empirical evidence. For example, Downs's theory, explored in Chapter 2, predicted that individuals would not vote, as voting is an irrational act, yet this prediction is not supported empirically.

Given this, the chapter will proceed as follows. Firstly, some of the criticisms and defences of the 'scientific status' of RCT will be investigated. Secondly, a variety of models that have been developed in order to supplement Downs's analysis of voting will be investigated, in order to assess their claims to scientific status. As some of these models modify Downs's model through appealing to ethical and norm following behaviour, the final section of the chapter will investigate to what extent such behaviour is compatible with models based on RCT.

Green and Shapiro's book *Pathologies of Rational Choice Theory* provides one of the more extensive, and well-researched, reviews of the relevance of RCT in politics.[1] Green and Shapiro are clear that they are not objecting to the claim that RCT provides a 'scientific' study of politics, or to the use of a mathematically based, deductive model of explanation, or even to the claim that RCT may be useful for heuristic purposes. Rather, Green and Shapiro are interested in the empirical status of RCT when used to explain political phenomena, arguing that:

> We contend that much of the fanfare with which the rational choice approach has been heralded in political science must be seen as premature once the question is asked: What has this literature contributed to our understanding of politics? . . . To date, a large proportion of the theoretical conjectures of rational choice theorists have not been tested empirically. Those tests that have been undertaken have either failed on

their own terms or garnered theoretical support for propositions that, on reflection, can only be characterised as banal. (Green & Shapiro, 1994: 6)

Essentially, their investigations are an extended study into the question raised earlier in the context of Downs's work: how can a theory that predicts x will occur (individuals will not vote) be confronted with numerous situations where this prediction is manifestly false (individuals do vote, in their millions) yet still claim to be useful in investigating political phenomena? Green and Shapiro detail a number of strategies developed by proponents of RCT in order to either avoid empirically testing the theory or to preserve the theory when the empirical evidence appears contrary. Some of these strategies are as follows:

POST HOC THEORY DEVELOPMENT

As noted earlier in the first chapter, there is no unified agreement amongst advocates of RCT as to what exactly constitutes the RCT 'model'. Hence if one formulation of the model does not appear to find empirical justification, the model can be modified in various ways until it does accord with the evidence. An example of this form of 'adjustment' was noted earlier with Downs, where the initial model was 'modified' in order to include 'preserving democracy' as a motive for voting. Although such modifications may be defensible under the notion of 'developing the theory', Green and Shapiro note how, when confronted with contrary evidence, proponents of RCT are highly reluctant to look at alternative ways of explaining political phenomena. The assumption is thus, if empirical evidence is not forthcoming, this does not indicate any problems with the RCT approach as such, merely that some of the parameters require modification.

FORMULATING TESTS

Green and Shapiro take it to be a requirement of testing a theory such as RCT means that the theory will generate predictions, which can then be confirmed or disconfirmed at the empirical level. However, they argue that RCT explanations are frequently constructed in ways that preclude any attempt at testing predictions. For example, the theories are developed at such a level that they are regarded as being 'too abstract' to generate testable conclusions. Further, RCT incorporates a variety of unobservable phenomena (tastes, preferences, beliefs, individual information) which can be manipulated in order to provide a 'satisfactory' result. For example, the 'centipede game' outlined in Chapter 3 predicted that individuals would end the game at the first chance. However, as explored in the following chapter, experimental evidence indicates that individuals generally do not actually play such 'games' in the way that game theory predicts and, in the case of the centipede game, do not in fact end the game at the first chance. How is this discrepancy between theoretical prediction and actual result to be explained? Well, it could be that individual players hold mistaken beliefs about what a rational strategy is for themselves or others, or do not possess sufficient information concerning the actual structure of the game. Hence deviations from the predictions are explained away by assuming some form of irrationality on the part of players which, if corrected, would result in them acting as the theory suggests.

Other strategies adopted by advocates of RCT include vague predictions (e.g. it is assumed enough individuals will act in the manner of the theory in order that an 'approximation' to the theory will result), only discussing evidence that appears to confirm the theory, interpreting evidence so that it does conform with the theory, and restricting the domain of the theory (e.g. by arguing that the theory is successful in most areas, but cannot provide explanations in some limited areas, such as voting behaviour).

Green and Shapiro's arguments attracted a number of responses, some sympathetic, some hostile. As an indication of the significance of the issues raised by Green and Shapiro, a special double edition of the journal *Critical Review* was devoted solely to issues raised by the authors, the various contributions being later published in book form (Friedman, 1996). Proponents of the use of RCT in political studies objected, in the main, to Green and Shapiro's characterization of what constitutes 'good scientific method', and hence to their argument that RCT failed to meet the criteria demanded in any work claiming to be scientific. Green and Shapiro thus stand accused of evaluating RCT according to standards that are 'derived from a view of empirical research that is deeply questionable' (Diermeier, 1996: 69). In contrast, critics of RCT reiterated the fact that experimental research indicated that individuals tend not to behave in the manner predicted by the theory (e.g. Abelson, 1996; Lane, 1996), an issue investigated further in the next chapter. For now, as the issues raised by defenders of RCT are significant in appreciating the status of the theory, it is worthwhile briefly considering these contributions.

Chong's chapter (1996) introduced two arguments frequently raised by defenders of the use of RCT in politics. Firstly, there is nothing necessarily wrong with 'ad hoc' modifications to theories. Such modifications may increase the empirical power of a theory (Chong, 1996: 45), and are commonplace in theories in the natural sciences (Diermeier, 1996: 61).[2] Secondly, as far as providing explanations of political phenomena is concerned, RCT really is the only show in town, and hence should only be rejected if a viable alternative is available which, at the moment, it is not (see also Shepsle, 1996). It was also pointed out that the alleged problem of 'domain restriction', whereby it is accepted that certain areas resist explanation, and appeals to 'unobservables' are also found in the natural sciences (Diermeier, 1996).

For example, Newton's theory is still utilized in the natural sciences, although it was and is incapable of providing an explanation for the orbit of the planet Mercury. Problems in explaining this orbit thus reveal a 'domain restriction' on the theory: the orbit of Mercury cannot be explained by the theory. Similarly, phenomena such as 'gravity' are used in formulating explanations and predictions in the natural sciences, although it is not observable. Other defenders of RCT were more willing to accept limitations, conceding that the theory is useful in explaining some, but not all, political phenomena (Lohmann, 1996: 131); is useful in guiding empirical research even if its explanatory success is questionable (Ferejohn & Satz, 1996: 72); or has explanatory power even if not very successful at producing predictions (Chong, 1996: 49).

Of these arguments, the claim that 'ad hoc' theory modifications are quite acceptable is probably the key issue and also, in the main, under-pins the other claims. Hence the issues raised above will be discussed in reverse order, starting with the claim that explanations based on RCT should be retained even if the theory's predictive power is weak. The reason why RCT is vulnerable to this objection concerns the claimed 'scientific status' of RCT. The ability to formulate predictions is often cited as a characteristic of theories in the natural sciences and hence the 'predictive power' of theories regarded as a desirable characteristic. It is worth noting in this connection that advocates of RCT frequently adopt, either implicitly or explicitly, a form of naturalism, whereby the methods of the natural sciences are seen as providing a 'model' for investigations in politics and the social sciences generally.

In order to illustrate the point that RCT is explanatory, even if not predictive, Chong refers to the example of a strike amongst major league baseball players in the USA during 1994–5. Chong admits that RCT is not capable of predicting what level of defection will take place through free riding (i.e. it cannot predict how many players will choose to break the strike). However:

> Although rational choice theory probably could not have told us the absolute level of free riding among baseball players, it could produce some insight into which categories of players would have been most likely to defect . . . in general, players who need the money most and who have weak relationships to other players. (Chong, 1996: 49)

However, this attempted endorsement of the potential explanatory power of RCT seems to run foul of another charge made by Green and Shapiro – the theory arrives at conclusions that are either trivial or obvious. Hence it might be objected that political scientists do not really need to employ the sophisticated mathematical modelling used in RCT to arrive at the conclusion that strike breakers are more likely to be those individuals most in need of the income supplied by their wages and feeling somewhat isolated from the group. The 'result' seems fairly obvious, and it is not at all clear in this example exactly what is being uniquely explained by RCT that could not be explained by any number of other approaches.

Next, consider the argument that, in contrast to Chong's claim, even if RCT has not attained explanatory success it has been successful in guiding empirical research. As an example of this success, Ferejohn and Satz offer the following:

> Consider, for example, the way that rational choice theories made the act of voting problematic in ways that it had not been in earlier theories. This shift meant that it was now voting rather than nonvoting that a successful theory need to explain. (Ferejohn & Satz, 1996: 72)

The logic of this argument appears to consist in the following:

1) In Western democracies, individuals, in the main, tend to vote;
2) Previously, this was not seen as raising any explanatory problems;
3) However, according to RCT the act of voting is irrational;
4) Hence we now need to explain why individuals do vote.

This argument appears to vindicate Green and Shapiro's argument that inquiries are frequently model led, rather than problem led. It is presumably only necessary to explain why individuals do vote because an RCT model, which assumes that such behaviour is irrational, is being deployed. However, leaving aside the RCT model, why is the fact that numerous individuals do vote in Western democracies a 'problem' that requires explaining? With this argument, a feature of the political process that RCT cannot adequately explain is turned into a 'problem' requiring explanation. There is no obvious 'problem of voting': rather, the activity of voting is an area of political activity that RCT cannot explain.

However, to be fair to advocates of RCT it could be argued that the theory does raise questions concerning an area that had frequently been regarded as 'obvious', not worthy of exploration. It was thus merely assumed that individuals would vote, and hence the increasing rate at which individuals tend to abstain from voting regarded as a major problem. From the perspective of RCT we should be more surprised that individuals vote in the numbers they do, rather than be concerned that voter turnout is becoming lower than it was.

The issue of voting is also raised in a paper by Lohmann who, although recognizing that RCT cannot explain all political phenomena, argues that voting does not cause any particular problems for RCT. Lohmann, citing in defence the model of voting developed by Palfrey and Rosenthal (1985), arrives at the conclusion that:

> There exists an equilibrium for which participation rates approximate one hundred percent – even if voters are purely self-interested and the electorate is 'very large' . . . Their result relies on the assumption that voters are completely informed about each other's preferences and costs of voting. Under incomplete information, the unique equilibrium involves vanishingly low (albeit strictly positive) turnout numbers. (Lohmann, 1996: 144)

Hence RCT can predict high turnout at elections, even where the act of voting is taken to be costly to individuals. However, this high turnout is only a result of the model if it is assumed that each individual knows the preferences and costs of all other individuals, which are highly implausible assumptions. So if a high turnout vote was observed in an election, does this RCT model explain why this has happened? Yes – *if* all individuals possess a phenomenal amount of information in the manner assumed by the model. Once these informational requirements are increasingly relaxed, it appears that the 'results' are more in accordance with the predictions of the basic RCT model on this subject: individuals will not vote.

This issue of voting can also be used to illustrate problems with the next point: that theories in the natural sciences exhibit domain restrictions, noted by Diermeier. In his account of scientific knowledge, Kuhn, to whom Diermeier refers, noted that scientists became increasingly concerned that Newton's theory was unable to explain certain scientific phenomena ('anomalies') (Kuhn, 1962). However, when Einstein propounded his theory, it was found that the theory explained the various phenomena that caused difficulties for Newton's account. Hence there are certain domains which are incapable of explanation in terms of Newtonian physics, although they can be explained by Einstein's theory. However, this does not result in Newtonian physics being completely discarded.

However accurate this might be as an account of theory explanation in the natural science, it is potentially misleading if claimed as an analogy regarding disputes concerning RCT. According to Diermeier's argument concerning the orbit of Mercury, 'Newton's theory never worked for this planet . . . [but] . . . Einstein's theory of general relativity could account for it' (Diermeier, 1996: 66). However, the fact that the orbit of Mercury could not be adequately explained by Newton's theory was only discovered by Newcomb in 1898, a considerable number of years after the publication of Newton's theory. In contrast, explaining voting behaviour was recognized as a problem for RCT from the start. The two cases would thus appear to be quite different. In the case of Newton's theory there was an increasing realization of explanatory problems, whereas with RCT explanatory problems were clear from the start.

Of course, it can be granted to Diermeier that just as adopting Einstein's theory in order to explain the orbit of Mercury does not require any wholesale rejection of Newton so rejecting RCT in the case of explaining voting behaviour does not necessitate that the theory thus cannot explain political phenomena. However, that is beside the point, which is that advocates of RCT *are very reluctant* to restrict domains when it seems clear that they should. If, after all the intellectual work that has been carried out, advocates of RCT are still incapable of explaining voter behaviour within their models, maybe they should agree that this is one area where the model is simply inapplicable.

The issue of voting is also relevant when introducing the next point made by advocates of RCT: that it is the only viable theoretical model available when investigating political phenomena. Thus Chong states that:

> The fact that rational choice theory has fallen short in explaining voter turnout, therefore, is no reason to abandon the theory. Until there is a rival theory that solves the paradox of voting, it will not be a problem that ate rational choice. (Chong, 1996: 41)

However, why should any other theory be able to 'explain the paradox of voting' when it only *is* only a paradox *because* of the assumptions embedded in RCT. If alternative explanations are offered as to why individuals vote, then there is no 'paradox of voting'. The fact that individuals vote when RCT declares this act to be irrational does not reveal that the act of voting is therefore paradoxical. Rather, the act of voting is an anomaly for RCT: it is an act that cannot be explained within the confines of the theory.

Advocates of RCT are frequently critical of anyone who rejects the theory without, as they see it, adequately understanding it. However, this argument cuts both ways, and surely it is incumbent upon advocates of RCT to adequately understand alternatives before deciding that RCT is 'the only show in town'.

As an example of this misunderstanding, take the view that 'social-science explanations must . . . be compatible with intentional descriptions of human agents' (Ferejohn & Satz, 1996: 74). This claim reflects the fact that 'rational choice explanations are typically formulated by reference to individual intentions' (Green & Shapiro, 1994: 20). As explored in the following chapter, it is in fact far from clear that RCT can provide intentional explanations in the form required. However, let us assume for now that explanations in politics must be conducted in terms of individual intentions, rather than, say, in terms of 'functions'. Assuming we accept the need for intentional explanations, does this mean we must necessarily adopt RCT? Chong provides the following contrast between sociological models and RCT models of explanation:

> In their ideal form, sociological explanations ground the motivation for behaviour in people's attachment to social norms rather than in their assessment of opportunity costs. Rational choice or economic explanations, on the other hand, focus on the intentions of the agent, who chooses among alternative courses of action depending upon the rewards promised by each one. (Chong, 1996: 39)

Hence we are given a contrast between a sociological explanation referring to norms and a rational choice explanation referring to individual intentions. Given this, then assuming we do want to speak of individual intentions, it seems that we are committed to adopting RCT, and rejecting any form of sociological explanation. However, the dichotomy proposed by Chong is simply false. To illustrate why, consider the following explanation conducted in terms of norms.

In Britain, barristers and judges almost invariably wear wigs when appearing in court. This 'fact' can allow me to make a prediction about the behaviour of barristers and judges. Hence if I choose to go to a courtroom in the Old Bailey tomorrow, I can predict that any barristers or judges present will be wearing wigs. So why do these individuals almost invariably wear wigs? According to RCT it is presumably because each individual weighs up the costs and benefits of wearing and not wearing a wig, and decides for the former. However, an alternative explanation may be that these individuals wear wigs because there is a norm of the form 'barristers and judges ought to wear wigs in court'. In other words, individuals wear wigs because they are following norms, not because they have undertaken some form of cost benefit analysis.

What constitutes norm-following behaviour, and why individuals follow norms, is a complex area, investigated later in this chapter. At this point, it is merely necessary to ask: if we accept the 'norm-following' explanation, does this indicate that we have thus rejected the intentional form of explanation advocated in RCT? This is not at all necessarily the case, as the norm may give the individual the reason, and thus the intention, to perform the act in question. Individuals thus wear wigs because they intend to wear wigs, and they intend to wear wigs because they intend to follow the relevant norm. Hence the fact that an explanation in terms of social norms, rather than in terms of RCT, has been offered in no way inhibits an appeal to intentional explanations.

In the above explanation, it was noted that the relevant individuals 'almost invariably' wear wigs. The qualification was introduced because, in recent years, it has become accepted practice for wigs not to be worn in court in cases where young children may be required to give evidence. However, this exception does not invalidate the above, as the relevant norm still allows predictions to be formulated. Hence if I go to the Old Bailey with the intention of attending a trial involving young children, then I would predict that the relevant individuals will not be wearing wigs.

Thus it seems perfectly possible to invoke intentional explanations, and offer predictions concerning behaviour, without relying on a RCT form of explanation. The main point following from this is that the claim that RCT is 'the only show in town' is frequently advanced because advocates of RCT misconstrue the nature of alternative forms of explanation. It does not seem unfair to demand that advocates of RCT should at least be aware of the alternative forms of explanation that are possible, and not reject these alternatives because of a set of false assumptions concerning the nature and scope of any such alternative forms of explanation.

This brings us to the last claim identified above: that 'ad hoc' theorizing should not be condemned, as it is an essential component of theory development. Hence if Downs's model of voting behaviour is modified in order to encompass, say, information about preferences and costs, as detailed above, does this represent an illicit modification, made in order to 'save' the model when confronted by conflicting evidence, or does it rather represent how RCT models of voting behaviour have become more advanced and sophisticated?

Although the discussion of the criticisms and defences of RCT conducted in this chapter have until now focused on general points, it would seem appropriate in investigating the 'ad hoc' theorizing claim to focus on developments concerning Downs's model of voting behaviour. What is thus of interest is to establish whether these developments represent theoretical developments that bring models more in keeping with available empirical evidence, or alternatively whether they reveal the 'ad hoc' theorizing that Green and Shapiro criticise.

As initially noted in Chapter 2, Downs argued that the act of voting was essentially irrational. Blais (2000) has provided the following list of seven main modifications that have been advanced to Downs's initial argument that voting behaviour is essentially irrational:

1) Individuals vote in order to maintain democratic institutions. This was the modification initially proposed by Downs and, as noted in Chapter 2, is incapable of resolving the claimed 'paradox of voting'.

2) Individuals vote out of a sense of duty. Riker and Ordeshook (1968) are two authors who have advanced a model of voting behaviour which incorporates the idea of 'duty'. According to this idea, the act of voting can be modelled as follows:

$$P \times NCD + D \geq C$$

Where P = the probability that an individual vote will affect the outcome of the majority rule decision,
NCD = the perceived net benefit of one candidate over another,

133

D = the individual's sense of civic duty, which is the utility that the individual derives from voting, regardless of the outcome,
C + costs associated, at the margin, with voting (e.g. time spent, weather conditions)

However, this explanation seems to rely more on an appeal to norm-following behaviour, rather than RCT. Further, as Blais points out, within the terms of RCT, the explanation is a tautology, as it is always possible to explain any behaviour by stating that the individual does what they do because they believe that the rewards outweigh the costs. Hence if the RCT model predicts that individuals will not act in a certain manner because the costs of so acting will outweigh any potential benefits, yet individuals do, in fact, so act, then all that is needed is to adopt the model by adding another factor – call it 'duty' – to the benefits side and, lo and behold, benefits now outweigh costs, and the behaviour is explained. As Mueller notes:

> This modification of the rational voter hypothesis does reconcile the act of voting with individual rationality, but does so by robbing the rational, self-interest hypothesis of its predictive power. Any hypothesis can be reconciled with any conflicting piece of evidence with the addition of the appropriate auxiliary hypothesis. (Mueller, 2003: 306)

Another problem with this appeal to 'duty' can be appreciated through exploring in what sense the term is being used. The idea of an individual having a 'duty' is frequently recognized as a correlative to the idea that another individual has a right. For example, if one individual has a right to life, other individuals have a duty not to harm or kill the individual. However, the idea of an individual having a duty might also be used where no other individual has a corresponding right. For example, an individual observing their neighbour attempting to push-start their car may feel that they have a duty to assist the neighbour. However, the neighbour does not have a right to this assistance, and cannot demand it if it is not forthcoming.

The use of the term 'duty' in the model detailed above clearly does not imply that any individual has a corresponding right. Consequently, the sense of duty entailed in the act of voting would appear to be analogous to the sense of duty felt towards the neighbour. However, whilst it might be easily understandable as to why an individual may feel a duty to help their neighbour, it is not at all obvious why an individual would feel that they had a 'duty' to vote. To whom do they feel they have such a duty? It would appear that this sense of duty is felt towards something like 'the civic culture'. However, in this case the explanation would appear to contradict the methodological individualism assumption, as a belief about duty towards a culture is not a belief about individuals.

A similar model claims that individuals vote because they value expressing support (Aldrich, 1997). According to this model, voting is an act of consumption, not investment. Hence if, say, a voter is asked to vote on a motion to increase the number of schools in an area the, on the expressive vote model, voting in favour of this motion merely indicates that the voter approves of the motion (Fails & Tollison, 1990). In contrast, in the economic model, the voter would take account of the costs of this outcome, if supported. Hence the gains from voting are seen as the 'act of voting itself and the opportunity for expression that this affords' (Mueller, 2003: 320).

3) Individuals are risk averse, and want to avoid the regret associated with not voting and seeing their preferred candidate lose by one vote. This argument, first propounded by Ferejohn and Fiorina (1974), assumes that individuals would adopt a 'minimax' strategy when considering voting. Hence individuals would compare how much regret they would feel if they voted and their vote was not decisive with how much regret they would feel if they did not vote and their preferred candidate lost by one vote. If the regret expected to be involved in the latter course of action is greater than that expected if the former course of action is undertaken, then the individual will vote. The individual is thus viewed as being somewhat conservative, adopting the strategy which involves minimizing the maximum regret they will feel ('minimax').

However, the theory appears to ignore the fact that individuals will probably have some idea as to how decisive their vote is likely to be. Further, as a number of commentators have pointed out (on this, see Mueller, 1993: 307–8), the theory seems to lead to some rather strange results. For example, say a voter is indifferent between the various candidates available for selection, and thus thinks they will stay at home and not bother to vote. However, the individual then discovers that, although previously unbeknown to them, a candidate for an extreme party, which the individual loathes, is also standing. The maximum regret would now be felt if the extreme candidate won by one vote, and hence the individual now votes, even if the extreme candidate has no realistic chance of winning the election. The theory would thus seem to predict that the presence of an extreme candidate should significantly increase turnout. A further point is that individuals adopting a minimax-regret strategy may well be advised to stay at home and not vote, as presumably being run down and killed by a car on the way to voting would elicit the most regret, even if the chances of this happening are minimal. (This issue also raises problems for Downs's model, as the probability of being run over by a car is probably just as great as the probability that one's vote will be decisive – see Mueller, 1993: 305.)

4) The fourth explanation relies on a modified form of game theory, arguing that individuals will vote because they expect other

rational individuals not to vote, and hence imagine that their vote will be decisive, a form of explanation already encountered during the discussion of Downs in Chapter 2. However, in this case, if an individual is not certain that all others will abstain, then they will themselves abstain. Also, the individual may reason that all others will adopt the same thought process, and hence all will vote, in which case abstention is again difficult. Aldrich notes that these models appear to be no more successful in predicting outcomes:

> They yield either virtually everyone or virtually no-one voting, and the real world situations to which the model corresponds are virtually always those that yield next to no-one voting. (Aldrich, 1997: 383)

5) A further explanation is that group leaders or politicians make it easier for individuals to vote. For example, politicians may mobilize voters or promise increased support for groups. However, again, the chance of an individual vote being decisive is still negligible.

6) The costs of voting are practically zero, so no great cost is incurred in voting. However, considerable costs may still be incurred in obtaining the information relevant to the act of voting, and any benefits resulting from the act of voting are also very low.

7) Individuals do not find it rational to calculate the costs and benefits of voting. This explanation essentially accepts that RCT is not relevant in explaining voter behaviour, hence accepting, at least, a 'domain restriction'.

Hence there are a variety of alternatives to Downs's original model that have been advanced in order to explain the claimed 'paradox of voting', although none can claim to command universal assent from those working in this area. Moreover, with the exception of the seventh alternative, all seem to involve attempted 'ad hoc' modifications of the theory, hence supporting the claims made by Green and Shapiro.

Mueller (1993: ch. 14) provides an overview of results that have been obtained from various surveys into voter behaviour, and it is worth noting some of the salient points. Firstly, Downs's model would seem to predict that turnout would be affected if the perceived result of the election was expected to be 'too close to call': the tighter the contest, the more likely an individual's vote will be decisive, hence the increased likelihood of the individual voting. However, the results of the various surveys concerned with investigating this issue were, at best, ambiguous on the issue. Secondly, as the 'costs' of voting are increased if the weather is bad, then it could be predicted that participation in voting would decrease in bad weather. However, a number of the surveys have concluded that this is not the case, although one study did conclude that individuals with a low sense of 'civic duty' did tend to be deterred by the weather (Mueller, 1993: 320). If this is the case, then modifying the theory by appealing to a 'sense of duty' would seem insufficient, as presumably the model would need to explain why some people, but not others, vote from reasons of civic duty rather than as a result of calculating costs and benefits in the manner of RCT models. Thirdly, individuals did not necessarily vote on issues in accordance with their own self-interest, and Mueller cites one survey which concluded that over 40 per cent of individuals voted in support of a change in tax policy even though this change was financially detrimental to them.

These last two points would seem to raise serious problems for RCT models of voting behaviour, as it would appear explanations as to both why and how individuals vote must incorporate ethical issues. Hence individuals decide to vote, in part at least, out of senses of duty and the votes they cast take into account considerations of issues such as fairness, not just self-interest. Although these factors may seem to indicate problems for the basic RCT model, especially regarding the assumption that individuals are self-interested maximizers. However, after reviewing the issues surrounding 'ethical voting', Mueller notes that 'What we normally describe as ethical behaviour is inherently no more or less selfish than what we call selfish behaviour' (Mueller, 2003: 325).

Hence if an individual braves bad weather in order to vote out of a sense of civic duty (Knack, 1994), realizing that their vote is unlikely to have any effect on the outcomes, and votes for a candidate whose policies, if implemented, would result in personal financial penalties, though they regard these policies as fair, is, after all, voting selfishly. Whereas initially the evidence that individuals vote for ethical reasons appeared to indicate that individuals do not vote as the RCT model suggests, it now appears that this evidence, rather than vitiating the model, merely confirms its validity.

So how does Mueller arrive at his conclusion that ethical acts are merely another form of selfish acts? The justification for this claim is of the following form:

> When one observes how man learns, it is difficult to reject the postulate that man is innately a selfish animal . . . Ethical behaviour is learned . . . When we commit acts that harm others we are punished by our parents, teachers, and other adult supervisors. Actions that benefit others are rewarded . . . ethical behaviour . . . is a conditioned response to certain stimuli governed by past reinforcement behaviour. (Mueller, 2003: 325; also Mueller, 2004)

Leaving aside the appeal to the somewhat contentious psychological theory underlying the above claim, let us assume that individuals are rewarded when they behave ethically and punished when they do not. If so, does this entail that ethical behaviour is this inherently selfish behaviour? Say an individual, when young, is 'rewarded' whenever they keep a promise and 'punished' whenever they break a promise. If this individual, in adulthood, attempts to always keep promises made, does this entail that this behaviour is simply the product of past rewards, and hence an example of selfish behaviour? According to RCT we are interested in providing explanations in terms of individuals and their intentions, and hence we are interested in the reasons why the individual attempts to keep promises.

Suppose that, on reaching adulthood, the individual reflects upon the practice of promise-keeping, possibly because they are tempted to break a promise and, on reflection (possibly for the Kantian reasons detailed below), decides that promises should, where possible, be kept. In this case the reason why the individual keeps the promise is because, on reflection, they believe that keeping promises is a sound ethical principle. Hence the fact that the individual was 'rewarded', when younger, for keeping promises is completely irrelevant when it comes to explaining this behaviour in terms of individual reasons.

Is it rational to keep a promise when it is in my self-interest to not keep the promise? According to RCT the answer is no. Recall the prisoners' dilemma from Chapter 1: even if the prisoners communicate and both promise to co-operate then, according to RCT, it is still rational for each to break the promise and defect. However, according to Kant, an individual should, where possible, keep promises made, even if instrumental rationality prescribes defection. Kant argued that our moral imperatives should be autonomous, not heteronymous. That is, they should be arrived at through the use of reason alone, and not be influenced by our desires. The 'Kantian test' as to whether we should or should not follow a possible moral imperative is that of universality: we should only follow those imperatives which we could rationally decide that all others should also follow.

So should we keep promises? The 'Kantian test' is to establish whether or not we could agree to the following imperative: individuals ought not to keep promises they have made. Kant argues that we cannot assent to this imperative because, if all others continually broke their promises, then the institution of promise-keeping will break down. A similar argument could be advanced to the question: should I vote? In other words, can I will a universal law of the form 'individuals ought not to vote'. The answer to the question has already been given by Downs, assuming that democratic institutions are valued. If no individuals voted, then democratic institutions would break down. Hence I have a duty to vote.

Several points flow from this brief exploration of Kant. Firstly, just because individual senses of 'civic duty' might have been rewarded, and because individuals vote out of a sense of civic duty, it cannot be concluded that they are thus voting because they have been so conditioned, and hence the act of voting is, in the end, a product of selfish behaviour. An individual may decide to vote, and vote the way that they do, because they are committed to a Kantian ethical code. For such an individual, considerations of self-interest are completely irrelevant. Even if an individual 'learns' to keep promises through being punished for not keeping them, it cannot simply be assumed that therefore this learning process explains why the individual keeps their promises. Secondly, Kant's argument reveals how individual behaviour based on self-interested considerations may be *parasitic upon* other forms of behaviour. Hence the reason why any individual can make a promise, then break it on self-interested grounds, is precisely because most other individuals do not break promises. If all individuals behaved in the manner of the self-interested individual, there would not be an institution or social practice of the form 'promise keeping'.

Thirdly, as its name implies, RCT is supposed to be a theory of individual choice. However, as noted in Chapter 3, in many situations it would appear that rational individuals do not, according to RCT, have much choice at all. For example, it would appear that individuals do not have a choice on whether to vote, as rationality dictates not voting; neither do they have a choice on co-operation or defection in the prisoners' dilemma. Mueller's appeal to conditioning behaviour appears to retain the flavour of this form of explanation: individuals act out of a sense of civic duty because that is the way they have been conditioned to behave. It seems somewhat peculiar to refer to 'rational choice' in situations where individuals, in order to act rationally, do not appear to possess much choice.

It consequently seems fair to conclude that Mueller's attempt to reduce ethical behaviour to self-interested behaviour is far from convincing. If the relevant surveys are correct, and individual voting behaviour is subject to ethical considerations regarding both the decision to vote and how the vote is cast, then we may well be interested in discovering how and why individuals hold these ethical views, and why they inform the act of voting in the way they do. However, it is far too early to assume that such ethical voting does not raise any questions for the RCT assumption that individuals act according to self-interest.

In its basic form, RCT does not appear capable of offering a satisfactory answer to either the question as to why individuals vote or to the question why individuals vote in the manner they do. Various modifications to the theory have been considered, none of which seem capable of commanding widespread support. Empirical evidence suggests that the act of voting is motivated, in part at least, by ethical concerns. However, it is not easy to appreciate how such concerns can be incorporated into the RCT model without considerable modifications to the model. Aldrich has noted that the question of the rationality of voting is the 'Achilles' heel of rational choice theory in political science', and continues by noting:

> The stakes are high. Voting is perhaps the most common and the most important decision faced by citizens in a democracy. If such a common

and important decision cannot be understood as 'rational', then how can our complex theories of politics, public choice, and even economics stand, if based on such unfirm ground. (Aldrich, 1997: 380)

It is thus perhaps not surprising that considerable work has been carried out by advocates of RCT in attempting to develop models that are capable of explaining voting behaviour. It is also not surprising that various methodological arguments have been advanced in order to attempt to minimize the potentially devastating effects of RCT models proving incapable of providing any coherent explanations of voting behaviour.

At various points in this chapter the issue of social norms has been raised. It thus seems appropriate to investigate in more detail what norms are, and whether the idea of norm-following behaviour provides an alternative explanation of human action to that provided by RCT.

NORMS, SOCIAL NORMS AND CONVENTIONS

In order to investigate social norms it is first necessary to differentiate between norms and conventions. For example, in Britain, students tend to go to lectures dressed in casual clothes, and individuals tend not to push in front of others when an orderly queue has formed. However, despite the fact that these examples both refer to the tendency of individuals to act in certain ways, are they both examples of the same sort of tendency and, if so, what is it? Probably the easiest way of indicating a difference between these behavioural tendencies is to ask: what if an individual did not behave in the specified way? For example, imagine a student attends a lecture dressed in a suit, shirt and tie. In this case fellow students may wonder why the individual has dressed in this manner or, if the behaviour is systematic, might regard the individual as being somewhat eccentric. However, it is highly unlikely that fellow students would display serious disapproval of the individual's choice of dress. This is not the case with the tendency to form orderly queues, as the behaviour of an individual who attempted to push in front of others would undoubtedly be met with disapproval, especially from those now behind the pushy individual in the queue.

The two examples offered provide an illustration of the difference between a social convention and a social norm. In the case of a social convention each individual tends to follow X and each individual tends to expect others to follow X. However, if an individual does not follow X they have not necessarily done something wrong. In the case of a social norm each individual believes that they ought to follow X and each individual expects all others to follow X because they ought to. A social convention is a generalized form of behaviour, possibly resulting from the socialization process that Mueller, as noted above, used to explain ethical behaviour. In contrast, social norms have, as the name suggests, a moral normative force. They refer to how individuals believe they and others ought to behave.

Social norms are thus enforced by individuals through expressions of approval and disapproval, and any individual who transgresses a social norm tends to feel guilty or embarrassed (Elster, 1989, ch.3). Not all norms are social: there are legal norms ('you ought to stop at a red light') whose transgression, if detected, involves punishment, and private norms ('I ought to abstain from smoking') whose transgression involves feeling of private guilt and failure. Similarly, not all conventions are social: an individual may always take the same route home, or carry a certain article around with them in order to bring them luck.

In the case of a social convention then, according to Lewis (1969), the following applies:

i)   most other members of P involved with me in situation S will conform to R;
ii) I prefer that, if most other members of P involved with me in S will conform, then I conform also;
iii) Most other members of P involved with me in S expect, with reason, that I will conform;
iv) Most other members of P involved with me in S prefer that, if most of them conform, I conform also;
v)   I have a reason to believe that (i) to (iv) hold.[3]

Take the case of the student X wearing casual clothes to the lecture. In this case most other student members involved in going to the lecture will also wear casual clothes; the student X prefers that, if others wear casual clothes, he or she does themselves; most other students expect student X to wear casual clothes; most students prefer, if they wear casual clothes, that student X also wear casual clothes, and student X believes that these conditions hold.

Hence what is particularly important in the case of social conventions and, likewise, social norms, is that they involve interlocking expectations characteristic of any social relation. Ruben (1985) thus defines a social relation as a relation involving a characteristic system of interlocking beliefs and expectations, and identifies the following four conditions:

i)   if there are any social relations between X and Y, then X and Y will have interlocking beliefs and expectations about actions;
ii) they will have interlocking beliefs and expectations about the beliefs and actions of others;
iii) there will be some descending reason-relation existing between them. Some of the beliefs and expectations about how others believe or expect an agent to act is part of the agent's reasons for acting in some way;

iv) that (iii) is generally believed to be the case. That is, X believes that Y sometimes does what they do for those reasons, and Y believes that X sometimes does what they do for those reasons.

Take, as an example, the social norm that individuals ought not to pick their noses in public places. This form of behaviour (i.e. not picking noses) involves a norm because if an individual does pick their nose in public, there is a good chance that others will express their disapproval of this form of behaviour, and the individual will hence feel ashamed. As Elster (1989) points out, examples such as this illustrate the *force* of norms: individuals tend not to pick their noses in public even in cases where they will probably never encounter the offended others again.

However, this norm is also social in the manner described by Ruben. That is, taking the final condition, I know that part of the reason that an individual will not pick their nose in public is because I (and others) expect them not to. The characteristic of social norms and conventions is such that they bear similarities to two features discussed earlier: interdependent preferences and Schelling's analysis of 'focal points'. Whereas interdependent preferences characterize situations where an individual's preferences are dependent upon the preferences of others, in social norms and conventions individual preferences are, to some extent at least, dependent upon the expectations of others. I prefer not to pick my nose in public because I know others expect me not to. Similarly, it can be argued that individuals choose certain 'focal points' because they expect others also to do so.

Having investigated the nature of social norms, is it possible to conclude that norm-following behaviour is different from the instrumentally rational action characteristic of RCT models? Mueller (1997) identified two ways that norms can be seen as compatible with the model. Firstly, norms may serve to deter short-run opportunistic behaviour in favour of long-term benefits. For example, as mentioned earlier, a shopkeeper might follow a norm such as 'individuals ought to behave honestly' because it brings long-term benefits, even if dishonesty might bring greater immediate rewards. Secondly, norms may arise as a form of adaptive behaviour, and explain why a particular Nash equilibrium is chosen. For example, recall the co-ordination game, where two individuals meet on a narrow path, and either both going to their left or both going to their right, constitute Nash equilibria. In this case, a legal norm such as drive on the left (in the UK) or drive on the right (in the US) serves to co-ordinate driving behaviour.

In both of these cases norm-following behaviour seems quite compatible with self-interested behaviour. However, is an individual who, say, joins the back of a well-ordered queue acting according to the RCT model? Acting in this manner does not seem to be easily explicable in terms of self-interested behaviour. Hence a young, fit individual might have their interests better served if they adopted a maxim such as 'the strong will prevail', and continually pushed to the front of queues. Given this, could queue-forming be explained as long-term self-interest, whereby an individual does not push in when young in order that they will not be pushed out when older?

Against this, Elster (1989) has strongly argued that many examples of norm-following behaviour simply do not consist in self-interested behaviour, and cites the case of potential queue jumping as one such example. For example, an individual in a hurry, arriving at the super-market checkout and finding long queues, might be tempted to offer another individual near the front of the queue a cash inducement in order to exchange places with them. Assuming that this individual is prepared to go to the back of the queue, taking the other's place, in exchange for the cash inducement, then it seems that the basis for an exchange where both parties feel they are gaining is possible. However, it is highly unlikely these two individuals will enter into the exchange, as both are aware that the other individuals comprising the queue will indicate strong disapproval, even though the exchange may well have no material effect on these others.

One possible response to the above would be to argue that feelings such as guilt and shame should be included in an individual's preferences. Hence the above individuals do not engage in the exchange because the costs of doing so involve feelings of guilt and shame, and hence the costs of the exchange outweigh the benefits. One reason this proposal is of doubtful validity is because it seems to indicate another ad hoc modification to the theory when counter-instances are raised. The theory predicts X, and, if X does not occur, then preferences are altered to include other factors.

A further problem with the proposal is that it assumes that all norm-following behaviour is subject to utility maximization considerations. However, as Vanberg notes:

> A viable social order seems not even conceivable if the rules on which it rests would only be obeyed in those instances where the particular social situational constraints render rule-compliance in fact the utility-maximizing choice. (Vanberg, 1994: 13)

Vanberg is reiterating a point that has been raised in the case of legal norms: laws are not the sort of things that are subject to continuous cost benefit calculations by the individuals who follow them. Individuals do not obey the law only because, in each case, they calculate that the costs of breaking the law outweigh the benefits of following the law. Hence the 'buying into a queue' example, as a situation where both parties to a transaction feel they will mutually gain through completing the transaction yet refuse to go through with the transaction, does appear to contradict the assumption of self-interested behaviour typically adopted in RCT models. It appears to be a form of behaviour, like law-following behaviour, that is simply not subject to cost benefit calculations.

However, even if norm-following behaviour cannot be always, if at all, explained as a form of self-interested behaviour, this would only appear to raise problems for some RCT models. This is because, as noted in Chapter 3, although RCT models tend to assume self-interest, they need not to do so. Yet even if this assumption of self-interested behaviour is relaxed, the problem raised by social norms for the RCT model is that norm-following behaviour does appear to loosen the RCT assumption that actions denote preferences. According to RCT, that a person strongly prefers x to y indicates that they will not choose y if x is available. However, in the queue example, an individual may strongly prefer paying in order to go to the front of the queue to not paying, yet still not pay. An individual with an itchy nose, may well prefer to pick their nose rather than it remains itchy and, if alone, may well pick their nose. However, if the same individual were in company they may well refrain from doing so.

This example could illustrate that the preference ordering has changed between the solitary and social situations. Alternatively, it could illustrate how an individual may have preferences over preferences, as mentioned in the course of the investigation into Downs in Chapter 2. The individual would prefer to pick their nose, but would prefer not to have this preference in social situations. However, the interlocking expectations characteristic of social norms suggest another possible explanation: in social situations, individuals prefer not to pick their nose because they know that others would prefer them not to. In this case preferences can no longer be taken as 'given' and 'independent', as they are now *formed* in response to the preferences of *others*.

Norm-following behaviour thus appears to raise a number of potential difficulties for the RCT model. On the one hand, such behaviour may be compatible with the model, as Mueller's two examples suggest. It is thus not necessarily the case that RCT models and norm-following models are incompatible.[4] However, on the other hand, in a number of cases it is difficult to appreciate how norm-following behaviour is compatible with self-interested behaviour in either the short or long term. In this case it is not clear how it can be claimed either that norm-following behaviour has evolved from self-interested behaviour or that norms are followed because they are compatible with self-interested behaviour. Hence, as Taylor (1993) remarks, it would appear that no single explanation for the emergence and evolution of norms is possible.

Yet norm-following behaviour does not merely question the self-interested assumption that tends to be made in RCT models, as it also raises doubts concerning the assumed relationship between preferences and choices. It would seem that either preferences change, depending upon contexts, and/or that preferences cannot, in these cases, be explained on an individualistic basis. That is, the preferences individuals may have in social situations may themselves be dependent upon the preferences that other individuals have.

It is thus perhaps not surprising that advocates of RCT tend to be suspicious of explanations of human action carried out in terms of norm-following behaviour. However, it seems dubious to assume that all actions can be explained in terms of RCT models, and apparent norm-following behaviour redescribed in some manner in order to appear compatible with the RCT model:

> Recognising that norms need to be analysed in their own right . . . one can redefine microeconomic analysis as the analysis of the results of behaviour by self-interested agents acting within constraints determined in part by . . . by the system of rules or norms confronted . . . or partici-pated in. (Field, 1984: 704)

However, why does Chong, cited earlier in this chapter, contrast norm-following explanations and RCT models in terms of the difference between non-intentional and intentional explanations? It seems plausible to suspect that part of the suspicion concerning norm-following explanations of human actions occurs because such explanations may suggest that individuals are following norms implicitly, not explicitly, and hence warrant the unfavourable contrast with RCT models in terms of the idea of intentionality. Hence take the rational voter who prefers candidate *A* to candidate *B* yet realizes that the chances of their voting affecting the result are minimal, hence the costs of voting outweigh the potential benefits. In this case, it can be stated that the individual decides that costs outweigh benefits, hence forms the intention not to vote. The individual does not vote because the individual calculated that the costs of so doing outweigh the advantages.

The case of an individual joining the back of an orderly queue can also be explained as an act of intentional behaviour: the individual intended to join the back of the queue. However, in this case it is not immediately clear as to why the individual formed the required intention. Say we explain the behaviour by assuming that the individual acted in the way that they did because they intended to follow the social norm that states that individuals ought not to push to the front of queues. However, this explanation, if correct, raises two issues. Firstly, it appears that the individual behaves in the way that they do because they have to, rather than because they choose to. The explanation appears to grant norms with a certain coercive power that may not sit comfortably with the claim that individuals choose. Secondly, individuals may appear to follow norms without explicitly knowing what the relevant norm is, or acting as they do because of the norm. When asked why they are acting in certain ways, individuals may respond by saying 'because I always do', not by specifying a relevant norm.

The two suspicions noted above concerning norm-following explanation can be summarized thus. Firstly, individual behaviour appears to be compelled, rather than chosen. Secondly, explanations of behaviour appear to be more opaque: it is not necessarily clear why individuals behave as they do, as norm-following behaviour may be ingrained and not reflected upon. Both of these suspicions are crystallized in the claim that social norms are analogous to linguistic rules (Giddens, 1979; Hayek, 1973).

When speaking a language, an individual must follow the linguistic rules constitutive of the language in question: an individual cannot simply make up their own linguistic rules and hope to be understood by others. However, individuals when speaking are undoubtedly unaware of all the linguistic rules applicable when they speak. An individual can know how to speak without being able to provide a comprehensive list of the relevant rules that govern sentence construction in the language. Hence if norms are the equivalent to linguistic rules, then norm-following behaviour is similar to linguistic behaviour. Individuals must follow the rules (hence have no choice) yet may not know the rules that they are in fact following (hence the opacity).

This objection on the grounds of choice assumes that RCT models do in fact offer, as their name indicates, a theory of choice, although this assumption was questioned in Chapter 3. Regarding the opacity problem, it has been noted in earlier chapters that one of the assumptions of the RCT model is that individuals can rank all alternatives. It was further noted that RCT models tend to assume that individuals have already formed beliefs about, say, the likelihood of certain events occurring. However, the example of linguistic usage reveals that it is very doubtful that individuals do *explicitly* perform in the manner assumed.

The philosopher John Searle has strongly argued that the truth conditions of sentences cannot be determined without assuming *implicit* contextual knowledge (Searle, 1980). Searle offers as an example an individual given the commands 'cut the grass' and 'cut the cake', arguing that there is nothing within these different commands that indicates grass is to be cut with a lawn-mower and cake with a knife. However, an individual given the command 'cut the cake' who proceeds to go and search out the lawn-mower is clearly doing something wrong. Moreover, as Searle notes, in certain contexts the command 'cut the grass' may require that a knife, not a lawn-mower, is required: the individual may be required in order to cut the grass up into sections in order to produce turf.

Searle maintains that these examples indicate that, in order to carry out these commands in the required form, individuals must rely on implicit, contextual knowledge. There are a host of interconnected beliefs that are brought into play when individuals understand language: however, these beliefs are not necessarily explicitly held: an individual may not be aware that they have these beliefs. For example, Searle notes that one of the beliefs held by an individual who responds to the claim 'cut the grass' by going to collect the lawn-mower is the belief that 'grass does not bite'. If grass did bite, then a lawn-mower may not be the appropriate tool for cutting the grass. However, as Searle indicates, how many individuals who cut grass with lawn-mowers are explicitly aware of this belief prior to cutting the lawn?

Searle's example indicates an opacity in the choice situation as individuals may not even be aware of the various beliefs that they hold yet which entail that the choice made is of a certain form. The problem, again, is that RCT models tend to make unreasonable demands on individual cognitive abilities. They assume that implicit beliefs – beliefs which individuals may hold without necessarily realizing what they consist in – are always held explicitly: the individual knows what beliefs they hold. Heiner thus refers to the 'broad spectrum' of views of human behaviour and choice:

> At one end of the spectrum are the kind of agents usually envisaged in economics. In particular, human agents are endowed with highly developed cognitive faculties. Such agents may use their thinking abilities to purposefully seek self-perceived goals, while in the process adjusting to expected future conditions . . . However . . . there is also systematic evidence that human behaviour is not uniformly governed by conscious mechanisms. The language of habits, rules of thumb, drives, passions, and the like is also pervasively connected with human decision making. (Heiner, 1986: 95)

Hence, in the case of norms, individuals may make choices, and behave in certain ways, without being explicitly aware of the various interlocking beliefs that ground and support these choices. Although the choice situation hence becomes more opaque, and such forms of explanation would, in all likelihood, be rejected by advocates of RCT, such explanations have two strong arguments in their favour. Firstly, they do seem to relate to how we understand ourselves as acting in certain situations: we do things without necessarily being aware of all the details relevant to, costs and benefits associated with, doing things in this way. Secondly, they avoid having to stipulate that the individual decision-maker is possessed of somewhat amazing cognitive powers, where all alternatives can be ranked and all beliefs are explicitly held and known prior to choices being made.

However, factors such as norms and implicit contextual knowledge do not provide the only examples where making choices may not be quite as transparent as is assumed in RCT models. In the prior discussion of Arrow's impossibility theorem in Chapter 3, it was noted that the assumption of an unrestricted domain may be too demanding as, in political communities, there may well be a sense that certain options simply are not permissible. However, such limiting factors may also arise because of an individual's personality. Hence an individual may not consider various options or alternatives because the individual does not consider them to constitute their understanding of their own personality. As noted, an individual may be honest because that is how they define and understand themselves, not because they have adopted the policy of honesty out of long-term considerations of self-interest.

If I suddenly started to dress in leather outfits, with accompanying metal chains as decorations, I doubt that my children would merely remark that my preferences appeared to have changed. Similarly, if my friend started to spend their spare money on purchasing heroin, rather than their previous preferred option of purchasing CDs, more than a 'preference change' would appear to be involved. There appears to be a more intimate link between our preferences and our sense of identity than is acknowledged in RCT models of choice. Hence I have never stolen a car, and I am pretty sure that I never will steal a car. However, this is not because I have calculated the costs and benefits of such actions, and decided against them. Rather, I do not consider 'someone who steals cars' to constitute part of my identity, hence would never seriously contemplate it as a possible option.

Similarly, an individual may vote in elections because they consider it to be inconceivable not to vote. That is, 'always voting at elections' is caught up with their sense of identity: it helps to define the sort of person that they are. Again, an individual's sense of identity serves to reduce the need for the complex cognitive abilities demanded in RCT models. Certain options or choices are simply not considered, because of an individual's self-understanding concerning what sort of individual they are.

It may be thought possible to ignore the issues raised by norms, contextual knowledge and individuality when applying the RCT model to economic phenomena. However, even in this case, this is doubtful, and the labour market again provides an example of a market where some of these factors may operate. For example, norm-following behaviour appears to be exhibited when unemployed individuals tend not to present themselves at potential work places, offering themselves at a lower wage rate than is currently being paid to those already working. Similarly, part of 'learning the job' involves mastering the contextual knowledge that informs various work practices.

Yet it is even more difficult to appreciate how these issues can be ignored when investigating political phenomena, as they appear fairly central components that must be acknowledged as important. Hence questions concerning identity would appear to be significant in investigating the various issues surrounding problems raised by ethnicity. For example, questions such as should governments be involved in actively encouraging the continued use of minority languages would only appear to be significant because these languages are important for groups that use them, and who fear for their continual survival.

CONCLUSIONS

Green and Shapiro raised a number of criticisms concerning the use of RCT in political studies. One of their primary concerns was that the empirical usefulness of such studies was questionable. It was noted in the course of the investigation of Downs's model of voting in Chapter 2 that the model lacked empirical validity. Hence Downs's claim that the act of voting was, on the whole, irrational, is not empirically supported by voting behaviour in most democracies.

However, despite providing various different models, recent explanations do not seem to have moved the debate on substantially since Downs's initial work: voting still seems to provide RCT models with a puzzling anomaly. In attempting to resolve this anomaly, it has been suggested that voters may be motivated by ethical factors, and as these factors can be explained as resulting from self-interested rational behaviour, they do not threaten the explanatory power of RCT.

However, certain key aspects of social and political life do not seem to be reducible to the form of explanation provided in RCT models. Individuals acting ethically are not necessarily following self-interest socialized behaviour, and norm-following is another case where individual behaviour does not appear to conform to the model. Norm-following does not seem to be reducible to self-interested maximizing behaviour. Indeed, norms may provide an instance where individuals are not fully aware as to why they act in certain ways.

Notes

1. For a complementary volume to Green and Shapiro, concerned predominantly with the use of RCT in the area of international relations, see M.E. Brown *et al.* (eds) (2000).
2. For a similar defence, see Herne and Sitala (2004).
3. For an alternative to Lewis's model, see Miller (2001).
4. Taylor (1993) criticizes Popkin's account of peasant society, examined earlier in Chapter 4, for precisely this assumption that norm and RCT models are necessarily incompatible.

CHAPTER 6

Rational Choice Theory: a Science of Politics?

We have noted on a number of occasions that according to its advocates one of the advantages of adopting RCT for the investigation of political phenomena is that it allows for the provision of 'scientific' explanations in politics. Although there is considerable dispute concerning exactly what constitutes a 'scientific' explanation, two factors that are frequently mentioned, and have already been alluded to, are empirical success and the identification of relevant causal factors. It has previously been suggested that the ability of models incorporating RCT to provide empirical explanations and/or predictions of political phenomena is, at best, contested, and hence the scepticism displayed by authors such as Green and Shapiro concerning the empirical validity of RCT in connection with political phenomena does appear justified. However, proponents of RCT, even if they accept that the empirical validity of RCT in explaining political phenomena is suspect, might counter with two arguments.

Firstly, it might be argued that this empirical failure merely indicates the need for developing more sophisticated models of political processes. The assumption here is that, because RCT has been found to be empirically valid in investigations in disciplines such as economics and decision theory, it is only a matter of time before this success is replicated in politics. Secondly, it might be argued that the main force of RCT does not derive from its empirical validity, but from its theoretical adequacy. Thus Shepsle argues that 'the comparative advantage of rational choice theorists lies in deriving theoretical propositions and advancing theoretical arguments; empirical assessment is a secondary matter' (Shepsle, 1996: 219. See also Johnson, 2003).

This chapter will critically evaluate both of these claims. The first section will examine the claim that RCT is empirically validated when explaining decision-making in general, and merely needs some modification when applied to political phenomena. It will be argued that, at this empirical level, RCT fails at both explanatory and predictive levels. Hence it is not the case that there is something peculiar about politics, revealing merely that modifications are needed to a model that has been successfully applied elsewhere. Rather, RCT models systematically fail to offer valid explanations or predictions concerning decision-making in general.

The second section of the chapter will focus on the claim that, even if the empirical validity of RCT models is not proven, the theoretical or conceptual coherence of these models is such that their ability to claim to provide a 'scientific approach' to the study of political phenomena remains unscathed. As noted, one of the main features frequently taken to characterize scientific research is the ability to offer causal explanations, hence providing explanations of the natural world through referring to causal laws, mechanisms, states of affairs, and so on. Consequently, advocates of RCT frequently argue that the theory, in order to claim the status of science, must also be involved in the search for causal relations in some form. Thus in the course of their defence of the use of RCT in politics, Ferejohn and Satz claim that:

> Accounts of empirical phenomena are *explanatory* (rather than merely predictive or descriptive) insofar as they show how those phenomena can be seen as instances of causal laws or *mechanisms*. Explanations, as distinguished from descriptions, identify causal mechanisms that are held to apply across all relevant similar contexts. (Ferejohn & Satz, 1996: 74, emphasis in original)

Clarification is needed here, as the claim that RCT is interested in providing causal explanations may appear initially puzzling. As noted on a number of previous occasions, RCT is interested in providing intentional explanations: it seeks to explain political phenomena through appealing in some way to the intentions of the actors involved. However, the attempt to provide both causal and intentional explanation may appear contradictory, as causal explanations of behaviour are frequently invoked when intentional behaviour is not involved. For example, the claim that 'the car backfiring caused Tom Smith to jump' offers a causal explanation, if correct, as to why Tom Smith jumped. However, it explains the behaviour of Smith jumping in terms of a reaction to something, rather than as a form of intentional behaviour. Immediately prior to jumping, Smith had not formed the intention to jump: his jumping was inadvertently caused by the backfiring.

Sometimes causal claims are initially ambiguous as to whether intentionality is involved or not. Thus the claim that 'Jack's fall caused his death' could refer to intentional behaviour, if Jack intended to fall to his death, or unintentional behaviour – Jack may have slipped. In this latter case, Jack's fall could be explained as an unintended consequence of Jack's intentional behaviour: 'Jack intended to climb to the top of the mountain but he lost his footing and unintentionally fell to his death'. However, in this case, do we want to assert that Jack's intention to climb was itself caused, that something caused Jack to intend to climb the mountain?

If this question is answered in the affirmative, it would seem we are denying that Jack has any freedom, as all of his actions appear to be caused by something external to him. In order to appreciate how causal and intentional explanations may be compatible, recall that the main 'building blocks' of models incorporating RCT consist in individual preferences, beliefs and actions. In order to provide a causal explanation, what is required is some form of causal explanation that incorporates these items. Using the terminology of Ferejohn and Satz, it appears that RCT models must provide causal laws, or identify causal mechanisms, that are instantiated in individual actions.

Although the exact nature of a 'causal law' is by no means easy to establish, let us assume that there is a claim of the form 'if an individual is rational, then they will stay at home rather than vote'. In this case a certain state of affairs – the individual staying at home and not going to vote – is explained in terms of the beliefs and preferences of the rational individual. Hence, put schematically, it is being claimed that the rational individual's beliefs and preferences are such that they cause the individual not to vote.

This example indicates how causal and intentional explanations may be compatible if an *internal* explanation of actions, or choices, can be given. Actions are to be explained as caused by processes or states that are internal to the individual, and not external, as was the case of the car backfiring. To appreciate how this might be possible, take the following:

> Peter intends to stay at home and not to vote because he has cal-
> culated that the chances of his vote affecting the outcome of the
> election are negligible, easily outweighed by the costs incurred in
> voting.

Here we are referring to an aspect of Peter's intentional behaviour – his intention to stay at home – yet the use of the term 'because' indicates how a causal explanation of Peter's action may be compatible with an intentional explanation of the same action. Peter's calculation that the costs of voting outweigh the benefits of voting give him a reason to stay at home, and this reason is the cause of his staying at home: reasons are causes. In this case Peter's intentional behaviour is not explained by something external to him, but something internal – his reasons.

In a simplistic form, there is Peter's preference for *A* over *B*: Peter prefers to stay in the comfort of his home rather than to get wet in pursuit of a hopeless task. Peter believes that going out to vote will entail getting wet in pursuit of a hopeless task, as the chances of his vote affecting the result of the election are negligible. Hence Peter's preferences and beliefs give him a reason not to vote, and this reason causes him not to vote. Hence Peter's action has been explained as being caused by his reasons and, ultimately, by his preferences and beliefs.

Given the desire to identify causal mechanisms, and hence provide scientific explanations, the possibility of characterizing reasons as causes appears to provide a convenient way of buttressing the claim that RCT provides causal, and thus scientific, explanations of political phenomena. Hence, as Hollis notes, 'for the rational agents of standard rational choice theory, reasons are indeed causes' (Hollis, 1996: 196). The desire to establish reasons as causes is thus frequently adopted as part of a *naturalistic* perspective on human agency (Mele, 1997: 3). That is, the identification of reasons as causes legitimizes the view that the social sciences, including politics, should model themselves upon the natural sciences. Not all models incorporating RCT are necessarily explicitly committed to the view that 'reasons are causes'. However, if causal explanations are being advanced, yet reasons are not viewed as causes, then there is 'a considerable cost from the standpoint of empirical testing. It then becomes exceedingly difficult for the researcher to pin down what the causal mechanism involved is or to know what would count as evidence in support of its existence' (Green & Shapiro, 1994: 21).

The following two sections of this chapter are thus related in the following manner. The first section will investigate to what extent RCT can explain decision-making in general. The theory attempts to explain why individuals make the decisions they do, and to predict how individuals will make decisions when presented with certain circumstances. In other words, the theory claims to explain the reasons why individuals behave as they do.

However, if individuals do not behave in the manner predicted in the theory, then there would appear to be something amiss in the way that RCT assumes that preferences, beliefs and actions are interlinked. For example, in the centipede game introduced in Chapter 3, RCT predicts that individuals will act in a certain way, by taking the money at the first decision point. However, if individuals do not act in this way, then it would appear that individuals do not have either the desires, or beliefs, or both, that the theory predicts. It could be, for example, that individuals are acting altruistically, rather than selfishly, or that they do not formulate beliefs in the way that the theory predicts. In this case then, the preferences and beliefs assumed to be 'rational' in RCT theory cannot be viewed as causing the actions.

Hence, at this empirical level, it may well be the case that a 'scientific explanation' of political phenomena can be given, in so far as reasons can be construed as causes, but the RCT model misidentifies what these reasons are. Thus in the case of the 'paradox of voting', then as individuals do tend to vote, they presumably perform this action because they have a reason to do so, and this reason may well cause their action. However, as RCT models predict, in the main, that rational individuals will not vote, then these models have misidentified the reason involved.

153

However, in claiming a scientific status for RCT, advocates need to be able to explain, at a theoretical level, how these reasons cause the actions that are the subject of investigation. It may be the case that, at an empirical level, the causes of actions have been misidentified, yet causal explanations in terms of reasons are still valid. The possibility of identifying reasons as the relevant causal mechanisms thus forms the subject of the second section of the chapter. The intention in this section is to rebut the naturalistic pretensions of RCT: the claim that RCT identifies causal mechanisms analogous to those discovered in the natural sciences.

RATIONAL CHOICE THEORY AND THE EXPLANATION OF DECISIONS

Decision-making in individuals and groups has been subject to a number of empirical investigations, most notably by Kahneman and Tversky and their associates. In a number of crucial ways, it has been found that decision-making differs from that predicted by models incorporating RCT. In this case, the problems germane to the 'voter paradox' may not be unique, but indicative of a systematic failure in explanation. This section will review some of these results.

One of the main assumptions in RCT is that preferences are asymmetric: an individual will not both prefer x to y and prefer y to x. This assumption is assumed to be 'self-evident', and its rejection a symptom of irrationality. However, take the following question (originally in Kahneman & Tversky, 1979, taken from Kreps, 1990):

Question One
As a doctor in a position of authority in the national government, you have been informed that a new flu epidemic will hit your country next winter and that this epidemic will result in the deaths of 600 people. (Either death or complete recovery is the outcome in each case.) There are two possible vaccination programmes that you can undertake, and doing one precludes doing the other. The first will save 400 people with certainty. The second will save no-one with a probability 1/3 and 600 with a probability 2/3. Which do you prefer?

Once you have determined an answer, try this question:

Question Two
As a doctor in a position of authority in the national government you have been informed that a new flu epidemic will hit your country next winter. To fight this epidemic, one of two possible vaccination programmes is to be chosen, where undertaking one

programme precludes doing the other. In the first programme, 200 people will die with certainty. In the second, there is a 2/3 chance that no one will die, and a 1/3 chance that 600 will die. Which do you prefer?

When Kahneman and Tversky posed these two questions to members of the medical profession, they found that the majority selected the first programme in the first question, and the second programme in the second question. However, the outcomes in each question are identical, the only difference consisting in how the questions have been asked, or how the questions have been framed. Respondents seemed to react positively to saving 400 people with the first programme in question one, yet negatively to the 'certain 200 deaths' with the same programme in question two.

Whatever the significance of the issues raised in economic theory by this 'framing effect', in the case of investigations in politics the potential effects are both significant and well known. As an example: in 1975 citizens in the United Kingdom were asked to vote in a referendum on the subject of membership of the European Community. The question asked was 'Do you think the UK should stay in the European Community (Common Market)', and the majority voted 'yes' to the question. However, it was claimed by opponents of membership that the wording of the question was such ('maintenance of the status quo') it revealed a bias in favour of membership.

The possibility of framing effects not only calls into question the assumption that preferences are asymmetric, it also raises grave doubts concerning the 'Harsanyi doctrine', referred to in Chapter 3. According to this doctrine, individuals confronted with the same information will draw the same conclusions. However, with framing effects, then the same individual may well draw different conclusions from the same set of information, depending upon how the information is presented.

The issue of consistency of choice, where choices may not be consistent if contexts differ, leads to the suggestion that we may need to understand the reasons why individuals make the choices they do. In the previous chapter it was suggested that social norms raise problems for RCT, and Sen (1982) has explicitly argued that consistency of choice may not occur where various social forces or norms are operating. Consistency of choice requires contradiction consistency, where an alternative chosen from a set must still be chosen if available when that set is reduced in size, and expansion consistency, where an alternative must be chosen if the set is expanded. However, an individual, offered a choice between two apples, may choose one of these apples (y), yet if offered a choice between this apple and nothing, may choose nothing (x), as it would be considered rude to choose the last apple. Hence the adherence to social norms may be such that consistency may not occur when the choice set is reduced in size. Similarly, an individual offered a choice between a large slice x and a small slice y of cake, may choose the small slice y, so as not to appear greedy. However, when an even larger slice of cake z is added to the choice set, then the individual chooses x.

Whereas the framing effect reveals that choices may alter, and hence appear inconsistent, depending upon how information is presented, these later examples reveal how choices may alter depending upon the social contexts within which they are made. However, are individuals in either case acting irrationally? In the case of the framing effects, it would seem that individuals are acting irrationally, in the sense that they are acting according to false beliefs, or not adequately 'processing' information. In the case of social norms, it has been suggested that rationality can be preserved through including the idea of 'social cost' (Dowding, 2002). Hence taking the apple when there is only one available involves a 'social cost' of appearing to be rude. However, the problem with this suggestion is that it would again seem to involve another *ad hoc* modification to the theory, introduced when it appears to be suitable. When are social costs to be introduced, and when not, except when the theory confronts choices that are problematic?

Alternatively, it may be possible to differentiate, or individuate, preferences in such a way that rationality can be preserved (Broome, 1991). For example, where the three slices of cake are involved, there is a choice between the small slice y, medium slice x and large slice z. However, when the large slice is removed, the choice is not now between the medium slice x and the small slice y, but between the small slice y and the 'medium slice and appearing to be rude' x'. As x is not the same as x', then no inconsistency is involved. The problem with this suggestion consists in how to justify the difference between x and x'. For example, could it simply be argued that, as the individual feels that the situations are different, and hence x and x' are indeed different, then this difference is justified? However, what if, in the case of the framing effect, an individual asserts that they feel the situations are different, and their choices consistent – could this claim be defended? It would seem that, with an increasing individuation of preferences, any choices can be viewed as 'consistent', and hence the consistency requirement loses any force.

There are a number of other cases where individual preferences do not exhibit the consistency that RCT assumes, and individuals appear sensitive to the contexts in which choices are made. Assume, for example, a fair lottery with a hundred tickets, with four gambles offering the prizes shown in Figure 6.1. Your first choice is between gambles A1 and A2. If you choose A1 you receive £5 million whatever ticket is selected. If you choose A2 you receive nothing if ticket number 1 is randomly selected, £5 million if a ticket between 2 and 11 is selected, and £5 million if a ticket between 12 and 100 is selected. As you receive the same prize whichever of these two gambles you select if

	TICKET NUMBERS		
	1	2-11	12-100
GAMBLES			
A1	£5 million	£5 million	£5 million
A2	0	£25 million	£5 million
B1	£5 million	£5 million	0
B2	0	£25 million	0

(After Savage, 1990)

Figure 6.1

tickets 12 to 100 are selected, then, intuitively, it would appear that your choice between gambles A1 and A2 cannot be influenced by the payout for tickets 12 to 100, as these are the same in both cases. Hence your choice is between A1 with £5 million if tickets 1–11 are selected, and A2 where you receive 0 if ticket 1 is selected, and £25 if tickets 2–11 are selected. This intuition is confirmed in the axioms of decision theory formulated by Savage, and is known as the 'independence axiom', or 'sure thing' principle.

Similarly, when choosing between gambles B1 and B2, then, as the payouts for tickets 12–100 are again the same in both cases (0), they should not influence the decision. Hence if you choose gamble A1 rather than gamble A2, you should also choose gamble B1 rather than gamble B2. (If you are choosing between a basket containing an apple and a banana and a basket containing a pear and a banana, and choose the basket with the apple, then faced with a choice between a basket with an apple and an orange and a basket with a pear and an orange, you should also choose the basket with the apple.)

However, faced with these gambles, the majority of individuals choose gamble A1 over A2, yet choose B2 over B1. Indeed, Savage himself, who formulated the axiom, also chose in this apparently inconsistent way (Savage, 1990). This paradox, formulated by Maurice Allais, hence known as the 'Allais paradox', has been replicated in a number of experimental situations. It suggests that individuals do not compare gambles in a state by state manner, but examine them as a whole.

The example can be taken to illustrate what has been termed the 'certainty effect': in the choice between gambles A1 and A2 individuals prefer the certainty of receiving £5 million than running the risk of receiving 0, even though this risk is small (1 per cent), and £25 million could be won. However, in choosing B2 over B1 individuals are aware

157

that they will also receive 0 if tickets 12–100 are selected, hence their assessment of the effect of receiving 0 if ticket 1 is selected is altered. This decision procedure has been characterized in terms of *regret*: the individual would regret their decision if they chose A2 rather than A1 and received 0 if ticket 1 was selected. However, if they chose B2 over B1, they would not regret receiving 0 if ticket 1 was selected, as they would also have received 0 if tickets 12–100 were selected. Hence, again, individuals differentiate between receiving 0 for ticket 1 in gamble A2 and receiving 0 for ticket 1 in gamble B2, even though ostensibly there is no difference between these cases.

Kahneman and Tversky (1990) cite another experiment which was conducted and appeared to indicate that there is a certainty effect in decision-making. The questions and resulting responses are shown in Figure 6.2. Hence, from 72 respondents, 78 per cent preferred the

Question One:

A. 50% chance to win a three-week tour of England, France and Italy

C. A one-week tour of England, with certainty

78%

22%

N = 72

Question Two:

B. 5% chance to win a three-week tour of England, France and Italy

D. 10% chance to win a one-week tour of England

33%

67%

N = 72

Figure 6.2

certain bet of the England trip to the 50 per cent chance of the Europe visit in question one, whilst in question two 67 per cent preferred the 5 per cent chance of Europe to the 10 per cent chance of England. Tversky (1996) indicates how examples such as the above threaten the assumption, often not made explicit, of invariance in RCT models. There are three aspects to this invariance assumption:

Descriptive Invariance

Preferences over options should not depend on the way in which they are presented. It has already been argued that this assumption is challenged by the problem of framing: however, Tversky offers the following example which introduces a further complication to RCT assumptions. Tversky gave a sample of 126 individuals the following options:

1) Assume yourself richer by $300 than you are today. You have to choose between i) a sure gain of $100 and ii) a 50% chance to gain $200 and a 50% chance to gain nothing. In this example, a majority of individuals (72%) chose the sure gain of $100 (option i).
2) Assume yourself richer by $500 than you are today. You have to choose between iii) a sure loss of $100 and iv) a 50% chance to lose nothing and a 50% chance to lose $200. In this case, the majority (64%) selected the gamble (option iv).

In both of these cases individuals are being offered the same choice: between $400 for sure and an even choice of either $500 or $300. However, the majority chose the $400 for sure when the question was posed in the form of question 1 and the gamble when posed in the manner of question 2. Why is there this 'framing effect'? Tversky argues that what is important to individuals here is their perceptions of their changes in wealth, not their states of wealth.

Procedural Invariance

Individual preferences between x and y can be established either by offering a choice between x and y or by comparing reservation prices. That is, if an individual prefers x to y, then this can be revealed either through the individual choosing x over y, or by the individual being willing to place a higher reserve price on x than on y: the result will be the same whichever procedure is chosen. Tversky disputes that this is, in fact, the case, citing the case of individuals choosing between two options, one involving issues of health care, one issues of animal conservation. In the first option, individuals are informed that farm workers are prone to skin cancer through their exposure to the sun, which can be alleviated through medical check–ups. In the

159

second option, individuals are informed that certain species of mammals are under threat of extinction, although this can be mitigated through providing safe breeding areas. Most individuals, when faced with a direct choice between these options, chose to provide medical check-ups for workers. However, it appears that individuals were generally willing to pay more, on average, in order to provide safe breeding areas.

Hence the preference ordering revealed through choice is different from that revealed through willingness to pay. In support of this, Bateman *et al.* (2000) conducted a series of experiments which differentiated between the willingness of individuals to accept options (WTA) and the willingness to pay for options (WTP), concluding that individuals did exhibit a divergence in preferences, depending upon how the issues were presented. In political terms this result is interesting because it raises the possibility of a disjunction between how individuals will reveal preferences, say, through being offered choices in opinion polls, and how they will reveal preferences through willingness to make financial contributions.

Context Independence

This issue is related to the problem of the independence of other alternatives raised in connection with the Allais paradox. In the first experiment, a group of 106 individuals were offered a choice between $6 in cash and an 'elegant Cross pen': 36 per cent of the individuals selected the Cross pen, 64 per cent the cash. In the second experiment, a group of 115 individuals were offered a choice between $6 in cash, the same 'elegant Cross pen', and another, less attractive, pen. In this case, 46 per cent of respondents now chose the Cross pen. Hence the introduction of a second, inferior, pen into the choice set resulted in a significant increase in the percentage of individuals selecting the Cross pen. Again, this supports the view that individual choices are influenced by the nature of the other options on offer, hence the context within which the choice is made.

In the above examples, the empirical evidence indicates that individuals do not act in the way assumed or dictated in RCT. Experimental evidence on free riding problems have revealed that individuals engage in this form of behaviour less than the theory predicts, and that 'subjects contribute even though non-contribution is a dominant strategy' (Ledyand, 1995: 172). This has led a number of writers to develop alternative theories of individual choice to RCT models. For example, Prospect Theory argues that (McLean, 2002):

1) Individuals assign values to changes in their situations, and thus gains and losses are perceived in relationship to a reference point.

2) Individuals tend to be averse to losses. Hence a) they tend to weigh perceived losses greater than perceived gains; b) most individuals are risk seeking where losses are concerned and risk averse in the case of gains.

3) The reference point from which changes are perceived is subject to framing effects.

Qualtrone and Tversky (2000) have indicated the relevance of some of these observations in the context of political choices. For example, the suggestion that individuals are risk averse in the case of gains and risk seeking regarding losses would have direct relevance in the case of election contests. This is because the party or individual already in power (the incumbent) is generally regarded as a less risky bet than the challengers. Hence if voters think that, say, economic conditions are improving, they will tend to vote for the incumbent (risk averse). However, if they think that the economy is likely to deteriorate, they will tend to vote for the opposition (risk seeking).

This explanation as to how individuals vote obviously differs from that offered by Downs, which focused on individual assessments as to how the opposition would have done if they had been elected. Qualtrone and Tversky explicitly confront the 'voter paradox', focusing on the tendency for individuals to confuse causal contingencies (acts that produce an outcome) with diagnostic contingencies (acts that are merely correlative with an outcome). Hence individuals tend to assume that, if they decide to vote, this decision will imply that individuals with similar political attitudes will also vote. Conversely, they assume that if they do not vote, then others with similar political attitudes will also desist from voting. Hence individuals tend to think that they should vote, as they regard this act of voting as diagnostic of millions of like-minded voters, hence their vote is seen as making a substantial difference to the result.[1]

Kahneman (2000) also notes that, in contrast to the assumptions in RCT models, individuals are not very good at predicting what their future preferences will be. For example, groups of individuals were shown a certain drinking mug, and asked, if they had the mug, what they would be prepared to accept in exchange for the mug. In this case, the mean predicted selling price was $3.73. However, when these individuals were actually given the mug, and asked how much they would be prepared to accept in order to give the mug up, the mean answer was $4.89. Hence Kahneman concludes that individuals appear unable to anticipate that actually possessing the mug would lead to a reluctance to give it up. On a general note in this regard:

> People do not always know enough about themselves to predict their future experiences. And . . . they sometimes make decisions that are inconsistent with their own beliefs about these experiences. (Kahneman & Varey, 1991: 158)

It was suggested in an earlier chapter that the empirical validity of RCT models in explaining and/or predicting behaviour regarding political phenomena was, at best, open to questioning. It can now be appreciated that this is perhaps not surprising, as RCT appears to fail to capture the nature of decision-making in many situations: individuals frequently simply do not behave in the way that RCT models claim that they will behave. Of course, it can still be claimed that these anomalies do not threaten the normative force of RCT models. The examples investigated above may indicate how individuals do make choices: however, these choices are irrational. Individuals would do better for themselves if they did behave according to the axioms of RCT.

However, whatever the validity of this argument in certain cases (and, at least in the case of the prisoners' dilemma, it appears to be highly dubious), the argument does not seem relevant to defenders of the use of RCT in investigating political phenomena. Advocates of RCT models in politics tend, as noted, to place considerable emphasis on the scientific status of their models, and consequently on the empirical reliability and usefulness of these models. However, the experiments cited above question this claim, as it now appears that individual decision-making in general simply does not subscribe to the RCT model. Individuals do make choices, but not, apparently, in the way described in standard RCT models.

However, it was noted at the beginning of this chapter that an advocate of RCT may appeal to another criterion in order to substantiate the claim that the theory provides a scientific basis for the study of political phenomena. According to this defence, what matters is the theoretical coherence of the RCT models. However, on its own, theoretical coherence is not sufficient to establish the scientific credentials of RCT models: what is needed is a coherent theory that can identify certain causal mechanisms. As already indicated, given the focus in RCT on individual choices, then the most readily available strategy appears to be that of connecting these choices to a causal theory of action. Hence the interest in identifying reasons as causes.

REASONS AND CAUSES

So far, the discussion of RCT has tended to be conducted in terms of desires or preferences, beliefs and actions. What is thus needed is a way of connecting these to reasons understood as causes. As the following investigation indicates, the conditions required in order to explain reasons as causes are fairly stringent, and it is not clear that RCT can meet these conditions. As a starting point, it is instructive to recall from Chapter 1 that actions can be regarded as the conclusion, following Aristotle, of a practical syllogism. Hence we have:

Major premise: I desire to eat something savoury;
Minor premise: I believe that eating this pork pie will be the eating of something savoury;
Conclusion: Therefore I eat the pork pie.

In this case, the action of eating the pie has been explained as an outcome of a deliberation involving only desires (or preferences) and beliefs. However, actions are not quite so simply explained. To appreciate why, assume that the pork pie in question is way past its sell-by date, and hence potentially harmful. In this case there is:

Major premise: I desire to refrain from eating anything potentially harmful;
Minor premise: I believe that eating this pork pie will be eating something potentially harmful;
Conclusion: Therefore I refrain from eating the pork pie.

Hence there are different desires and beliefs resulting in opposed actions: which action do I undertake? Do I eat the pork pie, or leave it alone? What is needed here is the idea of *weighted* desires (Elster, 1986): we need to evaluate our desires, and hence decide which action to take. Hence we evaluate our desires, and form an intention to perform a certain action. Note that the intention is made in the present, but involves my intending to perform an action in the future. Davidson refers to an intention as an 'interim report' where 'given what I now know and believe, here is my judgement of what kind of action is desirable' (Davidson, 1980: 100).

One problem here is that there seems to be no component in the RCT model capable of carrying out this weighting: desires cannot evaluate themselves, and, as noted in Chapter 1, beliefs cannot directly affect desires.[2] A further problem is that RCT models do not appear to include the idea of 'intending to X' within the features that characterize individuals making choices. This claim might seem strange, given the fact that RCT models claim to provide an account of intentional action or behaviour. However, there is a difference between intentionally doing X and intending to do X: the former characterizes our actions and the latter our mental states. However, the only mental states that RCT models admit are beliefs and desires, and hence our intentional action is explained *solely* in terms of our beliefs and desires. Yet it is precisely because of the fact that we may want to evaluate our desires that philosophers such as Davidson argue that any coherent account of human action must take account of the fact that individuals intend to do certain things, and intentional actions do not simply flow from desires and beliefs.

However, assuming for now that such problem can be resolved, how do we move from weighted desires to reasons as causes? Elster offers the following account, based on the ideas of the philosopher Davidson.

163

Elster defines (B) as behaviour, (C) as the set of cognitions held by the individual and (D) as the desires held by the same individual (taken to be weighted desires). Elster offers the following three conditions required in order to derive a causal explanation of behaviour.

Given C, B is the best means to realize D

This may initially seem uncontroversial. Assuming that I do not believe the pork pie is harmful, then if my cognitive state is such that I believe eating the pork pie is the best way of realizing my desire to eat something savoury (and assuming that this action is judged desirable, as above), then I eat the pork pie. Can it thus be concluded that my act of eating the pork pie was caused by my beliefs and desires? No, the condition above is not sufficient in providing a causal explanation of the behaviour.

Say a person is in dire financial straits and knows that their grandmother will provide them with money when she dies. The individual thus forms the belief that killing their grandmother is the best means to achieve their desire to alleviate their current financial circumstances. However, the individual also believes that their grandmother controls a sinister terrorist group, originating on the planet Mars, which is committed to overthrowing the government, and desires that all members of terrorist groups from Mars so committed be shot. The next day, the individual shoots the grandmother, resulting in her death.

There is thus one form of behaviour – the shooting of the grandmother – which was the best means of realizing two different sets of cognitions and desires. However, the police force is very interested in which set of cognitions and desires resulted in the actual behaviour. In other words, all the first condition provides us with is *a* reason for the action, whereas what is of interest is *the* reason for the action. It could be that the individual had tripped over when walking with a loaded shotgun, which accidentally went off, killing the grandmother. In this case, the individual had two different reasons for killing his grandmother, but neither of these reasons were the cause of the killing of the grandmother, which was completely accidental.

Although these examples are rather fanciful, they can become extremely important in legal cases, which may well revolve around questions of intention and accident, 'of sound mind' and mental disturbance. In order to establish reasons as causes it is necessary to know more than a variety of reasons which might explain the action: what is needed is knowledge of *the* reason the action was undertaken, where this reason is the cause of the action. Hence Elster introduces a second condition:

C and D caused B

The introduction of a causal relation into the formulation is thus introduced in order to distinguish between a reason and the reason for an action, whereby only the latter has a causal relation to the action. What is thus needed is knowledge of the actual reason why the action was undertaken, where this reason is the cause of the action. However, there remains a problem with the argument that reasons can be causes. In appreciating what this problem is, it is necessary to introduce the third condition specified by Elster:

C and D caused B *qua* reasons

Elster introduces this condition because he believes that it resolves a possible problem in explaining reasons as causes. Unfortunately, Elster's condition, although introduced to resolve a certain problem, does not in fact succeed in doing so. The problem Elster is trying to resolve with this third condition is that of 'wayward causal chains', which can be classified as either external or internal. As an example of the former, Bennett offers the example of an individual trying to kill someone by shooting at them (Davidson, 1980). However, the shot is way off target, misses the individual, but stampedes a herd of wild pigs that tramples the intended victim to death. Here the individual desired the other's death, believed that shooting at the other would result in this death, and shot at the other, resulting in the death. However, there is something wrong with the causal connection between the firing of the gun and the death of the victim: the model does not seem to provide enough leeway to differentiate between the death as a result of being directly shot and the death as a result of being trampled by the herd of pigs.

As an example of an internal chain, consider an individual who is driving along the road and recognizes a sworn enemy who has started to cross the road ahead on foot. The individual realizes that they would like to knock over and hopefully kill their sworn enemy and realizes that if they suddenly accelerated they could run the enemy over, thus hopefully accomplishing the task. Shocked at this thought, the individual inadvertently puts their foot down on the accelerator, hence knocking the enemy over. Here, there is a desire to knock the individual over, a belief that pressing the accelerator will achieve this effect, this action is undertaken, and the individual is subsequently knocked over. Consequently, as the individual had the reason to do the action, and did the action, then the requisite desires and cognitions caused the action qua reasons.

In the example above, the required desires, cognitions and action are present: however, the action cannot be described as intentional, as the knocking over of the individual was inadvertent (Moya, 1990: 115ff). Elster's third modification above hence does not 'rescue' the attempt to explain reasons as causes through eliminating the problem of wayward causal chains. However, apart from indicating that Elster's formulation requires modification, if possible, to accommodate these instances, the problem of wayward causal chains raises problems for the claimed 'scientific status' of RCT. As Davidson observes:

> Since there may be wayward causal chains, we cannot say that if attitudes that would rationalise *x* cause an agent to do *x*, then he does *x* intentionally. It is largely because we cannot see how to complete the statement of the causal conditions of intentional action that we cannot tell, if we got them right, the result would be a piece of analysis or an empirical law for predicting behaviour. (Davidson, 1980: 79–80)

The issue of 'wayward causal chains' thus raises problems for the claim by advocates of RCT that the theory can provide a scientific analysis of political phenomena, capable of predicting outcomes, and can do so through identifying beliefs and desires/preferences as constituting 'causes' of actions. A related problem concerns instances of 'weakness of the will'. An individual may desire to live as long as possible, and believe that smoking cigarettes will lead to an untimely early death, and hence ought not to smoke. However, a considerable number of individuals do have this form of desire and belief, yet continue to smoke. Here again the relevant desires and beliefs cannot be construed as causing the action.

The suspicion is thus raised that there may well be something amiss with the simple desire and belief model of action that underpins RCT. Searle (2001) draws attention to the 'gaps' prevalent in moving from beliefs and desires to actions. For example, even if I make my mind up to undertake an action, there is still a 'gap' between making my mind up and committing the action, which may result in my 'changing my mind'. Similarly, there is a 'gap' between my starting an action and continuing with the action, where I may pause in the course of undertaking an action, change my mind, and perform a different action (Searle, 2001: 12ff). The relationship between our desires, beliefs and actions thus appears to be considerably looser than the view that the former two can be unequivocally construed as causes of the action in question.

Searle thus draws attention to the fact that our actions appear to be the result of deliberations about our desires and beliefs, and do not automatically flow from these desires and beliefs. The problem that actions seem to be the result of deliberations, yet this idea is not incorporated in RCT models, has already been alluded to in the case of 'weighted desires' above. A further argument that has been levelled against the basic belief/desire model is that it does not take account of the idea that individuals formulate plans (Bratman, 1999). Unlike RCT models, Bratman argues that a coherent account of human action must take account of the fact that individuals form intentions to do things.

However, he further argues that, in order to understand the role of intentions, they must be situated in the context of larger plans. Some of the relevant issues can be illustrated in the following example.

Say an individual, in term time, always attends the lecture at three o'clock on Thursdays. However, one Monday morning in term time, the individual's friend suggests that they go to the cinema on Thursday afternoon, in which case they would miss the lecture. On reflection, the individual decides to go to the cinema with the friend, hence missing the lecture. In this case, it could be said that the individual forms an intention to go to the cinema and thus miss the lecture. This example reveals various aspects relevant to forming intentions prior to actions.

Firstly, intentions must be compatible. Hence the individual cannot intend to be both at the lecture at three o'clock and in the cinema at three o'clock. Secondly, intentions are what Bratman terms 'conduct-controlling' (Bratman, 1999: 16). Thus if the individual intends to go to the cinema on Thursday afternoon, then they will presumably not undertake actions that are incompatible with this action. Thirdly, and relatedly, intentions involve commitment. An individual who intends to X is committed to doing X. Of course, this intention may be revised – the individual may change their mind. Nevertheless, once the individual has formulated the intention to X, they tend not to continually consider alternatives. Fourthly, intentions may form parts of larger plans. For example, the individual may decide to go to the cinema because they know they can look at their friend's lecture notes for the missed lecture and, on deciding to go, will try to ensure they have enough money to pay the cinema ticket fee. These things, in turn, may require them buying some form of present for their friend, and cancelling the social drink the previous evening.

Bratman thus argues that theories such as RCT do not recognize that we form future intentions as parts of larger *plans* whose role is to aid the co-ordination of activities over time.[3] Consequently, Bratman argues that the desire/belief/reason model can only have relevance if it is situated within the context of plans. Practical reason thus has two levels. On one level there are prior intentions and plans, which both pose problems and provide filters on options as potential solutions. On another level are desires, beliefs and reasons, which enter as considerations to be weighed in deliberating between relevant and admissible options.

Hence Searle argues that models of action such as RCT cannot account for the idea that we deliberate over desires, beliefs and actions, whilst Bratman argues that actions require the formation of plans, which provide 'filters' on possible actions. These ideas of deliberation and planning are closely linked to another component of action that is omitted in RCT – the idea of commitment (Piekoff, 2003; Taylor, 1996). An appreciation as to how ideas of deliberation, planning and commitment indicate a view of individual action that differs from that embedded in RCT is possible through a brief consideration of Kavka's 'toxin puzzle' (Sugden, 1991).

An individual is offered the choice of consuming a drink that, although it will not result in their death, will make them rather ill for a few days. In exchange for consuming the drink, the individual will be offered £1 million. After due deliberation, the individual decides that the benefits of receiving the money outweigh the costs of consuming the drink, and hence decides to consume the drink in exchange for the money. However, the individual does not receive the money after consuming the drink. Rather, the drink is to be consumed at midday the next day, and the individual will receive the money at midnight today *if* they can convince a panel of experts armed with a variety of lie detectors that they will indeed consume the drink tomorrow. Hence if at midnight the individual can convince the experts that she definitely will consume the drink tomorrow at midday, then she will receive the money at midnight, prior to consuming the drink at midday tomorrow.

If the individual is a follower of RCT then, even although she has decided to consume the drink and receive the £1 million, it is not possible for her actually to achieve this end. Recall that, in the prisoners' dilemma, defection is dominant even if both agree to confess. In the toxin puzzle, the individual following RCT knows that, if they do receive the money at midnight, then it is completely irrational to consume the drink the next day, as they will already have the money. Hence when meeting the panel of experts, the individual will know that they are lying if they claim they will consume the drink after receiving the money. Assuming that the experts can clearly differentiate between truth and lying, then the individual following RCT will never obtain the money.

However, this is not so if the basic RCT model of action is replaced or supplemented by the inclusion of ideas such as deliberation, planning, commitment or Kantian morality.[4] Hence the individual may deliberate over the options, and form the plan or commitment to consume the drink even after they receive the money. Alternatively, the Kantian would arrive at the moral consideration that lying was wrong, hence also receiving the money and consuming the drink. So who in this example is behaving more rationally, the individual following RCT or the individual adopting plans and commitments?

It may be instructive to take stock here of the inferences that can be drawn from the above examples. Firstly, the claim that RCT can emulate natural sciences in identifying causal mechanisms or regularities seems misplaced in the case of 'reasons as causes'. The example of 'wayward causal chains' indicates that stipulating the relationship between desires, beliefs and actions may not be as straightforward as the causal theory would require. This is not to deny that hence the search for causal factors is mistaken, merely that it is difficult to enlist reasons as one of the causal factors that can be readily identified. However, the identification of the possibility of the wayward causal chains is not the only way that the relationship between desires, beliefs and actions appears to be more complex than suggested in RCT models.

According to Searle, the relationship between our desires, beliefs and actions is mediated through processes of deliberation. The idea of deliberation had already been introduced in connection with the account of weighted desires: we do not simply act on desires, but deliberate about and weigh our desires. However, even after this process of deliberation there still remains a 'gap' between the outcome of this deliberation and actually undertaking any action concerned to satisfy these weighted desires. Further, if an action is commenced, there remains a 'gap' between the commencement of an action and its conclusion. It would thus appear that there is no necessary direct form of 'causal' relationship between our desires and beliefs and the actions we eventually carry out.

Indeed, according to Bratman, an individual acting according to RCT would encounter problems in formulating future intentions. In contrast, individuals are viewed as formulating plans to which they are committed, and which guide courses of action over an extended time-horizon. Bratman's arguments complement Searle's observations, in so far as they indicate why the various 'gaps' identified by Searle do not lead to continual revisions to courses of action. Thus individuals form plans to which they are committed until actions have been completed. Of course, plans may be revised: however, they provide a way whereby individuals are initially committed to certain actions.

The toxin puzzle reveals how an individual committed to following a plan can achieve a successful outcome which appears to elude a follower of RCT. The puzzle also reveals how RCT fails at the normative level. An individual following RCT would not receive the money, and it is difficult to appreciate how following a procedure that fails to secure the model can be termed the most rational model to follow. If I want the money, I ought not to act according to RCT.

This raises another question: is the instrumentally rational action which forms the basis of RCT the only form of human action? Many advocates of RCT appear to think so, and the position has been explicitly defended in economics (e.g. Mises, 1949). However, the sociologist Max Weber famously argued that there were four types of action, of which instrumentally rational action consisted of one type. Although acknowledging the importance of instrumentally rational action, Weber also identified value-rational, affectual and traditional action (Weber, 1978: 24ff).

According to Weber, value-rational action is action orientated towards considerations such as duty, loyalty or a religious calling, where the individual does not consider the costs incurred to themselves in carrying out the action. In contrast, affectual action is essentially action governed by emotional states, for example acts of revenge or sensual gratification. Finally, traditional action is action conducted according to habit which, as Weber recognizes, may be undertaken almost automatically, without prior thought or later reflection.

It is difficult to appreciate how these types of action identified by Weber can be reduced to some form or forms of instrumentally rational action. For example, in the case of value-rational type action, Weber is suggesting that an individual may, at least, act in ways that are not self-interested. Hence an individual may realize what course of action is less costly to themselves, yet not undertake this action, out of a sense of duty. For example, in the toxin puzzle, an individual may believe that, given their promise to drink the toxin, they have a duty to do so. However, as Weber recognizes, if an individual is not acting according to the norm of instrumental rationality, then it becomes difficult to predict their behaviour:

> The question of the appropriateness of the means for achieving a given end is undoubtedly accessible to scientific analysis . . . To apply the result of this analysis in the making of a decision, however, is not a task that science can undertake; it is rather the task of the acting, willing person; he weighs and chooses from among the values involved according to his own conscience and his personal view of the world . . . The act of choice is his own responsibility. (Weber, 1949: 52–3)

An individual hence may be aware that, according to instrumental rationality, a certain act is 'irrational', yet still perform the act. Hence an individual may realize that the costs of voting outweigh the potential benefits, yet still vote, out of a sense of duty. Of course, as noted previously, RCT of voting behaviour has been modified in order to take account of ideas such as 'civic duty'. However, these *ad hoc* modifications have been advanced in order to increase the predictive power of RCT in this area. Weber's point is that, if individuals are not acting in line with instrumental rationality, it may be impossible to predict their behaviour.

Schmidtz (1995: ch. 3), amongst others, has also argued that not all actions are instrumentally rational. Take the example of an individual going for a swim. The individual may be engaging in this activity in order to become healthy, in which case the swimming is a 'means' undertaken in order to realize the 'end' of becoming healthy. However, alternatively the individual may undertake the swimming as an end in itself, not as a means to anything else (the swimming is a 'final end'). Indeed, the individual may engage in the activity simply because swimming constitutes getting exercise: it is not a means of getting exercise, but is itself exercise (the swimming is a 'constitutive end'). Indeed, Schmidtz also notes how the conscious attempt to be instrumentally rational may be counter-productive:

> If Tom is getting involved in a new romantic relationship, for example, he might be well-advised to relax and let things happen. Thinking too hard

about how to achieve his goals could make him look unromantic, and this
be precisely what stops him from achieving his goals. (Schmidtz, 1995: 21)

It would thus appear that, contrary to the assumption in RCT, not
all actions are instrumentally rational. Further, in certain situations,
attempting to act according to the precepts of instrumental rationality
may indeed be counter-productive. Given this, it is worthwhile considering now the subject of 'choice' in RCT. As its name implies, RCT
is concerned with explaining how individuals make rational choices.
Yet Weber is claiming that individuals may make choices, dependent
upon factors such as their consciences, which do not subscribe to the
RCT model.

Similarly, the economist Shackle has observed that 'rationalism, the
belief that conduct can be understood as part of the determinate order
and process of Nature . . . is a paradox. For it claims to confer upon men
freedom to choose, yet to be able to predict what they will choose'
(Shackle, 1972: 239). Shackle is explicitly raising this criticism in connection with economic theory: however, given the deference to this
theory in the majority of RCT models, it seems plausible to explore its
relevance in this connection. Shackle is pointing out that economic
theory claims to investigate individual choice: however, it also claims to
be able to predict how individuals will choose. Yet if the choices that
individuals will make can be predicted, in what sense can it be claimed
that they have a choice?

This issue can be explored in connection with Downs's original
model of voting behaviour. The assumption is roughly that, as the
chances of an individual's vote being decisive in an election is
negligible, and there are costs associated with voting, the theory predicts (incorrectly) that individuals will 'choose' to abstain from voting.
However, in what sense is the individual regarded as having a choice?
The decision concerns whether to go and vote or abstain from voting,
and given the potential costs and benefits involved, the rational
individual will not vote. Hence the only 'choice' available to the individual is that between acting irrationally (by voting) or acting rationally
(by not voting), and, in these terms, the decision does not really seem
a 'choice' at all. It seems that the individual *must* act in a certain way
(abstaining) if they are to comply with the canons of rationality.

Shackle is indicating the tension between the claims that a theory
can predict how individuals will behave and yet this predicted
behaviour can also be viewed as involving 'choice'. An engineer, with
full knowledge of all relevant factors, can no doubt predict with some
accuracy the path that a missile fired from a gun will follow. However, it
would seem rather strange to say that the missile 'chose' which path to
follow, although this is precisely the claim made by advocates of RCT.
On one level, the observations of Weber and Shackle make a similar
point. RCT claims to be able to predict the choices that individuals will

make: however, it does not consider the fact that one aspect of the choices made by individuals may involve choosing whether or not to act in an instrumentally rational manner. RCT assumes that individuals *will* act in an instrumentally rational way, and claims to be able to predict how, therefore, they will make choices. However, it does not take into consideration the fact that an instrumentally rational action may itself involve an element of choice, where other forms of acting are available.

Shackle's implicit criticism of the claim in RCT that choices can be predicted ranges further than this, as he directly connects his views with the idea of radical uncertainty, introduced in Chapter 3. According to RCT models, individuals choose from a set of available alternatives. However, if radical uncertainty is admitted, then individuals may be viewed, not merely as selecting from given alternatives, but as actually *creating* these alternatives, as 'the future is not so much unknown as it is non-existent or indeterminate at the time of the decision. The agent's task is not to estimate or discover, but to create' (Littlechild, 1986: 29).

However, if individuals create the future through their choices, then how can the result of these choices be predicted by anyone else? Buchanan, sympathetic to Shackle's arguments, hence remarks:

> We must acknowledge that in many aspects of their behaviour, men conform to laws of behaviour such that such behaviour becomes subject to scientifically testable prediction and control through the external manipulation of constraints. But we must also acknowledge that men choose courses of action that emerge only in the choice process itself. (Buchanan, 1982: 17)

The problem for the advocate of RCT here is that, in order to be able to predict how individuals will choose, they need to be able to predict, not just how individuals will choose between 'available options', but what options individuals will create through their actions. In other words, RCT would need to be able to provide a model of creativity, yet it is far from clear how creativity can be modelled. Buchanan's comment thus seems to indicate that, in contrast to the claim made by advocates of RCT, there cannot be *a* theory of human choice, as creative actions cannot be scientifically predicted.

Shackle's ideas are controversial amongst economists. However, he does seem to be voicing ideas that can be intuitively grasped. For example, the winner of the chess game or the battle may be the individual who devises moves or strategies that no-one else has ever thought of, or, if they have considered them, regarded them as impossible. Similarly, the successful entrepreneur may be the individual who can successfully persuade individuals that they desire something they had not previously even contemplated the existence of. Although Shackle's criticisms were levelled at economic theories, they have, if anything, even more pertinence when directed at the use of RCT to explain political phenomena.

It was noted in the first chapter that RCT adopts the convention from economic theorizing of assuming that preferences, desires or tastes are 'given'. This assumption may be (although it probably is not) innocuous in economics: however, it is far from innocuous when political phenomena are being investigated. However, according to Shackle's view of decision-making, 'tastes are not previously given: they have to be created' (Littlechild, 1986: 54). However, if preferences or tastes are created, then with political phenomena they may well be created by the political process itself. If this is the case, then the possibility of isolating preferences from the political process in order to analyse this process simply collapses. This problem is analogous to that of justifying institutions in terms of existing preferences, discussed in Chapter 4.

Hence take the argument, noted earlier, that political parties will tend to adopt policies that favour the median voter. However, what if the distribution of voters that yields this 'median voter' is itself a product of the party system? In that case, we are explaining the behaviour of political parties by appealing to preferences that they themselves produce. Whatever the rationale for neglecting the question of preference formation in economic theory, any such rationale appears highly dubious when investigating political processes. As an illustration, Taylor offers the following observation:

> Preferences change over time as a result of the activities of the state. Now if the state is in part the cause of changes in individual preferences, then clearly it cannot be deduced from the structure of preferences in the absence of the state that the state is desirable. (Taylor, 1982: 57)

CONCLUSION

The advocacy of adopting RCT models in order to investigate political phenomena is frequently made in terms of the claimed scientific credentials of these models. If RCT models are used in explaining political phenomena, then the study of politics would therefore be placed on a secure scientific basis. Two related aspects to this claim have been investigated. Firstly, RCT models can help provide a scientific basis for explaining decision-making, and, secondly, they can provide this basis through providing causal explanations of political phenomena. However, it appears that RCT models are not well equipped when it comes to the issue of explaining decision-making. Empirical evidence indicates that individuals frequently do not make decisions in the manner predicted in RCT models, hence it is difficult to appreciate in what ways it can be claimed that the models are thus useful in explaining choices.

However, neither does the RCT model appear theoretically well equipped in providing causal explanations. Indeed, the desire or preference and belief model which forms the heart of RCT not only has difficulties in identifying causes, it appears theoretically inadequate in explaining decision-making. Hence at both empirical and theoretical levels it seems difficult to substantiate the claimed scientific status of RCT. Further, although claiming to offer an account of rational choice, it is contestable to what extent a 'choice' is being made if this choice can also be predicted.[5]

Notes

1. I must admit that, although here and elsewhere the authors cite a number of studies to support this claim, and these studies seem convincing, I, for one, find this apparent confusion in the minds of voters somewhat puzzling.
2. This problem is analogous to the one raised concerning transitivity: what ensures that preferences are transitive?
3. The significance of planning in acting according to instrumental rationality was recognized by Weber – see Weber, 1978: 63.
4. Bratman specifically discusses this example in relationship to his ideas – see Bratman, 1999: 101ff.
5. Green and Shapiro (1994: 21ff) draw attention to one strategy that has been adopted by advocates of RCT in politics when confronted with such difficulties. This is to forgo any attempt to explain political phenomena in terms of individual beliefs and desires in favour of explaining these phenomena through postulating individuals who act 'as if' maximizing. Hence there is no need to refer to intentional behaviour. An analogy with evolutionary theories in biology is invoked here: just as animals can be viewed as maximizing reproductive output without it being assumed that they do so intentionally, so individuals can be viewed as maximizing utility without appealing to their intentions.

   Green and Shapiro point out that one problem with this strategy is that animals may evolve in a number of different ways, and it is difficult to predict what will be the outcome of any 'evolutionary development'. However, there seems to be a further fairly fundamental problem with this strategy. Evolutionary theory does not claim to be a theory of choice – quite the opposite. Hence giraffes have not evolved long necks because they chose to do so. However RCT, as its name implies, is intended to be a theory of choice, and of rational choice.

Conclusion

The previous chapters have examined the basis of rational choice theory, investigated how the theory has been used in the study of political phenomena, and indicated some of the potential problems with the theory. Given this, what general conclusions can be drawn concerning the use of RCT in providing explanations in politics? Firstly, it seems neither advisable nor possible to simply reject the theory as being deeply flawed in some irredeemable way. Such rejections might take the form of indicating a mistaken adherence to a modernist idea of rationality, arguing that the economic theory underpinning it is fundamentally mistaken, or arguing that, say, focusing on social norms or problems of meaning are the only correct way of proceeding in political studies.

However, neither does it seem possible to concur with the judgement that RCT has been an undeniable success when applied to the study of political phenomena. The explanation of certain significant political practices, such as the activity of voting, appears to remain an intractable problem within the RCT framework. Neither does it seem plausible to claim that whenever an author is addressing politically salient issues then these issues can always be better understood if reinterpreted into the framework of RCT: not all issues relevant to collective action can be reduced to 'free rider' problems.

Yet there are undoubtedly areas and topics where the application of models utilizing RCT have been both insightful and interesting. In particular, studies of the differing outcomes possible with different voting systems, issues in agenda-setting and logrolling, issues relevant to revolutionary action, and problems in social choice, are particularly revealing. Indeed, if nothing else, the promotion of models based on RCT has forced proponents of alternative explanations of political phenomena to defend their own views, and indicate exactly how they differ from the assumptions of RCT models.

The advantages and disadvantages of the models investigated can possibly be summed up by stating that the very term 'Rational Choice Theory' is something of a misnomer. The theory claims to offer an account as to how individuals either do, or ought to, make choices. However, the theory also claims to be able to predict what choices individuals will make, which implies that individuals do not, in fact, have any choice concerning how to act. Further, the theory does not consider that 'acting in accordance with RCT' may itself be the *result* of an act of choice.

There are no doubt a wide variety of situations where it would seem eminently rational for individuals to behave in the manner that the theory predicts. For example, a politician may be very interested in a certain policy option being passed as legislation, and might strongly support this policy because they know that it is strongly supported by the majority of their constituents. Hence, the individual believes that, if the policy becomes law, the chances of successfully achieving re-election will be considerably enhanced. In this case it could be considered quite rational if the individual engages in, say, the activity of logrolling in order to attempt to secure a successful outcome.

However, it would also appear perfectly reasonable for the politician to refuse to engage in this behaviour because they believed that the policy in question was distasteful, entailing a conflict with certain strongly held ethical principles. A politician acting in this way may well be risking their chances of achieving re-election. However, they have chosen to act in accordance with ethical considerations, and refuse to trade these principles in order to gain electoral advantage.

Alternatively, the politician might have already given a commitment to support an alternative policy option. Although this option will not be anywhere as popular with constituents, the politician feels that they are obliged to honour the previously given commitment, hence refuses to support the alternative, more popular, policy. It is difficult to appreciate why, of these three forms of action, only the first can be considered 'rational'. Alternatively, it does not seem convincing to believe that, if only costs and benefits or preferences are adjusted in some way, then all three can be taken as representatives of actions in accordance with RCT.

What would be of considerable benefit would be studies investigating how, and under what conditions, individuals act in the manner predicted in RCT, and under what conditions they do not act in this manner and, further, why they do not act in the predicted manner. It is no doubt possible, by adjusting informational requirements, or costs and benefits, or preferences, to build a number of RCT models explaining how voting is rational. However, it could also be the case that at least some voters are aware that the act of voting is irrational according to RCT, yet vote anyway.

It thus seems possible to conclude that the adoption of RCT in political studies has been useful and instructive, although only up to a point. The theory does not seem capable of explaining all the choices made by political actors, and, in certain crucial respects, offers a woefully simplistic model of individual choice. To any readers remaining completely unconvinced that RCT offers any benefits whatever, or still remain convinced that RCT offers the only way to study political phenomena, I can only offer the following consolation: at least, hopefully, you now have better knowledge of your adversaries.

Bibliography

Abelson, R.P. (1996) 'The secret existence of expressive behaviour', in J. Friedman (ed), *The Rational Choice Controversy*, New Haven: Yale University Press.

Akerloff, G. (1970) 'The market for lemons: quality uncertainty and the market mechanism', *Quarterly Journal of Economics*, 89, 488–500.

Aldrich, J.H. (1997) 'When is it rational to vote?', in D.C. Mueller (ed), *Perspectives on Public Choice: a handbook*, Cambridge: Cambridge University Press.

Anderson, L.R. (2001) 'Public choice as experimental science', in W.F. Shughart & L. Razzolini (eds), *The Elgar Companion to Public Choice*, Cheltenham: Edward Elgar.

Archer, M.S. & Tritter, J.Q. (2000) 'Introduction', in M.S. Archer & J.Q. Tritter (eds), *Rational Choice Theory: resisting colonization*, London: Routledge.

Arrow, K.J. (1951) *Social Choice and Individual Values*, New York: Wiley.

Arrow, K.J. (1974) *The Limits of Organisation*, New York: Norton.

Arrow, K.J. (1977) 'The foundations of social choice theory', in K.J. Arrow, A. Sen & K. Suzumura (eds), *Social Choice Re-examined: Volume 1*, Basingstoke: Macmillan.

Arrow, K.J. (1984) 'A difficulty in the concept of social welfare', in K.J. Arrow, *Selected Papers of Kenneth J. Arrow: Volume IV: Social Choice and Justice*, Oxford: Blackwell.

Arrow, K.J. (1994) 'Methodological Individualism and Social Knowledge', *American Economic Review*, 84, 2, 1–9.

Attfield, C. *et al.* (1985) *Rational Expectations in Economics*, Oxford: Blackwell.

Audi, R. (1990) 'Rationality and valuation', in P.K. Moser (ed), *Rationality in Action*, Cambridge: Cambridge University Press.

Barry, B. (1978) *Sociologists, Economists, and Democracy*, Chicago: University of Chicago Press.

Bateman, F. *et al.* (2000) 'A test of the theory of reference-dependent preferences', in D. Kahneman & A. Tversky (eds), *Choice, Values, and Frames*, Cambridge: Cambridge University Press.

Becker, G. (1976) *The Economic Approach to Human Behaviour*, Chicago: University of Chicago Press.

Berger, J. & Offe, C. (1982) 'Functionalism vs. rational choice?', *Theory and Society*, 11, 521–6.

Blais, A. (2000) *To Vote or not to Vote: the merits and limits of rational choice theory*, Pittsburgh: University of Pittsburgh Press.

✳ Booth, W.J. (1993) 'Marx's two logics of capitalism', in W.J. Booth *et al.* (eds), *Politics and Rationality*, Cambridge: Cambridge University Press.

Bowles, S. & Gintis, H. (1976) *Schooling in Capitalist America*, London: Routledge and Kegan Paul.

Boyne, G.A. (1998) *Public Choice Theory and Local Government: a comparative analysis of the UK and the USA*, Basingstoke: Palgrave.

Bratman, M.E. (1999) *Intention, Plans, and Practical Reason*, Stanford: CSLI Publications.

Broome, J. (1991) 'Rationality and the sure-thing principle', in G. Meeks (ed), *Thoughtful Economic Man: essays on rationality, moral rules, and benevolence*, Cambridge: Cambridge University Press.

Broome, J. (2000) 'Are intentions reasons? And how should we cope with incommensurable values?', in C.W. Morris & A. Ripstein (eds), *Practical Rationality and Preference: essays for David Gauthier*, Cambridge: Cambridge University Press.

Brown, M.E. *et al.* (eds) (2000) *Rational Choice and Security Studies: Stephen Walt and his critics*, Cambridge, Mass.: M.I.T. Press.

Buchanan, J.M (1954) 'Social choice, democracy, and free markets', *Journal of Political Economy*, 62, 114–23.

Buchanan, J.M. (1969) *Cost and Choice*, Chicago: Markham.

Buchanan, J.M. (1982) 'The domain of subjective economics', in I.M. Kirzner (ed), *Method, Process, and Austrian Economics*, Lexington: Lexington Books.

Buchanan, J.M. (1989) *Explorations into Constitutional Economics*, Texas: T&M University Press.

Buchanan, J.M. & Tullock, G. (1962) *The Calculus of Consent: logical foundations of constitutional democracy*, Ann Arbor: University of Michigan Press.

Cain, M.J. (2001) 'Social choice theory', in W.F. Shughart & L. Razzolini (eds), *The Elgar Companion to Public Choice*, Cheltenham: Edward Elgar.

Calvert, R.C. (2001) 'Models of imperfect information in politics', in J. Ferejohn (ed), *Positive Political Economy I*, London: Routledge.

Carver, T. & Thomas, P. (1995) (eds), *Rational Choice Marxism*, London: Macmillan.

Chong, D. (1996) 'Rational choice theory's mysterious rivals', in J. Friedman (ed), *The Rational Choice Controversy*, New Haven: Yale University Press.

Cohen, G.A. (1978) *Karl Marx's Theory of History: A Defence*, Oxford: Clarendon Press.

Colman, A.M. (1995) *Game Theory and its Applications in the Social and Biological Sciences*, (2nd ed), London: Butterworth & Heinemann.

Colomer, J.P. (2001) *Political Institutions: democracy and social choice*, Oxford: Oxford University Press.

Craven, J. (1992) *Social Choice: a framework for collective decisions and individual judgements*, Cambridge: Cambridge University Press.

Davidson, D. (1980) *Essays on Actions and Events*, Oxford: Clarendon Press.

De Serres, A. (2003) 'Structural policies and growth', *OECD Economic Working Papers*, no. 9.

Diermeier, D. (1996) 'Rational choice and the role of theory in political science', in J. Friedman (ed), *The Rational Choice Controversy*, New Haven: Yale University Press.

Doran, G. & Krovick, R. (1977) 'Single transferable vote: one example of a perverse social choice function', *American Political Science Review*, 21, 303–11.

Dowding, K. (2002) 'Revealed preference and external reference', *Rationality and Society*, 14, 3, 259–84.

Downs, A. (1957) *An Economic Theory of Democracy*, New York: Harper Row.

Downs, A. (1991) 'Social values and democracy', in K.R. Monroe (ed), *The Economic Approach to Politics*, New York: Harper Collins.

Dryzek, J.S. (2000) *Deliberative Democracy and Beyond: liberals, critics, contestations*, Oxford: Oxford University Press.

Elster, J. (1985a) *Making Sense of Marx*, Cambridge: Cambridge University Press.

Elster, J. (1985b) 'The nature and scope of rational choice explanation', in E. LePore & B.P. Mclaughlin (eds), *Actions and Events: perspectives on the philosophy of Donald Davidson*, Oxford: Blackwell.

Elster, J. (1986) 'Introduction', in J. Elster (ed), *Rational Choice*, Oxford: Blackwell.

Elster, J. (1988) 'Marx, revolution, and rational choice', in M. Taylor (ed), *Rationality and Revolution*, Cambridge: Cambridge University Press.

Elster, J. (1989) *The Cement of Society: a study of social order*, Cambridge: Cambridge University Press.

Elster, J. (2000) 'Rationality, economy, and society', in S. Turner (ed), *The Cambridge Companion to Weber*, Cambridge: Cambridge University Press.

Fails, R.L. & Tollison, R.D. 'Expressive versus economic voting', in W.M. Crain & R.D. Tollison (1990) (eds), *Rethinking Politics: essays in empirical public choice*, Ann Arbor: University of Michigan.

Ferejohn, J.A. & Fiorina, M.P. (1974) 'The paradox of not voting: a decision theoretical analysis', *American Political Science Review*, 68, 525–36.

Ferejohn, J. & Satz, D. (1996) 'Unification, universalism, and rational choice theory', in J. Friedman (ed), *The Rational Choice Controversy*, New Haven: Yale University Press.

Field, A.J. (1984) 'Microeconomics, norms and rationality', *Economic Development and Cultural Change*, 32, 683–711.

Fishburn, P.C. (2001) 'Interprofile conditions and impossibility', in J. Ferejohn (ed), *Positive Political Economy I*, London: Routledge.

Friedman, J. (1996) 'Introduction', in J. Friedman (ed), *The Rational Choice Controversy*, New Haven: Yale University Press.

Gauthier, D. (1986) *Morals by Agreement*, Oxford: Clarendon.

Giddens, A. (1979) *Central Problems in Social Theory*, London: Macmillan.

Goodin, R.E. (1996) 'Institutions and their design', in R.E. Goodin (ed), *A Theory of Institutional Design*, Cambridge: Cambridge University Press.

Green, D.P. & Shapiro, I. (1994) *Pathologies of Rational Choice Theory*, New Haven: Yale University Press.

Grossman, S.J. & Stiglitz, J.E. (1976) 'Information and competitive price systems', *American Economic Review*, 66, 246–53.

Grossman, S.J. & Stiglitz, J.E. (1980) 'On the impossibility of informationally efficient markets', *American Economic Review*, 70, 393–408.

Hahn, F. (1982) 'On some difficulties of the utilitarian economist', in A. Sen & B. Williams (eds), *Utilitarianism and Beyond*, Cambridge: Cambridge University Press.

Hampton, J. (1986) *Hobbes and the Social Contract Tradition*, Cambridge: Cambridge University Press.

Hardin, R. (1997) 'Economic theories of the state', in D.C. Mueller (ed), *Perspectives on Public Choice: a handbook*, Cambridge: Cambridge University Press.

Hargreaves Heap, S. *et al.* (1992) *The Theory of Choice*, Oxford: Blackwell.

Hargreaves Heap, S. & Varoufakis, Y. (1995) *Game Theory: a critical introduction*, London: Routledge.

Hayek, F. (1949) *Individualism and Economic Order*, London: Routledge and Kegan Paul.

Hayek, F. (1973) *Law, Legislation and Liberty: Volume 1: rules and order*, London: Routledge and Kegan Paul.

Heiner, R.A. (1986) 'Uncertainty, signal–detection experiments, and modelling behaviour', in R.N. Langlois (ed), *Economics as a Process*, Cambridge: Cambridge University Press.

Herne, K. & Sitala, M. (2004) 'A response to the critique of rational choice theory', *Inquiry*, 47, 1, 67–85.

Hinich, M.J. & Munger, M.C. (1997) *Analytical Politics*, Cambridge: Cambridge University Press.

Hollis, M. (1996) *The Philosophy of Social Science: an introduction*, Cambridge: Cambridge University Press.

Hollis, M. & Hahn, F. (1979) 'Introduction', in M. Hollis & F. Hahn, *Philosophy and Economic Theory*, Oxford: Oxford University Press.

Horn, M.J. (1995) *The Political Economy of Public Administration*, Cambridge: Cambridge University Press.

Johnson, J. (2003) 'Conceptual problems as obstacles to progress in political science', *Journal of Theoretical Politics*, 15, 1, 87–115.

Johnston, R. *et al.* (2001) *From Voting to Seats: the operation of the UK voting system since 1945*, Manchester: Manchester University Press.

Jones, C.I. (1998) *Introduction to Economic Growth*, New York: Norton.

Kahneman, D. (2000) 'New challenges to the rationality assumption', in D. Kahneman & A. Tversky (eds), *Choice, Values, and Frames*, Cambridge: Cambridge University Press.

Kahneman, D. & Ritov, I. (1994) 'Determinants of the stated willingness to pay for public goods: a study in the headline method', *Journal of Risk and Uncertainty*, 9, 1, 5–38.

Kahneman, D. & Tversky, A. (1979) 'Prospect theory: an analysis of decision under risk', *Econometrica*, 47, 263–91.

Kahneman, D. & Tversky, A. (1990) 'Prospect theory: an analysis of decision under risk', in P.K. Moser (ed), *Rationality in Action*, Cambridge: Cambridge University Press.

Kahneman, D. & Varey, C. (1991) 'Notes on the psychology of utility', in J. Elster & J.E. Roemer (eds), *Interpersonal Comparisons of Well-Being*, Cambridge: Cambridge University Press.

Keynes, J.M. (1973) *The Collected Writings of John Maynard Keynes: Volume VII: The General Theory of Employment, Interest and Money*, London: Macmillan.

Kincaid, H. (1996) *Philosophical Foundations of the Social Sciences*, Cambridge: Cambridge University Press.

Knack, S. (1994) 'Does the rain help the Republicans? Theory and evidence on turnout and vote', *Public Choice*, 79, 187–209.

Kreps, D. (1990) *A Course in Microeconomic Theory*, Hemel Hempstead: Harvester Wheatsheaf.

Kuhn, T. (1962) *The Structure of Scientific Revolutions*, Chicago: University of Chicago Press.

Lane, R.E. (1996) 'What rational choice explains', in J. Friedman (ed), *The Rational Choice Controversy*, New Haven: Yale University Press.

Laver, M. (1997) *Private Desires, Political Action: an invitation to the politics of rational choice*, London: Sage.

Ledyand, J.D. (1995) 'Public goods: a survey of experimental research', in J.H. Kagel & A.E. Roth (eds), *The Handbook of Experimental Economics*, Princeton: Princeton University Press.

Leibenstein, H. (1950) 'Bandwagon, snob and Veblen effects in the theory of consumer demand', *Quarterly Journal of Economics*, 183–207.

Levacic, R. (1990) 'Public Choice', in J.R. Shackleton (ed), *New Thinking in Economics*, Aldershot: Elgar.

Lewis, D. (1969) *Convention: a philosophical study*, Cambridge, Mass.: Harvard University Press.

Lichbach, M.I. (2003) *Is Rational Choice Theory all of Social Science?*, Ann Arbor: University of Michigan.

Littlechild, S. (1986) 'Three types of market process', in R.N. Langlois (ed), *Economics as a Process*, Cambridge: Cambridge University Press.

181

Lohmann, S. (1996) 'The poverty of Green and Shapiro', in J. Friedman (ed), *The Rational Choice Controversy*, New Haven: Yale University Press.

McLean, D. (2002) 'Some morals of a theory of non-rational choice', in R. Gowda & J.C. Fox (eds), *Judgements, Decisions, and Public Policy*, Cambridge: Cambridge University Press.

McLean, I. (1981) 'The social contract in Leviathan and the prisoners' dilemma super-game', *Political Studies*, 29, 3, 339–51.

McLean, I. (1987) *Public Choice: an Introduction*, Oxford: Blackwell.

Mandler, M. (2001) 'A difficult choice in preference theory: rationality implies completeness or transitivity but not both', in E. Millgram (ed), *Varieties of Practical Reason*, Cambridge, Mass.: M.I.T. Press.

Mele, A.R. (1997) 'Introduction', in A.R. Mele (ed), *The Philosophy of Action*, Oxford: Oxford University Press.

Menger, C. (1892) 'On the origin of money', *Economics Journal*, 2, 239–55.

Miller, S. (2001) *Social Action: a teleological account*, Cambridge: Cambridge University Press.

Mises, L. (1949) *Human Action*, Chicago: Contemporary Books.

Monroe, K.R. (ed) (1991) *The Economic Approach to Politics*, New York: Harper Collins.

Moya, C.J. (1990) *The Philosophy of Action: an introduction*, Oxford: Polity.

Mueller, D.C. (1993) 'The future of public choice', in C.K. Rowley *et al.* (eds), *The Next 25 Years of Public Choice*, Dordrecht: Kluwer.

Mueller, D.C. (1997) 'Constitutional public choice', in D.C. Mueller (ed), *Perspectives on Public Choice: a handbook*, Cambridge: Cambridge University Press.

Mueller, D.C. (2003) *Public Choice III*, Cambridge: Cambridge University Press.

Mueller, D.C. (2004) 'Models of man: neoclassical, behavioural, evolutionary', *Politics, Philosophy and Economics*, 3, 1, 59–76.

Munger, M.C. (2001) 'Voting', in W.F. Shughart & L. Razzolini (eds), *The Elgar Companion to Public Choice*, Cheltenham: Edward Elgar.

Niskanen, W.A. (1973) *Bureaucracy: servant or master?*, London: Institute of Economic Affairs.

Niskanen, W.A. (2001) 'Bureaucracy', in W.F. Shughart & L. Razzolini (eds), *The Elgar Companion to Public Choice*, Cheltenham: Edward Elgar.

North, D.C. & Thomas, R.P. (1973) *The Rise of the Western World: a new economic history*, Cambridge: Cambridge University Press.

Nozick, R. (1990) 'Newcomb's problem and two principles of choice', in P.K. Moser (ed), *Rationality in Action*, Cambridge: Cambridge University Press.

Olson, M. (1965) *The Logic of Collective Action*, Cambridge, Mass.: Harvard University Press.

Olson, M. (1982) *The Rise and Decline of Nations*, New Haven: Yale University Press.

Ordeshook, P.C. (1997) 'The spatial analysis of elections and committees', in D.C. Mueller (ed), *Perspectives on Public Choice: a handbook*, Cambridge: Cambridge University Press.

Palfrey, T.R. & Rosenthal, H. (1985) 'Voter participation and strategic uncertainty', *American Political Science Review*, 79, 62–78.

Parsons, S. (2003) *Money, Time and Rationality in Max Weber*, London: Routledge.

Peters, B.G. (1999) *Institutional Theory in Political Science: the 'new institutionalism'*, London: Pinter.

Pettit, P. (1996) 'Institutional design and rational choice', in R.E. Goodin (ed), *A Theory of Institutional Design*, Cambridge: Cambridge University Press.

Piekoff, A. (2003) 'Rational action entails rational desire: a critical review of Searle's "Rationality in Action"', *Philosophical Explanations*, 6, 2, 124–38.

Popkin, S.C. (1988) 'Political entrepreneurs and peasant movements', in M. Taylor (ed), *Rationality and Revolution*, Cambridge: Cambridge University Press.

Popkin, S.L. (1979) *The Rational Peasant: the political economy of rural society in Vietnam*, California: University of California Press.

Qualtrone, G.A. & Tversky, A. (2000) 'Contrasting rational and psychological analyses of political choice', in D. Kahneman & A. Tversky (eds), *Choice, Values, and Frames*, Cambridge: Cambridge University Press.

Rasmusen, E. (1989) *Games and Information*, Oxford: Blackwell.

Riker, W.H. (1982) *Liberalism against Populism: a confrontation between the theory of democracy and the theory of social choice*, San Francisco: Freemont.

Riker, W.H. & Ordeshook, P.C. (1968) 'A theory of the calculus of voting', *American Political Science Review*, 62, 25–42.

Ruben, D.-H. (1985) *The Metaphysics of the Social World*, London: Routledge Kegan Paul.

Sass, T.R. (2001) 'The autonomy of political representation', in W.F. Shughart & L. Razzolini (eds), *The Elgar Companion to Public Choice*, Cheltenham: Edward Elgar.

Savage, L.J. (1990) 'Historical and critical comments on utility', in P.K. Moser (ed), *Rationality in Action*, Cambridge: Cambridge University Press.

Schelling, T.C. (1963) *The Strategy of Conflict*, New York: Oxford University Press.

Schmidtz, D. (1991) *The Limits of Government*, Colorado: Westview Press.

Schmidtz, D. (1995) *Rational Choice and Moral Agency*, Princeton: Princeton University Press.

Schumpeter, J.A. (1976) *Capitalism, Socialism, and Democracy*, London: George Allen & Unwin.

Searle, J.R. (1980) 'The background of meaning', in J.R. Searle *et al.* (eds), *Speech Act Theory and Pragmatics*, Dordrecht: D. Riedel.

Searle, J.R. (2001) *Rationality in Action*, Cambridge, Mass.: M.I.T. Press.

Sen, A. (1970) 'The impossibility of a Paretian liberal', *Journal of Political Economy*, 78, 152–7.

Sen, A. (1982) *Choice, Welfare and Measurement*, Oxford: Blackwell.

Sen, A. (1986a) 'Behaviour and the concept of preferences', in J. Elster (ed), *Rational Choice*, Oxford: Blackwell.

Sen, A. (1986b) 'Foundations of social choice theory: an epilogue', in J. Elster & A. Hylland (eds), *Foundations of Social Choice Theory*, Cambridge: Cambridge University Press.

Shackle, G.L.S. (1972) *Epistemics and Economics: a critique of economic doctrines*, Cambridge: Cambridge University Press.

Shepsle, K.A. (1996) 'Statistical political philosophy and positive political theory', in J. Friedman (ed), *The Rational Choice Controversy*, New Haven: Yale University Press.

Shepsle, K.A. (2001) 'Models of multiparty electoral competition', in J. Ferejohn (ed), *Positive Political Economy II*, London: Routledge.

Shepsle, K.A. & Boncheck, M.S. (1997) *Analyzing Politics: rationality, behaviour and institutions*, London: Norton.

Stiglitz, J.E. (1987) 'The causes and consequences of the dependence of quality on price', *Journal of Economic Literature*, 25, 1, 1–48.

Stratmann, T. (1997) 'Logrolling', in D.C. Mueller (ed), *Perspectives on Public Choice: a handbook*, Cambridge: Cambridge University Press.

Sugden, R. (1981) *The Political Economy of Public Choice: an introduction to welfare economics*, Oxford: Robertson.

Sugden, R. (1991) 'Rational choice', *Economic Journal*, 101, 751–85.

Taylor, M. (1982) *Community, Anarchy, and Liberty*, Cambridge: Cambridge University Press.

Taylor, M. (1993) 'Structure, culture, and action', in W.J. Booth *et al.* (eds), *Politics and Rationality*, Cambridge: Cambridge University Press.

Taylor, M. (1996) 'When rationality fails', in J. Friedman (ed), *The Rational Choice Controversy*, New Haven: Yale University Press.

Tullock, G. (1976) *The Vote Motive*, London: Institute of Economic Affairs.

Tullock, G. (1988) *Wealth, Poverty and Politics*, New York: Blackwell.

Tversky, A. (1996) 'Rational theory and constructive choice', in K.J. Arrow *et al.* (eds), *The Rational Foundations of Economic Behaviour: proceedings of the IEA conference held in Turin, Italy*, Basingstoke: Macmillan.

Vanberg, V.J. (1994) *Rules and Choice in Economics*, London: Routledge.

Walt, S. (2000) 'Rigour or rigor mortis', in M.E. Brown *et al.* (eds), *Rational Choice and Security Studies: Stephen Walt and his critics*, Cambridge, Mass.: M.I.T. Press.

Watkins, J. W. (1973) 'Historical Explanation in the Social Sciences', reprinted in J. O'Neill (ed), *Modes of Individualism and Collectivism*, London: Heinemann.

Weber, M. (1949) *The Methodology of the Social Sciences*, New York: Free Press.

Weber, M. (1978) *Economy and Society: an outline of an interpretative sociology*, G. Roth & C. Wittich (eds), Berkeley: University of California Press.

Williamson, O.E. (1986) 'The economics of governance', in R.N. Langlois (ed), *Economics as a Process*, Cambridge: Cambridge University Press.

Wintrobe, R. (1997) 'Modern bureaucratic theory', in D.C. Mueller (ed), *Perspectives on Public Choice: a handbook*, Cambridge: Cambridge University Press.

Zagare, F.C. (2004) 'Reconciling rationality with deterrence', *Journal of Theoretical Politics*, 16, 2, 107–42.

INDEX